HISTORY OF BROADCASTING: RADIO TO TELEVISION

HISTORY OF BROADCASTING: Radio to Television

Marconi

The Man and His Wireless

ORRIN E. DUNLAP, JR.

ARNO PRESS and THE NEW YORK TIMES

New York • 1971

Reprint Edition 1971 by Arno Press Inc.

Reprinted from a copy in The Newark Public Library

LC# 72-161142
ISBN 0-405-03563-2

HISTORY OF BROADCASTING: RADIO TO TELEVISION
ISBN for complete set: 0-405-03555-1
See last pages of this volume for titles.

Manufactured in the United States of America

MARCONI

THE MAN AND HIS WIRELESS

"Who says Italia holds a dying race
And all the glory of her line is spent?"

MARCONI

THE MAN AND HIS WIRELESS

by

ORRIN E. DUNLAP, Jr.

Radio Editor, "The New York Times"
Marconi Operator, S.S. Octorara; U. S. Navy Operator
Member, Institute of Radio Engineers

NEW YORK
THE MACMILLAN COMPANY
1937

SET UP BY BROWN BROTHERS LINOTYPERS
PRINTED IN THE UNITED STATES OF AMERICA
BY THE FERRIS PRINTING COMPANY

TO

LOUISE

"If my slight Muse do please these curious days,
The pain be mine, but thine shall be the praise."

One of the first of the immortals in the Italian Royal Academy instituted by Mussolini in April, 1926, in the Farnesina Palace at Rome, is Guglielmo Marconi, inventor of wireless, President of the Academy, and Italian plenipotentiary of science and peace.

He has drawn "the most distant places and many forgotten lives into the orbit of civilization"; annihilated space, shriveled a planet and girdled its earthly sphere ere the pulse beat twice!

To whom has been granted the almost superhuman power to give wings to words, music and pictures that they may fly to the uttermost parts of the earth bearing messages from and to the heart of man, and whose name has already become a common noun.

PREFACE

Books have long been one of the strongest allies of civilization; so is communication. Both liberate ideas, spread knowledge and knit human kinship. It is pleasing to me that Mr. Dunlap, an editor possessing a wide background of practical experience in radio, has authored this story of Marconi wireless, recording the historic steps of science, and the part that I have had the honor to play in it.

In revealing to the world the significance of wireless and its influence on the lives of the people, I hope that this book in English will further cement the friendship of Italy and the Anglo-speaking nations, and that this story of wireless will be an inspiration to youth in science. The achievements of wireless illustrate the truth that where there is a will there is a way. There are no limits in science; each advance widens the sphere of exploration. It was that way in 1895; it is that way now. Radio is a symbol of progress.

Guglielmo Marconi.

APPRECIATION

It has been the good fortune of the author to have had Guglielmo Marconi's friendly interest in the writing of this story. For his kindness in thoroughly reading the final proofs that the book would be accurate in facts about wireless and historically correct in personal detail, the author is deeply indebted.

Trails of research have led far, from the nooks of old magazine shops to the time-yellowed newspaper files now tucked away in dark chambers. Recognition must be given to the observers and reporters, especially those of *The New York Times*, *McClure's Magazine* and the *Scientific American*, who at the turn of the century reported the drama of Marconi and his wireless. Those interviewed directly and by correspondence have been many, and to all who have been so helpful, sincere appreciation is expressed.

The author is grateful to Dr. Max Jordan for the interesting information relative to Senatore Marconi's early life, which, with his facility to converse in Italian, he uncovered among several old residents of Bologna.

INTRODUCTION

SEVERAL meetings with Senatore Marconi inspired the idea to write a "profile" of him—an impression of his personality. But the portraiture lengthened into a book. Face to face he is radically different from the world's general picture of him as a scientist. He is more English than Italian; shy and mysterious, punctual but not easy to meet.

Marconi the man and Marconi the inventor are two individuals with the outstanding characteristic of simplicity linking the two into one personality. Simplicity is the keynote of his everyday life and of his scientific triumphs; it is the secret of his wizardry. The simplicity of his mind protected him from complex technical ideas quite as Edison's deafness shut off noises and chatter which would have disturbed him by contamination of clear thinking. Marconi's simplicity of thought enabled him to accomplish what skilled mathematicians and theorists had failed to do because they became entangled in deep technical approaches.

"Nothing is more simple than greatness; indeed, to be simple is to be great," observed Emerson. Marconi stands with Edison in testifying to this truth.

Jotting down impressions of the man is comparatively easy, but almost before the author realizes, wireless has crept into the fabric of the personal story; Marconi and wireless are synonymous and inseparable. One cannot be told without the other. His life is a chapter in the history of civilization. What he has achieved—what he has said—all interwoven with his inspiring personality and the genius of his soul, make an impressive, almost incredible, story of accomplishment within the span of a lifetime.

Marconi sowed electric sparks to the winds. He ploughed electrically beyond the frontiers of science in search of elusive waves and reaped a wondrous system of lightning-like communication. He discovered new truths.

The very simplicity of Marconi's nature makes it possible for wireless to overshadow everything else in his life. The man is dwarfed by his own scientific creation. The human-interest yarns and lively anecdotes of his career have vanished as shadows in the brilliant glare of the wireless legend.

Even Marconi completely absorbed in wireless seems to have forgotten interesting little happenings of his boyhood and manhood. In all the records of his career, wireless predominates—always it is wireless, wireless, wireless! And that may explain why those who have talked with him along the march of life have generally overlooked the traditional fables usually recorded about great men. Nine times out of ten those who met him encountered him in hours of wireless triumphs and they naturally covered the big news of the day which eclipsed the man who made it possible. Marconi the inventor, of course, figured in the news but Marconi the man modestly stepped aside.

The unfathomed, unlimited wireless teases him in the sixties as it did in his teens to penetrate and to solve the ever-present riddles of the infinite. So steeped is he in the lore and craftsmanship of wireless—those who know him are aware—its enchantment will follow him to the gates of the Great Beyond. Indefatigable is the energy of this dynamic Italian, never content to rest on his laurels. Within sixty-three years he has crossed the Atlantic eighty-nine times on voyages of scientific research and good will. Once the ocean was his boldest challenger. It defied his magic.

Thoroughly familiar with the scientific aspects of wireless the author has endeavored to present impartially, with thoroughness and befitting brevity, the significant facts as he has seen and understood them; to interpret Marconi's role as revealed by a study of scientific and historical evidence much of which has been related to the author by veterans in wireless who have been with the inventor in hours of disappointment and triumph.

This is the life story of Marconi; a story of ingenuity. The emphasis is on the man's work and on his personality; on his life full of romance and historic interest quite as human, even humanitarian, as it is scientific. This is the story of Marconi as he came into the news. And once he came into it he remained, for Marconi crowned by wireless, is always news, generally front page. Today broadcasting bespeaks his genius; television illustrates it.

O. E. D., Jr.

New York, 1937.

CONTENTS

ILLUSTRATIONS

PART I

I

THE BIRTH OF A WIZARD

GUGLIELMO MARCONI is an Italian who speaks English as fluently as his wireless "talks" all the languages of mankind. He is the last survivor of a romantic age in science; the last of the dramatic Edison era in which a man's invention bore his name as did his child.

Marconi's triumph lives with the radio; Morse's with the telegraph; Bell's with the telephone. They pioneered in the nineteenth century—in the Victorian era, when rugged individualism was a potent force in science. There may never be another genius to whom science will award the sole honor of a great discovery and historically link his name with the invention. Mass effort in the twentieth century's highly specialized era of mass production has put an end to such single-handed achievements.

Invention is now developed, promoted, commercialized and merchandized by specialists, but in Marconi's day the complete problem belonged to him who nurtured the idea. His invention was the mere beginning; "selling" the idea was the herculean task, testing every ounce of the inventor's stamina and courage. He stood alone!

Today the glory of discovery is divided. No one man wears the crown. Invention is a laboratory product; a complex mathematical offensive, no longer the evolution of a simple idea born in the solitude of some visionary youth's attic workshop. Science now scatters and shares the inventive laurels; it emblazons the name of no lone inventor. The new instrument emerges from the perfectly equipped,

3

highly financed realm of research in which the worker's identity is lost amid plans, formulas, slide-rules and machines.

Already the forces of progress threaten to divorce Marconi's name from the ever-expanding invention, as is invariably the case when the originator's fame is dwarfed by the perpetuity of his achievement. Once it was always "Marconi wireless"; he personified wireless, and wireless was his life electrified. But when wireless gave way to the word "radio," and then radio to "broadcasting" and "television," the name Marconi was spoken less. Time, it can be seen, has a way of glorifying an invention, but the man who invented it shrinks into the ages which year after year dim the power of his name with the eventuality that he becomes almost a myth and his creation a commonplace thing.

Already the next generation may be heard inquiring who invented radio; who invented television? Old-timers and history books will tell them that Marconi discovered wireless, and from that as the root, the communication tree spread its branches. Now it's nobody's radio; nobody's television, but it is Marconi wireless! Those who remember the *Titanic* will never forget!

Guglielmo Marconi brought everlasting glory to Italy. He was one of two Italians possessed of the idea of encircling the earth; one with sails, the other with sound.

Three hundred and eighty-two years after Christopher Columbus excited the imagination of the fifteenth century, Marconi was born, destined to thrill the twentieth century to the utmost as did the Genoese sailor before him. Columbus voyaged in the age of silence. His was an adventure of dangerous solitude on an ocean believed to be flat. From Spain, scoffing mariners watched his sails drop over the edge of the earth, gone forever, but like some phantom he returned over a rounded sphere to tell the strange story of new lands over which he had unfurled the royal banner of Spain. He lived unaware that he had stepped upon a new continent. He died believing that he had sailed around the world to Asia.

Now, across an invisible sea of "ether" there lay hidden an unexplored continent in science. He who discovered it would find a short path to the Indies and to every city and hamlet on the face of the globe. The scoffers said no; by mathematics they attempted to show how the curvature of the earth, the very thing that Columbus proved, would stop such signals if ever hurled against the horizon by some man-made machine. They argued the world would have to be flat if such waves were to go far; they knew, however, the earth was an inter-stellar ball.

Science called upon Italy for a genius.

Had not the gifted Roman, Strada, fascinatingly antici-pated that from Italy would come wireless, when in 1617, he published his "Prolusiones"? He envisaged two friends corresponding by the aid of "a certain loadstone, which had such virtue in it that if it touched several needles one began to move, the other, though at never so great a distance, moved at the same time and in the same manner." Each owner of such a needle-device was portrayed adjusting it to a dial plate with the letters of the alphabet disposed around its rim. When they wished to converse one of them spelled the words, and they were reproduced at any distance by the sympathetic needle of the other.

Significant prophecy!

In the ancient city of Bologna lived the dignified Giuseppe Marconi, an able business man and gentleman of inde-pendent means, known among his neighbors as "the lightest-hearted and best-natured man in the town." [1] His first wife was of the Renoli family. She lived only long enough after

_____
[1] Died, March 27, 1904, Palazzo Albergati, Bologna (winter home).

her marriage to bear a child—a son, Luigi. In later years as a public servant he won the esteem of his native city in various capacities, finally being elected councilman on the strength of his personal charm and popularity among the people. By trade he was "an expert agriculturist."

Giuseppe Marconi's second marriage in 1864 at Boulogne-sur-Mer was with a blue-eyed, keen-witted Irish girl, Anna Jameson, youngest daughter of Andrew Jameson of Daphne Castle and Fairfield, Enniscorthy, County Wexford. The Jamesons were well-known whiskey distillers of Dublin. On the other side of her family she was related to the Scottish family of Haig. Anna went to Bologna to study music at the conservatory; she found love also.

Two children were the issue of this union: Alfonso, born November 22, 1865,[2] and Guglielmo, who nine years later first saw the light of day on April 25, 1874, in the massive, heavily shuttered Marescalchi Palace (now Orlandini Palace), Via Tre Novembre 5, near the center of Bologna and not far from the city hall. Guglielmo was baptized a Catholic in the Church of St. Peter at Bologna; his father was of the Catholic faith, his mother of the Protestant.

"Che orecchi grandi ha!" (What big ears he has!) exclaimed an old servant of the house on seeing the little stranger for the first time. And what historic sounds they would hear when science tapped on their drums!

Time was all he needed. Here was an Italian born with a secret; in that drowsy bambino's dreams and in the solemn silence of the ether, wireless was lost. The world in 1874, plunging toward a century of greater speed and tumult, was more concerned with current schemes in the minds of men. What mattered another Italian baby born of an Irish mother? That was not news. Here's what the telegraph clicked on that day for the presses to print:

[2] Died, April 24, 1936, heart attack in London.

April 25, 1874—President Grant vetoed inflation. That was the big story of the day in America. . . . Then more dots and dashes, "the King of the Fijis formally ceded the islands to England." . . . In New York, "Very respectable clergymen were discussing the temperance movement and the nature of wine used at the feast of Cana." . . . Over in London Victoria was Queen; Mr. Gladstone made a speech reviewing the budget; Disraeli spoke about war rewards in the House of Commons. . . . In New York the Italian opera "Don Giovanni" was sung at the Academy; Barnum's New Roman Hippodrome was in full swing "lit up with a galaxy of lights, a dazzling appearance." . . . A surveying expedition was examining the proposed route for an inter-ocean canal across the Isthmus through the State of Nicaragua. . . . Britain was building twenty-seven vessels-of-war, the largest the *Inflexible*, 11,165 tons, and the *Fury*, 10,950. . . . From Albany came the news that the Senate passed the Brooklyn Bridge bill. . . . Sermons of Henry Ward Beecher were published in New York. . . . In Washington Congress appointed a committee to report on the desirability of establishing a postal telegraph system in the United States. . . . Opposition was rife in the forty-third Congress against a proposed item of $2,000 to provide horses and carriages for the Department of Justice; a Senator recalled an old Spanish proverb, "Put a beggar on horseback and he will ride to the devil." . . . Two widely discussed topics in the news were cremation as a great reform, and the "invention" of oleomargarine as a threat to butter.

Such was the world and its problems on the day Guglielmo Marconi first cried, cooed and whimpered a bit.

Columns and columns of news, long stories about people and things soon to wither in the news; not a single sentence about that boy born at Bologna, Italy. Too many others born the same day, and no way of telling if any one would leave more of a mark upon the world than greenbacks, rapid transit or Gladstone oratory. Time gripped the answer in a babe's clenched fist, which only the years could open.

No soul in all Italy had the slightest inkling of what was inscribed in the book of Life for this boy, else some fortune teller might have hastened to read the stars. But, it was just as well, for no one would have believed the tale could the lad's path have been charted from the cradle to the grave. It would have been too unreal; too unlike anything that had ever gone before in science. No one dreamed that the germ of a great scientific truth was hidden in that tiny head, back of those little blue eyes. Yet, Italian parents might well envisage accolades of science for each cradled son, for had not Italy presented Galileo, Galvani and Volta!

Who could have suspected that this babe "with no language but a cry," when grown to manhood would turn to the Pope in Vatican City and dramatically exclaim, "Be pleased, I pray you, let your voice be heard all over the world!"

The canopy of the heavens, the very emptiness of space far and beyond the spinning stars would be his laboratory as some day he moved to unmask a new science.

The story of this youth who hitched wireless to Italy's star is not that of the poor boy who climbed by sheer grit through misfortune and poverty. His life is no Horatio Alger from "rags to riches" yarn. It is the opposite; evidence that the rich man's son can strive and succeed.

Whether heredity or environment counts most in life matters not in this case, for Guglielmo Marconi was endowed with a richly balanced quality of both. Italo-Hibernian heritage is a rare combination which largely accounts for independent action, intensity and vision. From his Gaelic mother he inherited persistence, alertness, initiative and musical refinement; from his Italian father, the power of conception, indomitable will and accuracy together with a good business sense.

Guglielmo was very fond of his parents and was particularly close to his mother, who was a guiding factor in his life. Hers was an immense influence. He does not remember that she ever scolded him for youthful impulses for she was lenient as a rule, while the father was rather strict. Always with serenity the mother encouraged him in his studies and work. From her he inherited blue penetrating eyes and a cold countenance which concealed strong sentiments and emotions.

Boyhood was passed in the country at his father's extensive estate in Pontecchio, near Bologna, except for an interlude in London where he went with his parents when three years old. Old residents remember him as a delicate lad who shrank from rugged play, and early found his chief delight in books. There was quite a complete scientific library in Villa Grifone, the family residence, and he reveled in reading about steam engines and electricity; he learned all he could about them. Chemistry attracted him and he attempted to extract nitrate from the atmosphere. That helped to lure him into space! In the history books, men who interested him most were, Napoleon, Garibaldi, George Washington and Edison.

Here was a boy of surpassing imagination, foreordained to venture far to the Antipodes and out across the frontiers of the planet. He would go off the beaten paths of science; his vision would influence the subsequent course of history and the lives of his fellowmen. But none of the neighbors suspected it.

Marconi never attended public school. His tutor on the parental estate was Germano Bollini, a grammar-school teacher of Pontecchio. When the family sojourned to Florence or to Livorno for the winter an instructor was engaged so the boy's studies would not be interrupted. When seven years old he attended the "Istituto di Cavallero Via delle Terme," at Florence. Some years later at Livorno he met Professor Vincenzo Rosa under whom he was initiated into the study of physics at the request of Signora Marconi, who was amazed at her son's passion for anything pertaining to electricity.

These winter migrations, made chiefly to dodge the severe weather at Bologna, because of Signora Marconi's health, were extremely educational for young Marconi. It was at Bologna, however, that he met Professor Augusto Righi of the University of Bologna, where Dante and Petrarch had studied and Tasso stood trial for his gall-dipped pen. Marconi was never a student at this or any other university. Nevertheless, both Rosa and Righi were attracted by the ardor the young man put into his studies, and by his intense interest in science.

After Marconi learned something of electromagnetic theories it did not take long for him to realize he was confronted with a jigsaw puzzle. All mixed up; all in tiny pieces, yet each fragment of utmost importance to some one who would fit ideas and devices into a finished picture—a practical system of communication for signaling through space without the use of connecting wires. Before this youth were strewn the pieces of a problem as cut out of electrical science by noted theorists and experimenters. A visionary with a practical mind was needed to put them together.

The young Italian observed a marked difference between Hertzian oscillations and ordinary alternating currents which had attracted the attention of several experimenters. This was the Marconi explanation:

An analogy may be found in the case of a sound wave in the air. The swing of a bell in a church steeple to and fro will produce no wave and further no sound. But if the rim of the bell is struck

Marconi, his father, mother and brother Alfonso in the park at Villa Grifone.

with a hammer, it affects the air with sufficient suddenness to make a sound.

Hence it appears absolutely clear to me that there is no Hertzian wave telegraphy without the essential feature for producing Hertzian waves, which is the Hertzian spark.

Static or atmospheric electricity aroused his curiosity. He had read about Benjamin Franklin's experiments with a kite during a thunder storm, and how Franklin proved lightning to be electricity. He studied Franklin's letter to the Royal Society of London, in 1750, in which he suggested, "electrical fire might be drawn silently out of a cloud before it came nigh enough to strike."

In a reminiscent mood he told how as an inquisitive youth, he once erected a spear-like zinc contraption on the roof and connected it to apparatus inside the house. When sufficient static electricity was collected a bell jingled. He was always on the watch for electrical storms, but when fellow students laughed at his bell-ringing alarm, Marconi "closed up like a clam and went fishing." That was his great sport; he had the patience of an expert angler. Next to fishing he liked to ride horseback and travel; they were his hobbies, so his brother Alfonso recalled, until wireless came along, but even that did not dim his love for travel, especially at sea.

This "fisherman" and traveler at the age of twenty was ready to embark on an invisible sea on which no bearded savant had ever traveled.

The summer of 1894 found Guglielmo and Luigi in the Italian Alps on vacation. While enjoying leisure in the mountains of Biellese, the younger of the two Marconis happened to pick up an electrical journal in which appeared an article describing in detail the work of Hertz, who had died in January of that year. The story told how Hertz radiated electromagnetic waves with an electric oscillator he had developed, and how little sparks appeared in the tiny gap of a metal loop across the room, although there was no connecting link except the air. There was the germ of an idea and Marconi had time up there in the mountains to think it over. Why not use these Hertzian waves for communication? If they could leap across a room they might cross a town, a country, a continent—perhaps the oceans!

"It seemed to me," said Marconi in a lecture years later, recalling those thought-provoking vacation days in Biellese mountains, where he worked the idea out in his imagination, "that if the radiation could be increased, developed and controlled it would be possible to signal across space for considerable distances. My chief trouble was that the idea was so elementary, so simple in logic, that it seemed difficult to believe no one else had thought of putting it into practice. I argued, there must be more mature scientists who had followed the same line of thought and arrived at almost similar conclusions. From the first the idea was so real to me that I did not realize that to others the theory might appear quite fantastic."

Throughout that summer in the Alps, Marconi's brother found him always figuring and sketching queer-looking diagrams that looked like the hieroglyphics of some unborn race, for Marconi was no artist; he had no talents for drawing or painting; in fact, his wireless hook-ups had to be supplemented by verbal or written explanations. All summer long the dream of wireless floated vaguely, ever changing like a chameleon. The idea that had shaped in his mind's eye made him restless. Dreaming day and night of signaling with electric waves, he confessed, "the idea obsessed me more and more in the mountains of Biellese." When he left for home he followed a vision embedded in his mind. Something new in electricity—a winged spectre had beckoned to a restless youth. Irresistibly he followed it.

Upon arrival early in the autumn at Villa Grifone in Pontecchio, he lost no time in going to his third-floor workshop —the first Marconi laboratory. Within a month or two he was ready to test the idea. The results, however, were not so spectacular as the dream.

The spark sputtered across the induction coil's gap faithful to the laws of physics, but there was no sign of electrical life at the receiver, as there had been in the scheme that buzzed in his mind. Some one with less confidence in science might have thought the idea but a mystification after all. Not so with this young man. He rearranged the instruments again and again for other tests but all were disappointments.

It was autumn in 1894. And looking back to those portentous days he declared, "Ma non mi persi di coraggio"— "But I did not lose my courage."

Work, work, work, day and night, in fact, he lost interest in everything else. His mother became worried at the drawn, wan face; his eyes revealed the need of sleep.

Alfonso was his assistant; so were the peasants on the estate. Alfonso always delighted in telling the story of the beginning of wireless. The years never dimmed his memory of those historic days in the Marconi "backyard." Only a few days before his sudden death in the spring of 1936, he recalled the story of how his brother actually made many different tests before the electric "buzzes" really indicated they were "going places."

After having worked for a month or more to perfect the instruments, Guglielmo invited his father and mother upstairs, and in Alfonso's presence too, the "wizard" demonstrated that he was able to ring a bell on the ground floor by pressing a button on the third floor without any connecting wires.

A few days later and signals were transmitted from one end of the house to the other; then from the house to the lawn. Wireless was on its way! Signora Marconi, although it was all a miracle to her, was firmly convinced that her boy was playing no prank. The father scratched his head; he wanted to figure it out. There was too much mystery in it for him. If there was any trick in it he would find out. He suggested that Guglielmo send the Morse letter "S"; he would go to the receiver on the lawn, and if the machine tapped off three dots he would be sure the magic worked through the air. And it did!

Signor Marconi was now more willing to lend financial assistance, so when prevailed upon by Signora Marconi, Giuseppe contributed 5,000 lire (about $1,000) to the cause of wireless. With this financial assistance from his father and the moral support of his mother, the "boy" inventor, in the spring of 1895, was ready to test wireless in the wide open spaces, and, if successful, offer it to the world.

On the work bench, close to the "laboratory" window of his father's villa, Marconi had built his first sending station. From that secluded spot, where he had spent hour after hour, had come the frequent requests for money to buy long lengths of copper wire, batteries, induction coils and other electrical gadgets. More than once the father had wondered what was going on up on the third floor of his home. He was by no means alone in doubting that messages could go through the air, nevertheless, he had grumblingly financed his son's queer notions. But now he had more faith; seeing and hearing were believing to him. He had seen the sparks; he had heard the clicks at the receiver!

Nothing could stop the Marconis now. Again and again Guglielmo tried to make the ether "talk" by using different arrangements of the instruments, but always utilizing the induction coil as the Hertzian wave emitter, and the ball discharger or gap described by Professor Righi in his scientific papers. It consisted of four brass balls separated by small gaps and immersed in vaseline oil. To control the electric discharge across the gap a telegraph key was wired in the primary circuit of the induction coil. This enabled him to cause sparks to leap the gap in dot-dash form, corresponding, of course, to the length of time the key was held down.

After the indoor tests across the length of the house, and then to the lawn, Marconi moved the paraphernalia further out in the garden, hopeful that experiments in the open might prove that wireless could cover a longer distance. This was a lucky step. In rearranging the equipment and in adapting it to outdoor conditions an important advance was made. Instead of employing the two rods of the Hertzian oscillator, one terminal of the "spark" discharger was connected to a metal cylinder or elevated conductor on top of a pole. The other terminal was attached to a metal plate on the ground. This gave Marconi an elevated aerial discharge across the gap to the earth, greatly increasing the signal strength, the range and reliability. Wireless by this step definitely went out of the "laboratory" and into the air. Now there seemed to be no limit to what the embryonic sparks might do and where they might go. The secret of covering greater distance was to "pump" more power into the waves.

Maxwell, of course, had "found" the ether; Hertz, the waves. Marconi enlivened the "ether" by making the waves more powerful, and he supplied a missing link in wireless— the receiving instrument.

Obviously, if the waves were to be utilized for signaling they would have to be converted into sound after having traveled through space. Maxwell had done nothing about that, neither had Hertz. The incoming impulses were high-frequency currents; vibrating many times in a second, so rapidly that the unaided human ear could not perceive them. A machine was needed to detect the waves; to rectify or change the signals into low-frequency currents capable of operating a device that would record them and put such mystic whispers of science within man's range of hearing. This called for even more ingenuity than flashing the sparks, the basic trick of which Hertz had revealed.

Marconi in his studies of electro-physics had learned that Edouard Branly, Professor of Physics at the Catholic University in Paris, had won distinction by studying the observation, first made by Calzecchi Onesti of Italy, that the conductive effect on metallic filings in a small glass tube, caused by an electric discharge in the vicinity, persisted after a comparatively long period, but quickly disappeared if subjected to mechanical shock. Sir Oliver Lodge called the device a "coherer." Marconi adopted it as a wireless detector. He erected an antenna at the receiving end, similar to the transmitter's elevated aerial, and connected the wire to the earth through the coherer.

As designed by Marconi it was a small, fragile-looking glass tube about the thickness of a thermometer and about two inches long. The silver plugs were so close together that a knife blade could scarcely pass between them; yet, in that narrow slit electrical magic was performed. Fine nickel dust nestled in the slit. These particles enjoyed the strange property of being alternately conductors and non-conductors for the Hertzian waves. They were good conductors when welded into a continuous metal path by a passing current. They were poor conductors when they fell apart under the blow of a little tapper, such as used to ring an electric door-bell. The tapper arrangement was known as a decoherer.

The practical operation is interesting: When the signals came down the antenna wire and struck the coherer the dust particles of metal cohered (hence the name); the tapper's tiny hammer hit against the glass tube. That blow decohered the metal particles, stopping the current flow from a local battery. Each successive impulse reaching the antenna

produced the same phenomena of coherence and deco-
herence, hence the recording of dots and dashes on a Morse
receiving instrument.

Marconi soon found the coherer was erratic. He realized
it would have to be improved or a more sensitive device
invented before wireless could hope to go very far and be
dependable. He sought a modification of the Branly instrument to improve the sensitivity. First, he tried a smaller
glass tube and shortened the slit in which the metallic filings were located. The mixture was changed by using
finely sifted particles, 95 percent nickel and 5 percent silver. Branly and others had concluded that copper, iron,
brass, zinc and similar metals responded best to the sudden
increase in conductivity. Marconi's new nickel-silver combination showed promise of being the most sensitive detector yet devised.

Now for a test across "long" distances—beyond the
garden!

The receiving station was carried out to a hill 1,700
meters from the window of the wireless room of Villa Grifone, so the inventor might keep an eye on the entire "expanse" he hoped to cover. At the receiver he stationed
Alfonso and told him to wave a flag should he see the
coherer's hammer tap three dots, the Morse letter "S."
Marconi touched the telegraph key and immediately his
brother's flag waved.

Jubilant, but, nevertheless, mindful that wireless to be
practical would have to pass through all obstacles such as
mountains and buildings, Marconi moved the receiver to the
opposite side of the hill beyond optical range. He instructed
Alfonso to take a gun and shoot, if he heard the coherer
tap out a cricket-like sound. Again Marconi touched the
key, and instantly from beyond the hill, which was about
three-quarters of a mile in thickness, came the "salvo"—

the first salute to wireless! Giuseppe Marconi was summoned for a repeat performance, and when he walked back across the fields to the house, he was entirely stripped of skepticism.

Right then and there Marconi was thoroughly convinced that no obstacle on the face of the earth or distance could stop his wireless.

"A problem is always simple—when solved," he once remarked in talking about his early experiments. "To radiate the electric waves was not easy; there seemed to be a thousand and one things in the way. But from the beginning I aimed at interfering with the radiation from the oscillator, breaking the emission up into long and short periods so that Morse dots and dashes could be transmitted. My first success with the radiation problem came in December 1895; and I continued to work all winter on it."

And so he did; but he took very good care not to whisper a word to anybody who knew anything about physics until his first patent was applied for in June, 1896.

Monsieur Branly, in the course of a communication to the "Société Française de Physique" in 1896, made the following statement: "Although the experiment which I have always prospected as the main experiment of my study of radio conductors (battery element, iron filing tube, and galvanometer, making a circuit where the current passes after an electric spark has been flashed at a distance) is the image of wireless telegraphy, I have no pretense to have made this discovery, as I never thought of transmitting signals." (Bulletin de la Société Française de Physique, Résume des Communications, seance du 16 decembre, 1896, p. 78 du volume de 1898.)

Later, in 1905, in the August number of the French magazine, "*Je sais tout*," Dr. Branly published an article on the "Marvels of Wireless Telegraphy," in which he said: "a young scientist, Mr. Marconi, conceived the idea that since it was possible to produce and transmit through space electric waves, it might be also possible, perhaps, to pick them up at a distance and 'talk' as diplomatists would say. Mr. Marconi deserves the credit of having devised ingenious apparatus for picking up these waves, and of having done so, in spite of the doubts and denials opposed to his daring idea, wireless telegraphy was born."

Distance—that was the goal. How to annihilate it—that was the problem.

Marconi utilized the idea of concentrating the waves into beams, like the flash from a lighthouse. He placed the discharge gap of the transmitter in the focal line of a cylindrical parabolic reflector. The detector was in the focus of a similar reflector. This was the alpha of the famous Marconi beam; the prelude of world-wide wireless which some day would flash powerful streams of energy in desired directions. All that, however, would transpire in the years to come, long after the early Marconi reflector patents expired. The inventor concentrated on the task at hand. He made the sparks snap with greater vigor; the signals were clearer and more consistent at the receiver.

But he did not rush to proclaim the genesis of wireless. Quietly he worked to strengthen the signals. Day after day the experiments were repeated with this new miracle called wireless, so named because no wires were used to link the sending and receiving stations.

The spark of a new era in communication had flashed. The scintilla was bewitching; Marconi saw no end to the dazzling beam that projected into the future.

From that day on, the workshop room in which wireless was nurtured and the home-made instruments fashioned by the hands of Guglielmo Marconi, were guarded as a sanctuary by his devoted mother, until her death on June 3,

1920, at Harley House in London. And on the spot where Alfonso waved the flag as a white ensign of scientific triumph that would spread the gospel of peace and good will among the nations of the earth, there happens to be erected a stone cross, which incidentally, stood there long before Marconi was born, as a remembrance of a monastery once located on the spot; there the crusade of wireless began.

Bologna, the scene of it all, might well be described as the Middle Ages still alive. It is a town of beautiful churches, and to a visitor it seems quite the same today as it might have been had he walked into the town 500 years ago. Now, however, the automobiles in the narrow streets, never planned to accommodate motorized traffic, offer a unique contrast with the sidewalk archways designed to shade pedestrians from Italy's summer sun; the atmosphere throughout the town is one of leisure.

Bologna is on the map near the top of the Italian boot, slightly above the knee of the long peninsula that swings down from the Alps to dip its toe in the waters of the Mediterranean. Pronounced Bo-lon-ya, in the Middle Ages the town was called "La Dotta," meaning "the Learned," because of its university; "La Libera," because of the democratic institutions; and "La Grassa," because of the fertile soils and abounding wealth.

Twitching frogs' legs brought fame to the town, however, long before Marconi wireless. It was the home of Luigi Galvani, who, while experimenting with electricity flowing through the legs of a frog observed galvanic or "animal" electricity, which led to the invention of the voltaic cell or battery by Volta. But the eighteenth century research pioneers never imagined that some day a son of Bologna would give wings to the perplexing electricity and send it fleeting around the world with messages, music and pictures.

Bologna is a town in which invention thrives!

Old-timers like to tell an interesting legend concerning

the stalwart warriors of that community. The hero of the
story is a butcher, described as "too fat to fight but keenly
alert to the tortures of hunger." He believed in Napoleon's
logic that "an army travels on its stomach." So as the
defenders sallied forth against the Milanese, this ingenious
butcher converted a notion into a clever idea. He chopped
up beef, pork and veal and stuffed the seasoned mixture into
the intestinal tubing of a pig. That was not all. He made
his invention practical for soldiers on the march. He linked
the sausage together so that long strings could be hung from
the neck or wound around the waist. He tied this portable
food supply into short lengths for convenient rations. As a
popular idea it swept the world; appropriately, to this day
it is called bologna.

Up the lane-like streets of this historic town visitors go to
see the old Marconi home, the Marescalchi Palace on the
façade of which is a marble epigraph bearing this inscription:

Qui nacque

GUGLIELMO MARCONI

che su le onde della elettricita
primo lancio la parola
senza ausilio di cavi e di fili
da un emisfero a l'altro
a beneficio della umanita civile
a gloria della Patria

.   .   .   .   .

Il Commune decreto

P

MCMVII

(Here was born Guglielmo Marconi, who
on the waves of electricity, first threw the human word
without the aid of cables and wires
from one hemisphere to the other, to
the benefit of the civilized world, for
the glory of the Fatherland.—By order of the
Municipality 1907)

At Pontecchio, one finds Villa Grifone, high on a hill over-looking the village, the same today as when wireless first sputtered beneath its rafters and through the thick walls. It is a heavy structure, three stories high with green blinds on the windows to keep out the heat of summer and the wintry blasts that sweep down from the Apennines. There is really no attic, in the American sense of the word, al-though fiction has pictured the boy Marconi toiling at his workbench under the shingles. That is not quite true.

The spacious, but now empty and neglected room on the third floor, used as the first Marconi laboratory, once served as a storage place for silk cocoons gathered on the sur-rounding farms and purchased by Marconi's father for profit. The chamber where Guglielmo slept as a boy may still be seen on the second floor, and from this room he could run up a back stairway to his workshop. From the windows he had a magnificent view of the Apennine ridges.

In the garden, facing the front entrance there is a large water fountain that adds a note of distinction to the place. The atmosphere is as peaceful and quiet as it can be. One hears the birds singing, and only once in a while a train is heard rumbling by on the Bologna-Florence tracks. From the distance the bells of a small Pontecchio parish church echo across the extensive estate.

Easy access to the Marconi home is gained from the main road. The visitor drives up to the top of the hill where house No. 126 is located. It is an imposing property, obvi-ously belonging to well-to-do people, although today the house is not so well taken care of as it probably was in the days of Giuseppe Marconi. Now, during the summer the old home is rented to vacationers from the city. The rooms are typically Italian with stone floors and only one large fire-place in the drawing room downstairs.

A marble commemorative tablet on the front wall of the
house, facing the village of Pontecchio, is inscribed:

Onore al merito di Guglielmo Marconi il quale in questa casa
facendo le prime prove ancora giovanetto col suo ingegno e collo
studio invento il telegrafo senza filo nell'anno 1895 ammirato dall'
Italia e dall' Europa.
(Honor to the achievement of Guglielmo Marconi who, still a
young man, making the first tests in this house, with his genius
and constant endeavor invented wireless telegraphy in the year
1895 admired by Italy and Europe.)

In this age only a few may be found in Bologna who remember Marconi as a youngster, among them a farmer
Antonio Marchi who, as an attendant on the Pontecchio
estate, helped Marconi carry the apparatus to various parts
of the garden during his first experiments. Now at the age
of ninety-three he lives with his wife, age eighty-seven, in
Calderara, Reno, near Bologna. He knew Guglielmo when
the lad was fourteen, and remembers him as "a very solitary
boy."

The patriarch never forgot how Guglielmo as a boy joked
and teased him, because he could not understand a word of
English, when he happened to be within range of conversation between Mrs. Marconi and her son. Signora Marconi,
however, could speak Italian quite well. And her son, even
in later life, is still familiar with the native Bologna dialect,
although there have always been slight traces of English
accent in his Italian. This is believed to explain partly why
he never associated much with other boys, besides being of
solitary character by nature. Those who know him intimately, and they are very few, say he has never changed
much in this respect.

Marchi, the old peasant, says that Marconi had few if any
school companions, in fact, he never seemed to have any
close friends in his boyhood years. Mostly he kept by

himself and enjoyed riding horseback over the hilly country and visiting neighbors. The old farmer remembers that Guglielmo would also climb the plane trees in front of his father's house and on several occasions was found asleep amid the heavy branches.

The boy, through manhood and fame, always had a warm spot in his heart for his old friend Marchi, who had done odd jobs to assist him put wireless in the air. As a mark of appreciation on the farmer's ninetieth birthday on July 15, 1935, Marconi sent a gift of 1,000 lire in cash, also his autographed picture.

And as Bassanio spoke to Antonio, the inventor of wireless might have inscribed, "I did receive fair speechless messages."

II

SECRETS OF MARCONI'S SUCCESS

THE trump cards of a new science had been put into Guglielmo Marconi's hands. He played them with the intuition of a genius. The prize he won was wireless.

It was in the '90's. Science challenged. Destiny dealt the cards. Opposite the unknown Italian, Marconi, at this electric gaming table was the Englishman, Sir William Preece, at his right another distinguished Briton, Sir Oliver Lodge, and at the left Professor Augusto Righi of Italy. All were intent. The game was near the final trick.

All were experts taught by Maxwell and Hertz to know that every coveted scientific honor on earth, fame and fortune lurked in the cards they held. No four men ever played for such a stake. Edison, Lord Kelvin, Popoff, Tesla, Branly, Fessenden, Crookes and Fleming stood by watching every move. They, too, were skilled at this electromagnetic game. For years these rival men of science had gambled their time in pursuing mysterious clues that in the air was hidden an invisible opportunity—a rich scientific prize.

But they had had their chances. Marconi in his teens had studied their errors in the game; he profited by the way they had flipped their cards without success. Fate stacked the cards for him. Lady Luck directed his every move. As if inspired by a vision the invincible Marconi confidently laid down every card with the persistence and foresight of a victor about to be crowned champion. The prize was his. It was engraved "Marconi Wireless."

With scientific cunning Marconi had played the cards that

ingeniously assembled the scattered parts of wireless. He offered the world a finished product to be accepted or rejected. It was accepted universally, for it was as universal as the air breathed by every race on the face of the earth.

Marconi assumed nothing. Modestly he presented civilization with a revolutionary system of quick communication. No statesman ever had such power; no dictator ever waved such a wand over the public domain. With invisible threads of electricity he proceeded to establish his empire in the sky to endure as long as the earthly sphere spins on its axis. Although heralded as "the King of Space"—that vast expanse of unfathomed "ether" reaching out to the planets and beyond—he was no hereditary monarch.

Timeliness is one of the sharpest tools with which destiny carves a man's career. Fame and fortune often are missed by a mere whim—by a twist of fate. Guglielmo Marconi did not miss. He did the right thing at the right time. He stepped upon the dais of Time when Fate held out the diadems of opportunity to make his name immortal.

Too soon is as ill-fated as too late whether the scene be in scientific research, exploration or in politics. That truth runs through history. There is Leif Ericson, believed to have visited the shores of Greenland between the fifth and ninth centuries. Nevertheless, Columbus is heralded as the discoverer of the New World. Wireless also has its "Vikings," and it would be amiss to leave them out of the story.

Dr. Mahlon Loomis, an American, in 1865, showed how to set up what he called "disturbances in the atmosphere" that would cause electric waves to travel through the air and ground, thereby establishing wireless communication between two distant points. He described and drew pictures of a so-called "aura" around the globe. He named it "the static sea." Later, others found the term, "the ether," more convenient.

Loomis knew what he was talking about. The United States Patent No. 129,971 dated July 30, 1872, proves it. In 1866, he sent signals from Cohocton Mountain, Va., to Beorse Deer Mountain, Va., fourteen miles apart, and later for two miles between ships on Chesapeake Bay. The patent covered "aerial telegraphy, employing an 'aerial' used to radiate or to receive the pulsations caused by producing a disturbance in the electrical equilibrium of the atmosphere."

The "Loomis Aerial Telegraph Bill" requesting an appropriation of $50,000 was presented to the American Congress on May 21, 1872. The principle of operation was described as:

. . . causing electrical vibrations or waves to pass around the world, as upon the surface of some quiet lake one wave circlet follows another from the point of the disturbance to the remotest shores, so that from any other mountain top upon the globe another conductor, which shall pierce this plane and receive the impressed vibration, may be connected to an indicator, which will mark the length and duration of each vibration; and indicate by any agreed system of notation, convertible into human language, the message of the operator at the point of the first disturbance.

What better conception could one have of wireless?

Loomis conducted experiments with "kites covered with fine light gauze of wire or copper, held with a very fine string or tether of the same material, the lower end of which formed a good connection with the ground by laying a coil in a pool of water." [1]

This all happened prior to the birth of Marconi.

And when Marconi was but a year old, Thomas Alva Edison, in November, 1875, while experimenting in his Newark laboratory, observed new manifestations of electricity through mysterious sparks. The true import and practical applicability of these phenomena, however, did not occur to

[1] *Washington Chronicle,* November 1, 1872.

him despite enthusiastic investigations. Nevertheless, he deduced correct conclusions that the impulses were of an oscillatory nature.

It was while experimenting with a vibrator magnet consisting of a bar of Stubb's steel fastened at one end and made to vibrate by means of a magnet, that Edison noticed sparks coming from the cores of the magnet. He had observed a similar effect while working with other devices but always passed it, believing induction to be the cause. But the action seemed so strong on the vibrator of the magnet that he wondered if he was witnessing some "true unknown force." Curiosity led him to connect the end of the vibrator to a gas-pipe, and when he drew sparks from the pipes in any part of the room, he considered it good proof of a new force, the sparks of which were tell-tale clues.

Edison then built what was popularly known as his famous "black box" inside of which two carbon points formed a micrometer gap across which the mysterious sparks could be seen through a "window." It remained for Hertz, however, a more profound student of mathematics than Edison, to prove the existence of electric waves in space.

Edison, having noticed the tendency of the strange force to diffuse or broadcast itself in all directions through the air, and through various objects, named it "Etheric." The idea was quite widely ridiculed. Nevertheless, he had discovered an unknown phenomenon—that under certain conditions electricity would pass through space and through matter entirely unconnected with the point of origin. He was on the threshold of wireless. Its history might have been different had Edison realized what he had discovered; had he injected more power into the waves and applied a coherer to detect them. But he didn't. Marconi did.

Laboratory notes dated December 3, 1875, captioned "Etheric Force," record how "Charley Edison hung to a gas pipe with feet above the floor and with a knife got a spark from the pipe he was hanging on." The note books reveal Edison tried all sorts of stunts with frogs' legs and various instruments in an effort to unravel the mystery of the sparks.

Dr. George M. Beard, noted physicist, devoted considerable study to Edison's "find," and in a discussion of priority claims by others said that "thousands of persons, probably, had seen this spark before it was discovered by Mr. Edison," but they failed to suspect its meaning, and thus missed an important discovery. To which Dr. Beard added, "The honor of a scientific discovery belongs, not to him who first sees a thing, but to him who first sees it with expert eyes; not to him even who drops an original suggestion, but to him who first makes that suggestion fruitful of results."

Marconi did just that.

Dr. Beard pointed out: "If to see with the eyes a phenomenon is to discover the law of which that phenomenon is a part, then every school boy who, before the time of Newton, ever saw an apple fall, was a discoverer of the law of gravitation. . . ."

Edison took out only one patent on long-distance telegraphy without wires. It involved the principle of induction, and while not exactly wireless in the sense that Marconi developed it, nevertheless, it was a step toward progress. The application was filed May 23, 1885, but the patent, No. 465,971, was not issued until December 29, 1891.

"I have discovered," said Edison in the specifications of his patent application, "that if sufficient elevation be obtained to overcome the curvature of the earth's surface and to reduce to the minimum the earth's absorption, electric telegraphing or signaling between distant points can be carried on by induction without the use of wires connecting such distant points.

". . . At sea from an elevation of 100 feet I can com-

municate electrically a great distance, and since this elevation or one sufficiently high can be had by utilizing the masts
of ships, signals can be sent and received between ships
separated a considerable distance, and by repeating the
signals from ship to ship communication can be established
between points at any distance apart or across the largest
seas or even oceans."

Edison further claimed: "Collision of ships in fogs can be
prevented by this method of signaling, by the use of which,
also the safety of a ship in approaching a dangerous coast in
foggy weather can be assured. In communicating between
points on land, poles of great height can be used or captive
balloons. At these elevated points, whether on masts of ships,
upon poles or balloons, condensing surfaces of metal or other
conductors of electricity are located. Each condensing surface is connected with the earth by an electrical conducting
wire." He called the receiving instrument an "electromoto-
graph."

Drawings accompanying the Edison patent showed his
conception of high-pole aerials, on either side of a stream,
connected to the signaling apparatus, which included a telephone receiver, telegraph key and batteries; his drawings
also illustrated how boats might be equipped. Edison is said
to have referred to his device as "grasshopper" telegraphy.

Convinced by the first transatlantic wireless signal that
Marconi was the logical man to wear the wireless crown, and
to pursue the research, Edison sold his "radio" patent to the
Marconi Wireless Telegraph Company for what was described as "a small amount of cash and quite a little stock."

Standing back of Marconi "four-square," Edison associates
recalled the friendship of the two inventors, and said when
Edison sold his patent to Marconi in 1903 he did so for "a
song." It seems other interests tried to acquire the patent
but Edison because of his faith in Marconi and his belief in

the fundamental nature of his experiments, flatly refused. Edison, engaged in other lines of research, side-tracked his investigations of "etheric force." The patent became a bulwark in Marconi's defense in the courts, in fact, early associates of Edison have remarked that this patent on more than one occasion in litigation helped to "save Marconi."

Edison's discovery of "etheric force" stirred scientific comment on both sides of the Atlantic. The later experiments of Hertz caused a spotlight to be put on Edison's early work and many wondered why such an important observation had been so generally overlooked.

At a meeting of the Institution of Electrical Engineers on May 16, 1889, in London, there was a wide discussion on the celebrated paper of Professor (Sir) Oliver Lodge on "Lightning Conductors," and the chairman, Sir William Thomson (Lord Kelvin), made the following remarks:

"We all know how Faraday made himself a cage six feet in diameter, hung it up in mid-air in the theatre of the Royal Institution, went into it, and as he said, lived in it and made experiments. It was a cage with tin-foil hanging all around it; it was not a complete metallic enclosing shell. Faraday had a powerful machine working in the neighborhood, giving all varieties of gradual working-up and discharges by 'impulsive rush'; and whether it was a sudden discharge of ordinary insulated conductors, or of Leyden jars in the neighborhood outside the cage itself, he saw no effects on his most delicate gold-leaf electroscopes in the interior.

"His attention was not directed to look for Hertz sparks, or probably he might have found them in the interior. Edison seems to have noticed something of the kind in what he called the etheric force. His name 'etheric' may, thirteen years ago, have seemed to many people absurd. But now we are beginning to call these inductive phenomena "etheric.'"

Britain wondered, and rightly, why Sir William Preece or Sir Oliver Lodge was not crowned sovereign of wireless.

Preece for a long time had been at work upon the problem of telegraphing through the air where wires were not available. When the cable broke between the mainland and the island of Mull in 1896, by laying lines of wire on the two shores, he telegraphed by induction over the water and through the air, the distance being four and one-half miles. He sent and received 156 messages in Morse code. But, Preece conceded in a lecture at Toynbee Hall that the Marconi system was superior. Furthermore, the Preece idea was not applicable on board ships.

Lodge, too, contributed to wireless. He verified the Hertz experiments, and in 1894 demonstrated the Branly coherer as a detector of signals up to 150 yards. His work was confined chiefly to the lecture halls. He took out a patent, however, that showed how undesired waves could be tuned out by adjustments of devices at the transmitter and receiver. (This patent was later acquired by the Marconi Company.)

Marconi's own appreciation of Sir Oliver Lodge and his work in wireless is found in the remarks he once made at Central Hall, Westminster, at a meeting in honor of the noted English scientist:

"Sir Oliver Lodge is, as we all know, one of our greatest physicists and thinkers, but it is particularly in regard to his pioneering in wireless, which should never be forgotten, that we are all here to welcome him tonight. In the very early days, after the experimental confirmation of the correctness of Clerk Maxwell's theory as to the existence of electric waves and their propagation through space, it was given to only very few persons to possess clear insight in regard to what was considered to be one of the most important hidden mysteries of Nature. Sir Oliver Lodge possessed this insight in a far greater degree than perhaps any of his contemporaries."

Sir Oliver explained why he had not pursued wireless in the '90's: [2]

"I was too busy with teaching work to take up telegraphic or any other development nor had I the foresight to perceive what has turned out to be its extraordinary importance to the Navy, the Merchant Service, and indeed, land and war services too."

Similar stories ran through the story of invention. There is always one, so it seems, whose conception surpasses all others, although to the layman in later years the differences may appear slight. For instance, Professor Samuel Pierpont Langley of the Smithsonian Institution, Washington, D.C., introduced a machine to fly in 1897. But it was not until 1909 that the airplane was developed for human locomotion. Wright brothers did the trick. Again the early pioneer did not win the inventive crown.

At the turn of the century it was remarked that it was difficult to invent anything basically new in radio, and still more difficult to invent anything which did not have some bearing on or had not been preceded by an invention of Nikola Tesla. In 1891, at Columbia University, Tesla demonstrated the principle of tuning. He obtained patents on tuned circuits and claimed more than 100 tuning inventions. Nevertheless, it is called Marconi wireless; not Tesla wireless.

Why was Marconi selected as the one to be immortalized?

He admits there were pioneers who blazed the trail. Yet Marconi became a synonym for wireless. Eventually, the others are likely to vanish in the mist of the past, forgotten or recorded as "a probable historic personage." They may

[2] *Wireless Weekly,* September 26, 1923.

have lacked business acumen or the subtle art of showman-
ship.

Marconi was treated kindly by fate and those uncanny
forces that sweep men in and out of the arenas of politics
and science to crown a few, and brush others aside although
they seem to be so near and deserving of the garlands of
victory.

Those inventors, who are uncrowned, lack some almost
mystic element. Glory calls for more than invention. Timeliness is a vital ingredient. So is money. So is courage, perseverance and the will to win. Drama is paramount!

Marconi had money. Back of his modest and retiring
manner was a flair for the dramatic. He was a master showman, although few suspected it by his actions. To some
extent he frowned upon publicity, but in so doing gained
bountifully of its fruits.

Marconi could get things done and reach a commercial
conclusion. There is where many inventors fail. Furthermore, he wisely realized from the beginning that wireless
was no one-man job. He surrounded himself with expert
electricians; such specialists as Dr. Erskine Murray, W. W.
Bradfield, Dr. W. H. Eccles, Dr. Ambrose Fleming, Andrew
Gray, C. E. Richard and C. S. Franklin of short-wave and
beam fame. With an inflexible will, when headed for a goal,
Marconi drove everything and everybody associated with
him toward it. No one thought of failure.

All were spurred by an intense interest in wireless; a tireless energy and love for long hours of work. Tested by ad-
versity and disappointments they never lost confidence in the
elusive signals. Marconi never gave up. Skeptics could not
dent the armor of his faith. Always he plodded ahead under
the slogan, "Occorre progredire!"—"We must progress!"
He was endowed with a plastic power; he mastered circumstances.

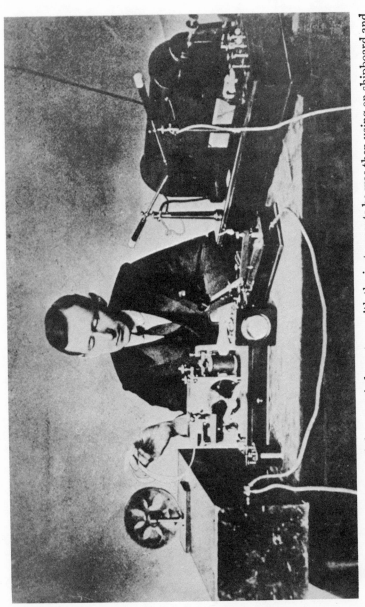

Marconi at the dawn of the twentieth century with the instruments he was then using on shipboard and at shore stations.

"Marconi's success may be summed up in patience and infinite persistence plus a great deal of natural ability," said one of his early associates. "I have seen him work thirty hours at a stretch. He hates routine business, and while he has a business sense he lacks administrative and organizing ability. He is no mixer; out of 700 on the Marconi staff probably not more than a half dozen knew him well enough to speak to him. He never cared for sports.

"I knew his brother Alfonso. He had none of Guglielmo's characteristics. He was a pleasant, amiable chap; a good-natured man, but you would never suspect they were brothers physically or mentally. Alfonso, however, was for years a director of all the principal companies of the Marconi organization. He was distinctly Italian; and so was Guglielmo, who possessed, moreover, a sharp inborn knowledge of the world.

"It was natural that an inventor of Marconi's personality and ability should attract the cream of the engineering crop. He had a fine collection of experts. George S. Kemp, an ex-Navy man, was his first assistant and remained with him until his death in 1933. Andrew Gray was Marconi's first chief engineer. R. N. Vyvyan, also on the engineering staff, was a graduate of a big university, perhaps it was Oxford or Cambridge; he was a society man with wide acquaintances in government circles. He jollied the officials when documents were delayed. We called him the red-tape breaker."

Marconi, himself, was credited with "opening new doors in the electric wing of the temple of truth." Dr. Jagadis Chunder Bose, the Hindoo, Professor of Physics in the Presidency College at Calcutta, and distinguished student of electrical radiation, foresaw, "all the special sciences marching abreast along the old Roman road of science which leads no one knows whither." And he espied an obstacle—a great high wall blocking the way in all directions. Upon the wall, as upon the wall in the palace of Babylon, he perceived "a strange and as yet unintelligible inscription—the mysterious word 'ether'.[3]

"What new and great discoveries lie beyond this wall no one knows," said Dr. Bose; "but more than one high authority believes that these discoveries will startle the twentieth century more greatly than the nineteenth has been startled. To suggest in the crudest possible fashion, how the ether is at present regarded by scientists, imagine that the whole universe, to the uttermost stars is a solid mass of colorless jelly; that in this jelly the stars, solar systems and space-worlds are embedded like cherries in a mould of fruit jelly. . . . In short, this jelly or ether is a universal substance so thin that it permeates everything in space on earth. Only by its quivering, only by the waves in it, which light rays and electric rays excite, are these rays enabled to travel and produce their various results.

"Strange to say, considering the number of brilliant electricians today, and the enormous amount of interest in electrical phenomena, it has been left to a young Italian scientist, Guglielmo Marconi, to frame the largest conception of what might be done with electric waves and to invent instruments for doing it."

> One ship drives east, and another west,
>   With the self-same winds that blow;
> 'Tis the set of the sails, and not the gales,
>   Which decide the way we go.

> Like the winds of the sea are the ways of fate,
>   As we voyage along through life;
> 'Tis the will of the soul that decides its goal
>   And not the calm or the strife.

REBECCA WILLIAMS.

[3] *McClure's Magazine*, March, 1897.

III

ACTS IN AN OCCULT DRAMA

QUICKLY the cry went up from several nations that Marconi was not the true inventor of wireless. The envious declared that the way had been paved for him; that he merely acquired and adapted what others had discovered. With their theories and devices, it was asserted, he had "invented" wireless.

The point they overlooked, however, was that no one despite all previous discoveries and instruments had ever assembled all the units to achieve Marconi's master stroke. He accomplished what no man had ever done; he had the courage and persistence to continue the conquest far beyond the initial invention. Experiments by others never fructified. Marconi was the perfectionist. He consecrated his life to wireless.

The law holds that it is no "black mark" against an invention if it is made accidentally, or in the course of experimenting with something else, provided only that the presence and nature of the thing is recognized. It is explained that "the patient labors of a lifetime and the unpremeditated flash of an original thought resulting in invention stand upon equal footing in character and merit in the realm of discovery." The wireless achievement, however, was no accident; it falls in the class of "patient labor" and "premeditated thought."

Marconi was quick to concede that wireless was no one-man job. He was mindful that the eternal quest to solve the

37

age-old riddle of light had led men of wisdom into the ethereal realm long before he was born. He never claimed that he discovered all there is to wireless, for he knew that before the world was ready for him, science had to disclose a clue that the pendent earth spins in a quivering mass of imperceptible jelly.

Some one had to observe that tapping with an electric finger would stir vibrations over a far-flung range—beyond the orbit of the moon. Genius had to discover in the Creator's plan a mysterious medium hidden until the twentieth century approached, when mankind's accelerated pace needed communication on a world-wide scale; more rapid than the mail carried by an ocean liner, faster than an airplane dispatch, quicker than the telegraph of Morse or the telephone of Bell.

"I have been an ardent amateur student of electricity," explained Marconi, "and for two years or more have been working with electric waves on my father's estate at Bologna.[1] I was using the Hertz waves from a modified form of apparatus for exciting the waves as used by Hertz. My work consisted mainly in endeavoring to determine how far these waves would travel in the air for signaling purposes. In September of last year (1896), working a variation of my own of this apparatus, I made a discovery.

"I was sending waves through the air and getting signals at distances of a mile, or thereabouts, when I discovered that the wave which went to my receiver through the air was affecting another receiver which I had set up on the other side of the hill. In other words, the waves were going through or over the hill. It is my belief that they went through, but I do not wish to state it as a fact. I am not certain. . . . I find that while Hertz waves have but a very limited penetrative power, another kind of waves can be excited with the

[1] Interview in *McClure's Magazine*, March, 1897.

same amount of energy, which waves, I am forced to believe, will penetrate anything and everything."

Several nineteenth century pedagogues had been entranced by what they called "the ether"—an invisible, odorless, tasteless substance believed to occupy all space. The original conception of this airy nothing is as old as Plato's time. Newton, Descartes, all the beacon lights of science through the ages, assumed its existence. It was a great convenience in bridging an infinite, unfathomed void.

By dropping fragmentary clues for man to behold science has a queer way of leading up to a master stroke. For example, Christian Huygens, a Dutch mathematician, in 1678, worked out a theory of undulation of light in an ether, which as a conveying medium might explain the phenomenon of light. Scientists and philosophers pondered over the problem. They wondered if inter-stellar space was filled with a substance, a sort of liquid-filling matter. Huygens seemed to strike a practical conception.

To pick up the long threads from which the odyssey of Marconi is spun it is interesting to note that a conservative Munich professor, K. A. Steinheil, predicted in 1837, "wireless communication will soon be possible." The prophecy was so startling that his colleagues are said to have questioned the sanity of the prophet. He added nothing, in fact, he refused to qualify or to retract his statement. Had he divulged further the thoughts running through his mind he might have gone down in history as the Jules Verne of space. And all because the alert professor accidentally discovered while experimenting with a telegraphic apparatus using two connecting wires, that the instrument clicked although one wire was disconnected.

Joseph Henry, an American physicist, developed an electromagnet as invented by William Sturgeon of England, and attracted considerable attention as an electrical experimentalist. The Henry magnet, incidentally, lifted 3,000 pounds. In 1842, at Princeton University, he observed that in the discharge of a Leyden jar the phenomenon was an oscillating one (alternating current), and further that the discharge would induce discharges in other circuits at considerable distances; he was observing the essential phenomenon of signaling through the air.

Then came the first big step toward wireless—Michael Faraday, in 1845, held to the Huygen undulatory theory by a firm belief in its eventual practical realization. Faraday began to experiment in order to seek definite proof of an all-pervading medium. He suggested the theory that the electrical action between two bodies was conveyed by lines of magnetic force through the ether. That was a radically new idea far removed from the old "elastic solid theory of light."

But Faraday did not mention wireless, and if there were any thoughts of such magic, they were overshadowed in 1858 when the Atlantic cable was dramatically proclaimed as the ultimate in communication between the continents, for how else could messages be transmitted unless a wire connected the two points? The cable was something more tangible than the ether, nevertheless, it was difficult for many to believe that such a long wire could be stretched on the bottom of the sea and enlivened with intelligence.

There were reasons for doubt. The first attempt to lay the cable in 1857 had been a failure; the next in 1858 was successful for a short time only, but long enough to permit President Buchanan of the United States to exchange greetings between the hemispheres with Queen Victoria of England. The third attempt to cableize the Atlantic in 1865 was a disappointment, but the next year the indefatigable Cyrus West Field succeeded.

The cable, however, did not distract all minds from the

"ether." Experimentalists who believed space might be set in vibration turned to the induction coil as a means of generating electromagnetic waves. The history of the induction coil goes back to November, 1831, when Faraday discovered the principle of induction. As time went on, various practical applications for the coil were foreseen.

H. D. Ruhmkorff, a Russian working in Paris, in 1853, added an automatic interrupter to the coil; insulated the secondary and increased the number of turns of wire, thereby minimizing the possibility of breakdown. Utilizing a battery as the primary source of power, high voltages could then be generated. Armand H. L. Fizeau shunted a condenser around the interrupter, increasing the length of the sparks that snapped across the induction coil's gap-like mouth. By the time 1867 arrived suspicions were being aroused that man might some day actually send signals through the air, but there were more who scorned the idea than believed in it.

The Faraday conception of a field of magnetic force inspired James Clerk Maxwell, Professor of Experimental Physics at Cambridge, and later at the University of Edinburgh, to evolve the famous equation from which he predicted, solely by mathematical reasoning, the existence of ether waves. In what was called a masterful treatise on the electro-dynamic theory of light, he proved that light is one form of electromagnetic waves.

His logical equations concluded that electric waves were propagated in space with sunlight velocity. As an expert mathematician he pointed the way to a new field of research, although in 1867 he had no method of generating or detecting the impulses.

Maxwell found the ether.

The task of causing the vast ethereal sea to ripple and wave under the influence of electricity remained for Heinrich Rudolph Hertz, born in 1857. At Berlin University, in 1878, he enrolled as a student under the distinguished scientist, Hermann L. F. Helmholtz, who developed the static or friction machine.

The youthful Hertz was attracted by the Maxwell theory and became convinced that if a conductor were charged or discharged suddenly, electromagnetic waves would radiate into space. He went to Kiel in 1883 as Professor of Theoretical Physics, and, while lecturing, he experimented with two flat coils linked by wire with a Leyden jar or condenser. He noticed the discharge of the jar through one coil, in which there was a tiny gap, induced a current in the other coil, despite the fact that they were not connected. This encouraged him to delve further into the mystery. He built a machine to generate and another to detect electromagnetic waves.

The transmitter was called an "exciter." It comprised two metal plates connected by rods to two metal balls about one-half inch apart. The rods were wired to the terminals of an induction coil's secondary. When the coil was electrified sparks jumped the gap between the balls.

The receiver or "resonator," as Hertz called it, was extremely simple, consisting of a circlet of wire the ends of the wire being connected to two small metal balls. This formed a loop with a micrometer opening in it. When the exciter was energized and sparks leaped across its gap, a spark was also seen to flow across the fractional gap in the resonator. Of course, the resonator was not far removed from the exciter, nevertheless, the simple experiment confirmed the Maxwell theory, and demonstrated the physical properties of electromagnetic waves.

Furthermore, Hertz observed that the law of this electrical radiation was the same as the corresponding law of optics. He proved Maxwell was right in his assertion that the velocity of electromagnetic impulses was the same as that of light.

Hertz had done much to prepare for the entrance of Marconi. Yet, this scientist, of whom Sir Oliver Lodge remarked, "He effected an achievement that will hand his name down to posterity as the founder of a new epoch in experimental physics," modestly stated: [2]

"The theory of electricity is so foreign to me, that I should almost like to chime in with the regular question: what is really the purpose of the whole nonsense?"

On a page of his diary, dated December 9, 1893, Hertz wrote: "If anything actually happens to me, you are not to sorrow but to be a little proud and to think that I belong to those especially selected, who live only briefly and yet live enough."

Four weeks later he died leaving behind a lasting monument to his memory—Hertzian waves. Of her son's innermost trait his mother said, "He was really not ambitious, only very eager."

Now, those who accepted the electro-dynamic theory of Maxwell were aware of an all-pervading ether. They knew from the work of Hertz that electric waves with a penetrative power could pass through the mysterious ether to be reflected and even polarized. They knew the waves traveled 186,000 miles in a second. But how could the trick be done if the transmitter and receiver were more than a few feet apart? How could it be done from room to room, from mile to mile, from city to city, from continent to continent? If Hertzian waves could cover all that territory and be converted into sound or print again at a distant point, then they could be used for signaling through space.

Conquest of the ether became international. Experimenters studied the scientific records of the past for clues that might lead to a device capable of detecting electric waves. They found that as far back as 1835 it was known

[2] *Short Wave Craft*, May, 1932.

that a mixture of tin filings and carbon were non-conductive of electricity but became conductive when the discharge of a Leyden jar passed through them. Also there were records to show that S. A. Varley, in 1852, noticed metallic filings when influenced by atmospheric electricity offered less resistance to the current. Several years later he made the first practical application of the principle in the construction of a lightning arrester designed to protect telegraph lines.

Professor David E. Hughes, in 1878, observed the discharge of a Leyden jar or condenser caused loosely associated zinc and silver filings in a glass tube, wired in series with a battery and telephonic earphone, to cling together or cohere.

Professor Calzecchi Onesti of Italy noticed that copper filings between two metal plates were non-conductors but quickly became conductive when under the influence of a high voltage discharge. Then, in 1881, Edouard Branly of France, contributed his famous filings tube.

A patent was awarded Professor Amos Emerson Dolbear, an American physicist at Tufts College, for a unique apparatus utilizing the induction principle to facilitate "electrical communication between two points, certainly more than one-half mile apart, but how much further I cannot say." That was in 1882.

Had not Professor Alexander Popoff of the Electro-Technical Institute of St. Petersburg, in 1895, used a coherer, battery, relay and tapper to detect approaching thunder storms? One end of the coherer is reported to have been attached to an elevated wire to intercept the "static," and the other terminal connected to the earth. When the metal filings cohered under the influence of the atmospheric electricity, caused by the lightning storm, they were automatically decohered by the tapper and restored to sensitivity. Popoff was close to wireless!

He expressed a hope that wireless telegraphy could be accomplished by the utilization of Hertzian waves, but as the courts later pointed out, "no one had described and demonstrated a system of wireless adapted for the transmission and reception of definite intelligible signals by such means."

Marconi did.

Edison had been witnessing another curious phenomenon inside an incandescent lamp. His curiosity was aroused by an electric current passing across the space between the hot filament and an adjacent cold metal plate. That was a breath of life for wireless; some day vacuum tubes would send streams of electrical energy circulating through the international arteries in the sky. And at the receiver this same sort of tube would detect and amplify the incoming impulses. Edison's patent stated a fact and suggested a tantalizing mystery, because even he did not pretend to know why the "effect" took place. His disclosure remained a laboratory problem for some one to apply to a new and practical field of usefulness. An English physicist—a wireless expert— would do it years later. But the principle went into history as "the Edison Effect."

When the calendar turned into the '90's more frequent predictions were heard from men of science that space might soon be used as a medium of invisible communication. Sir William Crookes contributed a remarkable prophecy to the London *Fortnightly Review* in 1892:

Here is unfolded to us a new and astonishing world, one which is hard to conceive should contain no possibilities of transmitting and receiving intelligence.

"Rays of light will not pierce through a wall, nor, as we know only too well, through a London fog. But the electrical vibrations of a yard or more in wave length . . . will easily pierce such mediums, which to them will be transparent. Here, then is revealed the bewildering possibility of telegraphy without wires, posts, cables or any of our present costly appliances.

Granted a few reasonable postulates, the whole thing comes

well within the realms of possible fulfillment. At the present time, experimentalists are able to generate electrical waves of any desired wave length from a few feet upwards, and to keep up a succession of such waves radiating into space in all directions.

This is no mere dream of a visionary philosopher. All the requisites needed to bring it within grasp of daily life are well within the possibilities of discovery, and are so reasonable and so clearly in the path of researches which are now being actively prosecuted in every capital of Europe that we may any day expect to hear that they have emerged from the realms of speculation to those of sober fact.

The stage was set in this occult drama for the entrance of a practical-minded scientist—a master magician who could juggle coils of wire, unleash electrical impulses and pull messages from the air, all in the twinkle of an eye. The queer-looking instruments and strange theories of the pioneers were but props assembled before the footlights of the scientific world. The trick was to make them work; to talk across the sea.

All very well to predict such miracles by mathematics. Theoretically, and on paper it might look quite feasible, but even the sages wondered what there was to prevent such electrical flashes from flying off the globe at a tangent like the sparks from a wheel? How could mute devices built by man cause the immensity of space to pulse with living sound; spoken words in any tongue—the symphonies of Beethoven; swirling images of people and places all criss-crossed through the sky at the speed of sunlight?

Impossible! But even so, by what fantastic chance could these waves be plucked from overhead to be turned back into the original sound and possibly into television pictures? At sunlight velocity they would be gone before man could snatch them. To do it would be witchery.

So reasoned those who called the idea but a whim-wham.

This thing called wireless was a miracle too wondrous for

Early receiving equipment which, with the simple coherer as a "heart," first felt the pulse of wireless.

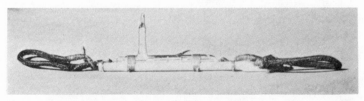

The coherer—first detector of Hertzian waves.

the mauve decade to grasp. The man to perform such wizardry in the span of a human life would be immortal.

In Italy a life had been shaping for the task. Tireless in play as a boy so was the youth in study and research. There was no end to his energy. Always he pursued the goal, no matter how puzzling or evasive. If Nature were ever caught off guard, this penetrating mind might go far to learn long protected secrets. The earth might be girdled in less time than the imaginative Puck in "A Midsummer Night's Dream," fancied it could be done in forty minutes! The unprecedented job cut out for this young Italian was to conquer space, shrivel the size of a 25,000-mile sphere and weave his fellowmen closer together in an invisible web of lightning-like communication; to make an international whispering gallery of the heavens.

IV

THE SCENE SHIFTS TO ENGLAND

MARCONI's youthful intuition and patience, his ambition and perseverance would carry him far. Having put the spark of life into wireless he offered it to the Italian Government, but the offer was not accepted. So following in the footsteps of Columbus, Marconi at the age of twenty-two left Italy to seek encouragement under a foreign flag.[1] Accompanied by his mother, whose method of doing things was English rather than Italian, he set out for London. Yet in their hearts both held a strong love for Italy.

"I first offered wireless to Italy," Marconi explained, "but it was suggested, since wireless was allied to the sea, it might be best that I go to England, where there was greater shipping activity, and, of course, that was a logical place from which to attempt transatlantic signaling. Also my mother's relatives in England were helpful to me. I carried a letter of introduction to Sir William Preece. Mind you, Italy did not say the invention was worthless, but wireless in those days seemed to hold promise for the sea, so off to London I went."

There he met Sir William Preece,[2] Engineer-in-Chief of the British Post Office, a man deeply interested in the possibilities of signaling without wires. Marconi told Sir William about the magic tin boxes or cylinders, and how he had discovered, "when these were placed on top of a pole two meters high, signals could be obtained at 30 meters from the

---

[1] First British patent, No. 12039 of 1896, described use of transmitter and coherer connected to earth and elevated aerial.

[2] Died, November 6, 1913.

transmitter"; and that, "with the same boxes on poles four-meters high, signals were obtained at 100 meters, and with the same boxes at a height of eight meters, other conditions being equal. Morse signals were easily obtained at 400 meters."

It began to look as if the higher the pole the greater would be the mileage. So the sky was the limit to this youth hot on the track of something stupendous. The urge for distance pushed wireless on to new goals just as it has enchanted explorers and astronomers.

Distance, distance, more distance, that has always been the call ringing amid the wireless signals since the beginning.

Now there were two gentlemen in London at this same time from different countries, to tell the same story—telegraphy needs no wires. And the messages will go through walls, houses, towns and mountains—even through the earth —on the wings of an electrical flash.

The Italian youth, aided by his cousin Jameson Davis,[3] was soon ready to begin experiments in London.

"When Guglielmo was a small boy, about six or seven years of age, I stayed with his parents for a short time in Italy," recollected Mr. Davis. "He was a bright, intelligent child, but, of course, no one suspected at that time or for a long time afterward that he would blossom into a genius.

"When he was twenty-two or three I was in considerable practice as an engineer in London, and his mother wrote asking if I could help him; I replied that I would be glad to do what I could if he came to London to see me. This he did very shortly after. His instruments were broken by the customs authorities, as they were not understood and were thought to be dangerous. New instruments had to be procured, and these we ordered on Marconi's specifications.

"When they were assembled and started to work, the pos-

[3] Died on Christmas Day, 1936.

sibilities of wireless telegraphy were very evident to me, and for some weeks experiments were conducted at my home in London; many prominent experts and others came to see them."

Among the notables was Sir William Preece. He welcomed Marconi and extended an invitation to use his laboratory. Britain was interested in this thing called wireless and was anxious to get to the root of it. This was fortunate for the Italian who otherwise might have encountered opposition from the British authorities. On the contrary, their cooperation was at his command and he installed apparatus at Westbourne Park.

Preece, in December 1896, lectured in London on, "Telegraphing without Wires." He described the Italian's magic and expressed complete faith in Marconi. He disclosed that he had been instructed by the Postal Department to spare no expense in testing the Marconi instruments and ideas to the fullest degree.

The Marconis, however, were not long in London when the Ministry of War in Rome declared that Guglielmo should do regular military service as all others. He had two choices: go to Italy and enroll for three years of military training and be completely distracted from his wireless experiments or remain in England and apply for citizenship papers, thereby evading Italian service. But he thought too much of Italy.

He went to General Ferrero at the Italian Embassy in London and explained the situation; he wanted to remain an Italian but he also wanted to continue the conquest of wireless. Ferrero was sympathetic and wrote to the Minister of the Navy, who luckily for Italy decided if the young man consented to conduct his tests under the auspices of the Italian Embassy, he could be attached to it as a naval student in training.

Marconi quickly agreed, and the demonstrations that followed for the benefit of the Post Office officials were highly successful. The signals first covered only 100 yards but later traveled between the General Post Office and the Savings Bank Department in Queen Victoria Street. Trivial distances, yes—but extremely important.

The next step was to establish stations at Penarth and Weston-Super-Mare. Between those two sites the sputter of wireless sounded more triumphant than ever as Marconi "pumped" more power into the mystic waves.

All of these English tests were so encouraging that the Wireless Telegraph and Signal Company, Ltd.,[4] was incorporated in England (July 1897), as the first commercial organization of its kind, the chief purpose of which was to install wireless on lightships and at lighthouses along the English coast. The capitalization, £100,000 was sufficient to acquire Marconi's patents in all countries except Italy and her dependencies. Marconi was given half-share of the capital and £15,000 in cash. Jameson Davis, who assisted in formation of the company, was appointed Managing Director, a position he held for two years.

Marconi, disappointed in Italy's lack of interest in his invention, nevertheless, did not yield the Italian patent rights to the English Marconi Company. More faithful to Italy than Italy was to wireless and to him, he wanted to be liberal to the land of his birth, the land over which wireless first vibrated. He felt that Italy in case of war might want to be independent of any foreign nation, so with his usual foresight he protected Italy in regard to wireless apparatus and patent rights.

The serious-mannered Italian youth, speaking with grave precision in his London home in Westbourne Park, made no claim whatever to being a scientist. He simply said that he

[4] Name changed to Marconi's Wireless Telegraph Co., Ltd., in 1900.

had observed certain facts and invented instruments to meet them.

"My work," he said, "consists mainly in endeavoring to determine how far these waves will travel in the air for signaling purposes. I am forced to believe the waves will penetrate anything and everything." [5]

Inquiry was made if fog would interfere.

"Nothing affects them," he replied. "My experience with these waves leads me to believe they will go through an ironclad."

What are you working on at present?

"Mr. Preece and I are working at Penarth, in Wales, to establish regular communication through the air from the shore to a lightship."

What length of waves have you used?

"Various lengths from thirty meters down to ten inches."

Why could you not send a dispatch from London to New York?

"I do not say that it could not be done," he continued. "Please remember wireless is a new field, and the discussion of possibilities which may fairly be called probabilities omits obstacles and difficulties likely to develop in practical working. I do not wish to be recorded as saying anything can actually be done beyond what I have already been able to do. With regard to future developments I am only saying what may ultimately happen; what, so far as I can now see does not present any visible impossibilities."

The interviewer concluded: "Such are the astounding statements and views of Marconi. What their effects will be remains to be seen. The imagination abandons as a hopeless task the attempt to conceive what—in the use of electric waves—the immediate future holds in store. The air is full

[5] *McClure's Magazine,* March, 1897.

of promises, of miracles. The certainty is that strange things are coming."

What is his magic? Proclaimed in a headline across the front page of the New York *World* [6] as "the boy wizard, an Italian lad of 23 years of age," Marconi described his invention and his faith in wireless:

"I am uncertain as to the final results of my system. My discovery was not the result of long hours and logical thought, but of experiments with machines invented by other men to which I applied certain improvements. These experiments were made principally at Bologna, Italy. I used the Hertzian radiator and the Branly coherer. The radiator was what would be known in telegraphers' speech as the sender and the coherer the receiver. Before I began the experiments these two instruments would send a message without wires a distance of from three to thirty yards, but there the power ended.

"The improvements which I made were to connect both receiver and sender with first the earth and second the vertical wire insulated from the earth. The latter was by all means the more important of the two innovations.

"At once instead of being limited to a few yards in results, I extended the distance over which a message could be sent without wires to about two miles. I found this principally due to the vertical wire, and speaking as simply as possible, I believe the following theory may explain why this was so.

"Everybody knows how sound is transmitted by means of vibrations of air. For instance, if you fire a cannon, the concussion produced by the explosion of the powder causes the air to vibrate, and so far as these vibrations of air extend just so far is sound audible. In other words, sound consists of vibrations of air. Well, my vertical wire carries the elec-

[6] August 8, 1897.

tric vibrations up into the air and produces certain vibrations in the ether, and these vibrations extend in every direction until they reach the receiving instrument. Thus a message can be transmitted through ether for as great a distance as you can cause vibrations to proceed.

"The original Hertz radiator worked on the same principle, but the vibrations its two brass spheres produced were very slight. My improvement magnifies them.

"An Italian scientist in speaking of the case said: 'The old Hertz radiator and old Branly coherer might be likened to the reed of an organ. By the Marconi improvements the pipe of the organ is added. The reed would make very little noise, but when you add the reverberant power of the pipe you get a great volume of sound. Marconi's connection of both receiver and transmitter, first with earth, second with air, supplies the pipe to the reed and makes the volume of vibrations great enough so that it will reach great distances.'

"As a matter of fact before I improved the receiver, it was impossible to end one pole of the transmitter with the earth and the opposite pole with insulated vertical wire. It was impossible to communicate intelligible messages even thirty yards, but after I had done these things, I succeeded in communicating from the Arsenal of San Bartolomeo at Spezia with an ironclad twelve miles away upon the water.

"I have no reason to suppose that this is the limit of the possibilities of the system. Indeed, I am sure that it is not the limit. What the ultimate limit will be I cannot say. I have no idea whether or not my system will ever be able to carry messages across the Atlantic, but for land purposes it will be a complete commercial success within a comparatively short time."

England still wondered what Sir William Preece, after association with this young man from Italy, really thought of him. Why should Britain be devoting so much attention to the foreigner when Preece and Lodge were already in pursuit of the mysterious waves?

Preece endeavored to clear up the matter when interviewed by the New York *World:* [7]

While I cannot say that Marconi has found anything absolutely new it must be remembered that Columbus did not invent the egg. He showed how to make it stand on end.

Marconi shows how to use the Hertz radiator and Branly coherer. He has produced a new electric eye, more delicate than any other known system of telegraphy which will reach hitherto inaccessible places. But enough has been shown to prove its value.

I have experimented freely with Marconi's instruments and I find for a certainty that they all proved of immense value to shipping and lighthouse purposes.

The next experiments, the historic dots and dashes on Salisbury Plain, proved the wisdom of Preece's remarks, and caused many others to agree with him. First, the signals flashed across 100 yards; then for a mile and a quarter; six miles and nine. Army and Navy officials were summoned to watch this demonstration. If any were skeptical when the tests began they left with plenty of evidence that wireless could speed through house and hill, and that neither brick, rock, earth nor wood could stop or block the subtle waves.

Surprisingly, Marconi was able to send the messages at Salisbury in a more or less definite direction. By aiming aerial reflectors he projected beam-like waves. The Hertzian energy was concentrated by a parabolic copper reflector or bowl, two or three feet in diameter, thereby shaping the waves into narrow strips, in much the same way that a searchlight stabs a streak through the darkness.

The waves measured about two feet from crest to crest instead of two or three hundred feet as previously used. The reflector results, however, were not so satisfactory as the results obtained with longer waves radiated from a pendant

[7] August 8, 1897.

wire. Naturally, at this time Marconi was more desirous of widespread coverage than limitation of range or area so he resumed his experiments with longer waves.

Lavernock Point and Breen Down, eight miles apart, were the scenes of the next demonstrations. One witness was Professor Adolphus Slaby, a German electrical scientist, who lost no time in carrying the news of what he had heard and seen back to his fatherland. In the summer of 1897, while Preece was busy bringing the attention of the Royal Institution to bear upon the miracles being performed, Professor Slaby was lecturing on wireless telegraphy before a royal audience that included the German Emperor and Empress, and the King of Spain.

Professor Slaby also contributed an article to the *Century Magazine* in 1898, from which these remarks are quoted:

In January 1897, when the news of Marconi's first successes ran through the newspapers, I myself was earnestly occupied with similar problems. I had not been able to telegraph more than 100 metres through the air. It was at once clear to me that Marconi must have added something else—something new—to what was already known, whereby he had been able to attain to lengths measured by kilometres. Quickly making up my mind, I travelled to England, where the Bureau of Telegraphs was undertaking experiments on a large scale. Mr. Preece, the celebrated Engineer-in-Chief of the General Post Office, in the most courteous and hospitable way, permitted me to take part in these, and in truth what I saw there was something quite new.

Marconi had made a discovery. He was working with means the entire meaning of which no one before him had recognized. Only in that way can we explain the secret of his success. In the English professional journals an attempt has been made to deny novelty to the method of Marconi. It was urged that the production of the Hertz rays, their radiation through space, the construction of his electric eye—all this was known before.

True; all this had been known to me also and yet I never was able to exceed 100 metres. In the first place Marconi has worked out a clever arrangement of apparatus, which by the use of the simplest means produces a sure technical result. Then he has shown that such telegraphy (writing from afar) was to be made possible only through, on the one hand, earth connection between the apparatus and, on the other, the use of long extended upright wires. By this simple but extraordinarily effective method he raised the power of radiation in the electrical forces a hundred fold.

Incidentally, Marconi had taken out German patents covering his invention. A year later, however, patents were granted to Professor Slaby, who had modified Marconi's aerial system, and developed in collaboration with Count Arco the Slaby-Arco system, which in 1903 was merged with other German wireless organizations into what was called the Telefunken system. There was bitter rivalry between Marconi and the Germans, but the former held the secrets of long-distance communication.

There was some talk by enthusiasts that wireless might replace the cables, which were expensive, and always in danger of destruction by upheavals at the bottom of the sea. And for the lonely lightships wireless was a boon. That had already been indicated. Wireless seemed to belong to the sea and its sailors.

"There must be a great saving by the wireless over cables," remarked a newspaper reporter.

"Judge for yourself," replied a Marconi engineer. "Every mile of deep-sea cable costs about $750; every mile for the land-ends about $1,000. All that we save, also the great expense of keeping a cable steamer constantly in commission making repairs and laying new lengths. All we need is a couple of masts and a little wire. The wear and tear is practically nothing. The cost of running, simply for home batteries and operators' keep."

While the controversy of wireless versus cable spread, strange antics were witnessed in various parts of England during 1897. Masts were temporarily abandoned while ten-foot balloons covered with tinfoil were sent up as "capacities." They might be efficient aerials, but they were heavy and required a strong wind. Gales, however, ripped them to slivers. Then long-tailed calico kites bedecked with tinfoil were entrusted to the winds. The atmospherics were none too favorable, nevertheless, signals broadcast from these lofty aerials covered about eight miles. The tests were made in the daytime, the experimenters being unaware that at night the range might be doubled if not tripled.

The kites offered interesting results, but Marconi soon realized such aerials bobbing up and down at the mercy of the winds were impractical, so in November 1897, at Needles on the Isle of Wight, he rigged up a stout mast to support a 120-foot aerial wire. It connected with a transmitter destined to radiate the first paid Marconigrams sent by Lord Kelvin to his friend George Stokes, and to Sir William Preece.[8]

Marconi, anxious to test the range of the Needles signals, hired a tug and went to sea with a receiving set fed by an antenna suspended from a 60-foot mast. For several weeks he tossed about on the water, all the time tinkering with the apparatus. When he returned to land the tests were reported successful, for he had heard the signals over a distance of eighteen miles.

Encouraged, Marconi built a new station at Bournemouth, fourteen miles west of Needles, but later moved it to Poole, which was eighteen miles away. The station was erected on the sand dunes of a barren promontory six miles from the town. Wireless from this transmitter vibrated with such strength that a Marconi engineer intercepted the signals at Swanage, several miles down the coast, by simply lowering an antenna from a high cliff, dispensing with the usual mast.

Marconi stations were visualized dotting the coastlines, because, even as the invention stood at this time, it would

[8] June 3, 1898.

be possible for all incoming and outgoing vessels within twenty-five miles of shore to broadcast position reports. So apparent were the advantages of the system that in May, 1898, the Lloyds Corporation negotiated for instruments at various Lloyd lighthouse stations; and a preliminary test was made between Ballycastle and Rathlin Island in the north of Ireland. The distance was seven and one-half miles, and the fact that a high cliff intervened made the communication all the more astonishing.

Wireless was on its way from England to the sea.

V

AS TRIUMPHANT AS A CAESAR

MARCONI'S renown was spreading. Newspapers were telling more and more about the young Italian and his work. New commercial possibilities were foreseen almost daily for the invention, in fact, the applications of wireless to business were featured in predictions as well as further scientific advances. For example, why should wireless not speed the news? It could flash dispatches from remote regions beyond the reach of telephone, telegraph and cable, and in more civilized areas the ether might supplement them.

Marconi saw the possibilities and he gave an inkling of what his invention might do in this respect, when in July, 1898, he accepted an invitation to wireless bulletins of the yacht races off the Irish coast.

Already he had conducted a series of experiments under the patronage of a French Commission between a station he built at Wimereux, France, another at South Foreland Lighthouse and a third on the French battleship *Ibis*. Both transmitters sent messages to the *Ibis*, the replies from which proved beyond doubt that messages could be sent and received from a station in motion.

It was the *Daily Express* of Dublin that introduced a new fashion in newspaper reporting by arranging to have the races observed from a steamer, the *Flying Huntress*, used as a mobile station from which Marconi should describe the progress of the yachts.

The wireless men were still laboring under the idea that the higher the aerial the better would be the results, so from a 75-foot mast they suspended an aerial wire, which they figured would radiate messages to Kingstown, even while the steamer was twenty-five miles off shore.

The receiving mast at Kingstown was 110 feet high. As fast as the bulletins were received they were telephoned to Dublin, enabling the *Express* to print full accounts of the contest as soon as the races were over, and while the yachts were far beyond the range of telescopes on shore. During the regatta more than 700 bulletins were broadcast to the printing press.

If wireless had failed in this test of its career the press might have lampooned it. But Marconi succeeded and won the backing of a powerful agency—the newspapers. Editors realized that wireless brought them news while it was still news on the spot where the event happened.

It was not long after this, that Marconi was invited by Queen Victoria to establish communication between Osborne House, on the Isle of Wight, and the Royal Yacht *Osborne* with the Prince of Wales aboard, in Cowes Bay. The Queen was anxious for frequent bulletins in regard to the Prince's injured knee. Marconi lost no time in installing the equipment. Within sixteen days more than 150 messages of a strictly private nature were transmitted with success, bringing new laurels to the young man from Italy and his so-called toy of the air.

By permission of the Prince of Wales several of the messages were made public:

August 4, 1898.

From Dr. Tripp to Sir James Reid.

H.R.H. the Prince of Wales has passed another excellent night and is in very good spirits and health. The knee is most satisfactory.

From Dr. Tripp to Sir James Reid.

H.R.H. the Prince of Wales has passed another excellent night, and the knee is in good condition.

These messages were intercepted by a vertical antenna suspended from a 100-foot mast at Ladywood Cottage on the grounds at Osborne House. The aerial on the yacht was attached to the mast, eighty-three feet above the deck. The lead-in wire ran down into the salon, one corner of which served as a wireless cabin.

Royalty aboard, notably the Prince of Wales, the Duke of York and the Princess Louise, anxiously watched the instruments that were talking back and forth with the shore. They marveled most at the fact that signals could be sent and answers received while the yacht was in motion. And even rain or fog did not stop them.

In the meantime the Needles station was becoming quite famous. Overhanging Alum Bay was the Needles Hotel alongside which towered Marconi masts braced against the winds as new symbols of safety for the men who went down to the sea in ships. From the halyard a wire dangled to a window of the wireless room, where seashore visitors caught their first glimpse of the flashing sparks as they enacted the mystery of talking through space.

Two matter-of-fact young men, whom a visitor described as doing something simple, adjusted the instruments. One of them worked a long, black-handled key up and down. Every time he touched it a bluish spark crashed and leaped an inch or more between two metal balls of a spark gap atop a large induction coil. He was saying something to the operator at Poole, eighteen miles away. It was a noisy machine but that seemed to add to the witchery and romance of wireless.

A short-lived spark jumped the gap when a dot was the

signal. The dash was a longer stream of the spark. One terminal of the induction coil was linked with the aerial lead-in and the other knob was connected with the "earth" to form the so-called "ground." Press a key, flash a spark and it was picked up miles away.

That's all there was to wireless in the beginning!

A guest at the station looked out across the water, which was dull under a gray sky. He found something uncanny in the thought that the young man at the key, who seemed as far as possible from a magician or supernatural being, was flinging his words across the waste of sea, over the schooners, over the feeding cormorants to the dim coast of England yonder down the map.

It all seemed so simple, but not so easy to teach the world how to do it.

Marconi was busy now at the Poole station, where he and Dr. Erskine Murray, one of his assistants, were trying to unravel more of the ethereal mysteries. It was there that Cleveland Moffett, an American correspondent found them; Marconi and his electricians granted one of their first interviews.

"How about the earth's curvature?" inquired Moffett.[1] "Or doesn't that amount to much just to the Needles station?"

"Doesn't it though," exclaimed an engineer. "Look across and judge for yourself. It amounts to 100 feet at least. You can only see the head of the Needles lighthouse from here, and that must be 150 feet above the sea. And the big steamers pass there hulls and funnels down."

"Then the earth's curvature makes no difference with your waves?"

"It has made none up to twenty-five miles, which we have covered from ship to shore; and in that distance the

[1] *McClure's Magazine*, June, 1899.

earth's dip amounts to about 500 feet," replied the electrician. "If the curvature counted against us then, the messages would have passed some hundred feet over the receiving station; but nothing of that sort happened. Therefore, we feel reasonably confident the Hertzian waves follow around smoothly as the earth curves."

"And you can send messages through hills" asked Moffett.

"Easily. We have done so repeatedly."

"And you can send in all kinds of weather?"

"We can."

"Then if neither land nor sea nor atmospheric conditions can stop you, why can't you send messages to any distance?"

"So we can, given a sufficient height of wire. It has become simply a question of how high a mast one is willing to erect. If the height of the mast is doubled, a message can be sent four times as far; if trebled the message will go nine times as far. In other words, the law established by our experiments seems to be that the range of distance increases as the square of the mast's height. To start with you may assume that a wire suspended from an eighty-foot mast will send a message twenty miles. We are doing about that here."

"Do you really think it would be possible to send messages from Eiffel Tower to New York through the ether and get an answer without ocean cables?"

"I see no reason to doubt it," answered one of the Marconi men. "What are a few thousand miles to this wonderful ether, which brings us our light every day for millions of miles?"

Royalty as well as news correspondents was becoming deeply interested in Marconi; wireless in war would be ideal for quick communication, unhampered by the enemy. Wires could be severed but there would be no means of cutting, shooting or blasting electromagnetic waves. Various nations were casting envious eyes on the Italian and his wireless.

Interviewers invariably asked, "In what direction do you expect your invention to be first utilized?"

"The first may be for military purposes, in place of the field telegraph system," replied the inventor. "There is no reason why the commander of an army should not be able to communicate easily with his subordinate officers without wires up to twenty miles. It would be equally useful for the admiral of a fleet."

Usually he was reminded that his system was not secret. The queries of the doubting public or military men, however, did not discourage him. He was aware that it was natural for many to believe lack of secrecy in his system was a drawback to its practical use on a large scale. Who would want their private messages eavesdropped upon by any one who owned a receiving set and understood the code? What good would such a blatant system be in wartime? The enemy could listen-in!

The inventor retaliated that Admirals, Generals and the public could always protect themselves by sending messages in cipher. Furthermore, the range of the signals might be restricted by lowering the aerial mast or by reduction of power output. On the other hand a boat in distress would want every one to hear its call. Laws might be passed to protect the contents of a commercial or even a private communication.

"I believe one of the greatest uses to which these instruments will be put, will be signaling in wartime," repeated Marconi, little realizing that in seventeen years a great conflict involving twenty-three nations would devastate the world while thousands of listening-in posts eavesdropped on every word and cipher that wireless carried through the heavens.

Do you use stronger induction coils as you increase the distance of transmission? he was asked.

"We have not up to the present, but we may do so when we get into the hundreds of miles. A coil with a ten-inch spark, however, is quite sufficient for any distances under immediate consideration."

Do you think you will be able to send directed messages very much farther than you have sent them already?

"I am sure we shall," replied Marconi. "It is simply a matter of experiment and gradual improvement, as was the case with the undirected waves. It is likely, however, that a limit for directive messages will be set by the curvature of the earth. This seems to stop the one kind but not the other."

And what will be the limit?

"The same as for the heliograph, fifty or sixty miles."

And for the undirected messages there is no limit?

"Practically, none. We can do a hundred miles already. That only requires a couple of high church steeples or office buildings. New York and Philadelphia with their skyscraping structures, might talk to each other through the ether whenever they wish to try it. And that is only a beginning. My system allows messages to be sent from one moving train to another moving train or to a fixed point alongside the tracks; to be sent from one moving vessel to another vessel or to the shore, and from lighthouses or signal stations to vessels in fog or distress."

Marconi foresaw one notable case where the directed waves might serve humanity.

"Imagine," he said, "a lighthouse or danger spot in the sea fitted with a transmitter and parabolic reflector, the whole kept turning on an axis and constantly broadcasting impulses in the ether—a series of danger signals.

"It is evident that any vessel equipped with a receiver could get warning, perhaps by the automatic ringing of a bell long before her lookout could see a light or hear a fog-horn. Furthermore, as each receiver gives warning only when its rotating reflector is in one particular position—that is, facing the transmitter—it is evident that the precise location of the alarm station would at once become known to the mariner. In other words, the vessel would immediately get her bearing, which is no small matter in storm or fog."

The English Lightship Service, having faith in Marconi's predictions, authorized in December, 1898, establishment of wireless communication between the South Foreland Lighthouse at Dover and the East Goodwin Sands lightship, twelve miles distant. The incentive was to test thoroughly the utility of the Marconi instruments. Those anxious for results did not have long to wait. A heavy sea battered the lightship on April 28, 1899, carrying away the bulwarks; the mishap was reported to shore and assistance was quickly dispatched. That might be called the first SOS. Two months later the steamer *R. F. Mathews* collided during a dense fog with the East Goodwin Lightship; wireless summoned life-boats to rescue the crew.

Practical and immediate applications of wireless were discussed far and wide. But there were still many skeptics. A professor at Clark University wrote to S. S. McClure and urged him to avoid announcing in his magazine such absurd-ities as wireless, for it made the periodical ridiculous. It was a source of relief for those who had confidence in Marconi to look back to the early days of the telegraph and tele-phone; they, too, had been ridiculed by doubting Thomases.

The astounding fact about Marconi is that he did not conceive wireless piece by piece or merely stumble upon each succeeding development. The very spark of his genius is embedded in his historic replies to interviewers in 1898. The answers he gave at this early date reveal that he foresaw wireless as it would be developed thirty or forty years later. And he would devote the next three decades of his life to polishing these ideas of the '90's and making them practical. He realized the importance of short waves and ultra-short waves. He had visions of the "wireless lighthouse," the radio direction finder and the radio beacon before the dawn of the twentieth century.

Reports went back to Italy, to the Government, to the Minister of Marine, to King Humbert and Queen Margherita. Italy, the land that sent its native son Columbus away to beg support from a foreign country would never make a mistake like that again. Yet, it was on the verge of doing so. The Italians foresaw the aggressiveness of the British and were quick to realize the folly of turning their backs on Marconi.

A "missionary" was dispatched to England to convince him that Italy had faith in him. Dinners were held in his honor and medals presented under Italian auspices, but by this time the Italian emissaries encountered resistance; jealousy on the part of the English Marconi Company to have Italy come upon the scene to capture the glory that had been nurtured under the Union Jack.

Eagerly, the Minister of the Navy dispatched a message to Marconi in England extending a flattering invitation to continue his research under the auspices of the Italian Government at the Naval Arsenal of Spezia. The cruiser *San Martino* was assigned to participate in the experiments.

Heeding the call, and delighted with the recognition of

his native land, the inventor of wireless, as triumphant as a
Caesar, returned to Italy.

> *Open my heart and you will see*
> *Graved inside of it, "Italy."*
> *Such lovers old are I and she:*
> *So it always was, so shall ever be!*
>
> BROWNING.

VI

FRANCE CALLS FOR PROOF

FRANCE called to Marconi in 1899. Could he send a message through the air across the English Channel? Marconi answered, "Yes," and left for France to prove it.

It was March, and all was ready for wireless to meet one of the most critical tests of its career. The "sparks" must leap from the little town of Wimereux, three miles out of Boulogne, to the cliffs of Dover. That was a long distance! Soldiers in ancient times had dreamt of digging a tunnel under the Channel to link the British Isles with the Continent, but no one had thought of talking back and forth across the water without the use of wires.

The French Government wanted Marconi to try this span. Electrical experts and government officials visited the station at Wimereux where Marconi and Jameson Davis met them and explained the installation, and what they believed could be accomplished.

Monday, March 27, was a momentous day in the history of wireless. At five o'clock in the afternoon Marconi pressed the sending-key that tapped out the first cross-Channel signal. There was nothing new in this for him except the distance! Months of work at the Poole and Needles stations had made wireless an everyday event in his life.

The transmitters and receivers used to spin the invisible thread to link England with the Continent were quite the same as utilized in previous experiments.[1] A seven-strand

---

[1] *McClure's Magazine,* June, 1899.

copper wire insulated from a sprit 150 feet high served as the aerial. The mast projected up from the sand at sea level, with no high cliff on the French side to aid in tossing the messages across the water.

Crack! flashed the spark under the master hand from Italy. All eyes seemed to glance anxiously out upon the sea as the spring gales lashed angrily against Napoleon's old fort that rose forsaken in the foreground. Would the message carry all the way to England? There was nothing in the confident, deliberate action of Marconi to reveal that it would miss the mark. Thirty-two miles seemed a long leap!

Suddenly, as if he sensed something in the air for him to lend an ear, Marconi signed-off with three Vs and stopped transmission. The room was silent. Every one was watching Marconi and their ears seemed to be strained more than his to catch some sound from the receiver. There was a pause but only for a moment, and then briskly the dots and dashes began to click as the tape rolled off the message.

"And there it was," said a guest who later described the historic scene, "short and commonplace enough, yet vastly important, since it was the first wireless message sent from England to the Continent: First 'V,' the call; then 'M,' meaning 'Your message is perfect'; then, 'Same here 2 CMS. V V V'; the *cms.* being an abbreviation for centimeters referring to the length of the spark, while V was the conventional finishing signal.

"And so, without more ado, the thing was done. The Frenchmen might stare and chatter as they pleased, here was something come to the world to stay. A pronounced success surely, and everybody said so as messages went back and forth, scores of messages, during the following hours and days, and all correct."

Marconi with a stroke of diplomacy was quick to acknowledge the debt of science to Branly, the Frenchman. He flashed this message:

Marconi sends M. Branly his respectful compliments across the Channel this fine achievement being partly due to the remarkable researches of M. Branly.

Two days later Robert McClure, magazine publisher, was at the Dover station. Cleveland Moffett was at the Boulogne terminal to hold cross-Channel conversation. To test the accuracy of transmission, Mr. Kemp who was operating the French transmitter, was handed this message which he clicked off the spark:

McClure, Dover: Gniteerg morf Ecnarf ot Dnalgne hgourht eht rehte—Moffett.

This meant, "Greeting from France to England through the ether," each word being spelled backward. The Dover operator may have thought something was tangled up but he copied just what he heard, and all were pleased when the Boulogne receiver intercepted:

Moffett, Boulogne: Your message received. It reads all right. Vive Marconi—McClure.

The operators flashed "Good-by" and the trial was over.

"How fast can you transmit a message?" Moffett asked Kemp.

"Just now at the rate of about fifteen words a minute; but we shall do better than that no doubt with experience," said the engineer. "You have seen how clear our tape reads. Any one who knows the Morse code will see that the letters are perfect."

"Do you think there is a field for the Marconi system in overland transmission?"

"In certain cases, yes. For instance, where you cannot get the right of way to put up wires and poles. What is a disobliging farmer going to do if you send messages right through his farm, barns and all? Then see the advantage in time of war for quick communication, and no chance that the enemy may cut the wires."

"But the enemy can read your dispatches."

"That is not so sure," replied Kemp. "Besides the possibility of directing the waves with reflectors, Marconi is now engaged in most promising experiments in syntony."

A great secret was out of the bag! Marconi had developed a method to separate stations on different wave lengths! His engineer referred to the invention as "syntony." He called it electrical tuning.

"I may describe syntony as the tuning of a particular transmitter to a particular receiver, so that the latter will respond to the former and to no other, while the former will influence the latter and no other," said Mr. Kemp. "That, of course, is a possibility in the future, but it bids fair soon to be realized. There are even some who maintain that there may be produced as many separate sets of transmitters and receivers capable of working only together as there are separate sets of locks and keys. In any event any two private individuals might communicate freely without fear of being understood by others."

Those skeptics who had always clamored that the weak link in wireless was the fact that if more than one station sent at the same time the messages would be a discordant jumble, now had no reason to scorn.

Tuning—a wireless miracle, protected by Marconi's famous patent No. 7777, solved the problem.

Little did the public realize in 1899 that their children would be using this magic tuning to separate great symphonies from talks by kings, weather reports from menus, and a funeral oration from jazz. Marconi had completely mastered the wild waves criss-crossed overhead.

New possibilities for wireless were seen overnight. Did not the wonder of tuning boom wireless as a powerful force? Indeed it did, and some inquired if the granting of a limitless number of distinct tunings for transmitter and receiver did not threaten the telephone, the cable, the telegraph and even the newspaper.

"Our newspaper system?" exclaimed a correspondent.

"Certainly," said a Marconi engineer; "the news might be ticked off tapes every hour right into the houses of all subscribers, who have receiving instruments tuned to a certain transmitter at the newspaper distributing station. The readers would have merely to glance over their tapes to learn what was happening in the world."

Great was the foresight of these pioneer Marconi men. Did they dream of facsimile broadcasts, photoradio or television?

Prophets were moved to point to the day when citizens would set wireless dials at a definite wave when retiring, so that during the night the machine could pluck a facsimile newspaper from the air. Should the owner of the machine prefer a New York paper he would tune to a specific wave; and another for Chicago. He would have a choice of tele-newspapers.

Wireless in its race to overtake print, however, runs in a circle. The only way it can catch up is to receive and record automatically what the air waves say. That gets back to print again. Wireless and print supplement each other. Both are needed.

Marconi had other things to think about without trying to compete with such a powerful force as the printed word.

The Marconi Company then started unaided to develop its own system of shore stations for communicating with ships at sea. This course was free to anybody and everybody, because no licenses were required and no permission had to be acquired for performance.

The "ether" was a gold field of science; Marconi was the main prospector.

VII

AMERICA BECKONS MARCONI

MARCONI was anxious to see America. His mother had often told him stories of the land across the sea. As a boy he had read the adventures of Columbus. He had heard of America's commercial enterprise and how intensely interested Americans were in his invention.

A representative of the *New York Herald*, Milton V. Snyder, was in Ireland when the Kingstown regatta was wirelessed. Snyder reported what he had seen and heard to James Gordon Bennett, an enthusiastic yachtsman and owner of the *New York Herald*. He told him how the *Dublin Express* had posted the wireless bulletins in the window. In the meantime Snyder went to Paris.

"Go back to London," cabled Bennett, "and make arrangements for Marconi to go to New York in September to report the America Cup races for the *Herald*."

In London, Snyder talked with Jameson Davis, chairman of the British Marconi Company. He was in favor of the proposal but Marconi hesitated. He was not sure he could send messages the distance required in following the yachts off New York Bay. Finally, the inventor agreed if the experiments he planned for the spring of 1899 in the English Channel were successful he would accept Mr. Bennett's invitation and go to America in September.

During the first half of that year, he increased the range of the wireless apparatus on a boat from eighteen to seventy-two miles, and boosted the speed of transmission to twenty

76

words a minute. That satisfied him, as did tests he was invited to conduct during the British fleet manoeuvres, so he decided to see America. The *Herald* attracted international attention when Marconi's acceptance was announced on September 12, 1899.

Sir Thomas Lipton's *Shamrock I* had been built on the Clyde, and then was taken to pieces, sent in sections to London for reassembly at the yard of the Thornecroft Ship and Boiler Builders on the Thames. Finally, after much mystery the *Shamrock* slipped into the Thames and headed for Manhattan Island.

Marconi, accompanied by William Goodbody, a London director of the Marconi Wireless Telegraph Company, Charles E. Rickard and W. W. Bradfield and William Densham, skilled operators, sailed on September 11 from Liverpool on board the Cunarder *Aurania,* which arrived in New York on the 21st. As he came down the gangplank Marconi confidently exclaimed, "We will be able to send the details of the yacht racing to New York as accurately and as quickly almost as if you could telephone them. The distance involved is nothing nor will hills interfere."

Sightseeing attracted Marconi for the next few days. After spending much time at the Custom House, he went to the top of the St. Paul building to get a bird's-eye view of New York's "monster" buildings; he was impressed with the swift moving "lifts," as he designated the elevators. And as he looked about he said, "I'm not frightened that your big steel buildings will stop wireless."

It was on this occasion that he had his first experience with New York reporters. Most emphatically he declared he did not like the ordeal. In fact, it took considerable persuasion to induce him to talk. At last he consented to see the reporters at his headquarters in the Hoffman House. His room was near the skyline, where the noise, turmoil and crowds, which he detested, could not disturb him.

The reporters were quick to observe that he was very sure of himself—a man convinced that he was destined to pass into history, else he could not have been so "glacial" and inflexible despite his modesty.

One news man referred to him as "a serious, somewhat self-centered young man who spoke but little but then always to the point."

"He is no bigger than a Frenchman and not older than a quarter century," wrote a reporter in the news. "He is a mere boy, with a boy's happy temperament and enthusiasm, and a man's nervous view of his life work. His manner is a little nervous and his eyes a bit dreamy. He acts with the modesty of a man who merely shrugs his shoulders when accused of discovering a new continent. He looks the student all over and possesses the peculiar semi-abstracted air that characterizes men who devote their days to study and scientific experiment."

That night there was an explosion in the hotel, and there were some who wondered if the wireless apparatus from Europe had anything to do with it. Marconi smiled and with his assistants began to unpack the trunks containing the equipment. One trunk was missing. It contained the coherers and other essential parts. Search by Custom officials was futile. The temperamental Marconi declared he would return to England on the next ship out of New York.

Bradfield, Marconi's chief assistant, recalled that another Cunarder had sailed from Liverpool for Boston on the same day that the *Aurania* left. He had a hunch that the missing trunk might be on that boat. Robert E. Livingston, a *Herald* reporter, was sent to Boston to search both ship and dock. Bradfield was right; the trunk was in Boston.

Quickly the work of installation proceeded. The Highlands of Navesink in New Jersey was selected as the site of the receiving mast. Lighthousekeepers and Signal Corps men on the lighthouse reservation at Navesink were frankly skeptical.

"When Marconi explained buildings and hills would not interfere with wireless," said Snyder in recalling the event, "the Signal Service men spat scornfully and gazed at the inventor as they would at a madman."

The steamship *Ponce* of the Porto Rico Line and the ocean-going steamer *Grande Duchesse* were chartered, and Marconi installed his apparatus while Bradfield manned the receiving station at Navesink.

Then came the day for the race. Public interest was at fever heat, chiefly due to efforts to keep secret the details of the challenging yacht. The first few meetings ended in a "becalmed" contest because of light winds. Marconi, however, flashed a few bulletins to silence the scoffers. They were sent by wire from the Highlands to the *Herald* office in Herald Square for display on bulletin boards. Broadway in sixty seconds knew what was happening off the New Jersey coast.

The "drifting contests" continued. Marconi was impatient. Admiral Dewey had cabled he would bring his flagship the *Olympia* up New York harbor on a certain day and the metropolis prepared to welcome the hero of Manila Bay. Some one with a news sense suggested "why not install wireless on a craft and meet the *Olympia* at sea, get the news and flash it back to the Highlands long before the *Olympia* could be boarded by newspapermen inside Sandy Hook?"

The idea pleased Marconi. An eight-foot mast was erected on the after deck of a Luckenbach ocean-going tug. The plan was frustrated because Dewey steamed into New York two days ahead of schedule. He had no wireless to report the ship's progress.

Attention was again directed on the *Columbia-Shamrock*. On the day of the first race 2,500 words were sent from the *Ponce* at an average speed of fifteen words a minute. From beginning to end, 1,200 messages, about 33,000 words, were sent through the air.

Eventually the *Columbia* won the series, and by that time Marconi was a national hero. The practical value of wireless at sea and as an agency for quick dispatch of news was apparent. No longer would the sea be a region of silence. No longer would ships sever communication with shore when they pulled away from the docks. Wireless robbed the ocean of much mystery, uncertainty and death.

Let us return to the steamer *Ponce* and see how a newspaper reporter observed the inventor:

When you meet Marconi you're bound to notice that he's a "for'ner." The information is written all over him. His suit of clothes is English. In stature he is French. His boot heels are Spanish military. His hair and mustache are German. His mother is Irish. His father is Italian. And altogether, there's little doubt that Marconi is thoroughly a cosmopolitan.

From where we sat we could hear sounds coming from the chart room, as if somebody in there were striking parlor matches as rapidly as possible one after another. That was Marconi's operator sending Columbia-Shamrock telegrams by the Morse code, but without wires to the receiving station at Navesink, many miles away.

The "Beware of Live Wire" sign was excused by the fact that such a wire actually did run from the chart room to the top of the mast, where the messages spread out into the air as Hertzian waves, after the fashion that ripples spread in a pond when a stone causes a splash.

"Fine day, Chevalier."

"Thanks," said the Chevalier. "That's the first time I've been given a title in this country. But mister's good enough for me."

"What do you think of New York?"

"Well, America may be all right but New York is simply purse-breaking. A New York cab costs me four times as much as a London cab. I guess I am not unlike tens of thousands of Europeans. I'd like to live here, but I cannot afford it."

Marconi's triumph was overshadowed in the news by the arrival of Admiral Dewey; that was the big story. Then, too, the steamer *Oceanic*, heralded as "the latest wonder and new giantess of the sea," had just reached New York on her maiden voyage. She was the biggest thing afloat, and measured 704 feet! Peary in an attempt to reach the North Pole also occupied columns of space.

There was plenty of news in 1899 other than wireless, the value of which many doubted, but the *Herald* declared: "The possibilities contained in the development of telegraphy without the use of wires are so important that any step tending to bring the system before the public and to show what it is capable of accomplishing in a commercial way must be of interest not only to those interested in science, but also to everyone who sends a telegram.

"The tests stimulate the hope that the man of the coming century may be able to 'halloo his name to the reverberate hills' and irrespective of distance or material obstacles 'make the babbling gossip of the air cry out' in intelligible speech."

The United States Navy became interested in the Marconi contraptions. Wireless was installed on the cruiser *New York* and on the battleship *Massachusetts*. Signals were exchanged up to thirty-six miles and that seemed to be about the limit! The earth's curve was blamed for restricting the range.

The United States Army was interested, too. The Signal Corps established communication between Fire Island and Fire Island Lightship, a distance of twelve miles, and later in 1899 between Governor's Island and Fort Hamilton.

England was busy too. The warships *Alexandra, Juno* and *Europa* exchanged messages at sea up to seventy-five miles. Perhaps wireless could skirt the earth's curve after all.

When the skeptics laughed at the feeble signals and derided the thought that from them might evolve a new communication system, competing with the dependable telephone and telegraph, scientists who recognized the possibilities of Hertzian waves smiled and "painted" a bright future for wireless.

Over in England Sir William Preece in a speech, on November 22, 1901, reviewed the progress of wireless:

An immense sensation has been caused in these days by the facility we have acquired of transmitting messages across space to ships in motion at great distances.

The completion of an electric circuit through water was effected by Morse in America in 1844, and by Lindsay in Dundee in 1854, and it has been in regular practical use in India, for bridging rivers, for many years. In 1884 the distance to which electrical disturbances upon telephone were conveyed attracted my attention, and I reported the result to the British Association at Montreal.

In 1893, at Chicago I was able to announce the transmission of messages across three and a half miles to Flat Holme, in the Bristol Channel. In 1894 I reported to the Society of Arts that speech had been transmitted by telephone across Loch Ness. My paper ended thus; "If any of the planets be populated (say Mars) with beings like ourselves having the gift of language and the knowledge to adapt the great forces of nature to their wants, then if they could oscillate immense stores of electrical energy to and fro in electrical order, it would be possible for us to hold communication, by telephone with the people of Mars."

In 1896 Mr. Marconi came to England, and the resources of the Postoffice were placed at his disposal for experiment and trial. They were successful.

The conclusion I came to was that while his system was practical, the field for its use was limited. In the navy it would be of great service and in lightship service it might be beneficial, but that it was going to dispense with submarine cables or with poles and wires was quite chimerical.

It is still quite in an experimental stage, but it has attracted an immense amount of attention in connection with the highly successful tour of the Prince and Princess of Wales.

It is impossible to predict what will happen in the twentieth century. Progress is slow; anticipations are wild. Mr. Marconi, personally, is to be congratulated on what he has already done, and everyone wishes him continued success.

For the indefatigable inventor there was much ahead. At odd moments in the solitude of his workshop his thoughts roamed across the ocean. Wireless across the Atlantic! That was a new goal.

"Do you think wireless messages will ever cross from the Old to the New World?"

"I see no reason why it should be otherwise," replied the pensive man from Italy, "providing the transmitter has sufficient power to hurl the waves across the ocean."

And it would take no longer to leap that 3,000 miles than to span the English Channel.

The Atlantic was the slogan of his hopes.

Marconi, in the words of Keats: "Doth tease us out of thought as doth Eternity."

PART II

VIII

THE FIRST TRANSATLANTIC SIGNAL

MARCONI at the dawn of a new century caught the vision of a dream. He saw men sitting on the edge of the North American continent listening to what a lambent spark was sputtering across 2,000 miles of broad, curving ocean.

New Year's Day, 1900, ushered in an electrical age of speed and scientific wonders—a Century of Progress.

The question in 1900 was, how can 20-kilowatts spread out to every point of the compass provide sufficient energy to traverse 2,000 miles in one direction? Would America and England be brought in touch with each other without the aid of the submerged cable costing from $4,500,000 to $9,000,000 or up to $2,500 a mile?

Marconi thought so, and was working feverishly toward that conclusion.

The cable secluded in the bed of the sea could carry dots and dashes, but the idea that thoughts might pass through the ocean air in less than a second was something to balk human credulity.

How less tedious, less expensive it would be to utilize a free right-of-way in the heavens instead of laying a cable in Neptune's dreary sanctum? The idea had possibilities calling for a miracle man. The skeptics, of course, were countless. It was true, this man Marconi had convinced the doubting world that wireless lifted messages for short distances, but the Atlantic—well, it was much wider than the English Channel.

It was not so difficult to comprehend, in view of Marconi's achievements, that a boat 250 miles off the English coast picked up a wireless signal from the shore. But that must have been a freak of nature aided by extraordinary atmospheric conditions. So argued the die-hards. It was eight times that distance from England to America!

Marconi, a conservative scientist, knew the Atlantic project was fraught with daring—a little too much for the public mind to grasp. He realized the significance of premature announcements.

Wireless across the sea meant the very shrinkage of the earth. It meant new and revolutionary communication between every nation on the face of the globe. Wisdom called for secrecy. If the dream turned out to be a bubble it would be a matter of disappointment only to the dreamer. If successful it would be a signal of progress for mankind. So he would work quietly, unassumingly, with plans unpublicized.

He was looked upon as a modern wizard whose human traits outwardly failed to betray any eccentricities of genius. Londoners who saw him in Piccadilly or Pall Mall observed a rather sad, keen-eyed, thin-lipped young man with unlimited capacity for work and a firm faith in his own ability. His brown hair was neatly trimmed and carefully brushed; sometimes he shaved twice a day. His attire, if anything, was a little too neat for a scientist. He was fond of a fur coat and was not above afternoon tea. One who passed him in the street would class him with the average club or city man, fond of the good things in life, yet his manner and step revealed he was by no means an idler. He looked like a man faithful to friendship but one who would give it rarely.

Divested of the fur coat he looked frail. His movements were slow and direct, yet there was an odd air of diffidence very apparent when he was in the company of strangers. This shyness was emphasized if wireless telegraphy was the topic. He appeared much younger than his twenty-six years, and more than one great scientist eyed him incredulously when seeing him for the first time.

Superficially, Marconi had little to distinguish him from the average man, but closer acquaintance invariably impressed one with his tremendous energy. The doctrine of strenuous life never had a more faithful follower. He labored under high pressure and expected his subordinates to feel the same intense enthusiasm that gripped him during experimental periods. He worked by night and day when a problem presented itself.

Such was the calibre of the man intent upon transatlantic wireless; the man who was preparing for what he termed, "the big thing"—wireless between the Old and New Worlds.

Marconi, accompanied by Major Flood Page, managing director of the Marconi Wireless Company, and R. N. Vyvyan, engineer, in July 1900, went to the barren southwest tip of England and selected Poldhu, near Mullion in Cornwall, as the site for a pioneer transmitter, 100 times more powerful than any station ever built. Construction began in October.

There history would be etched electrically on the blue canopy of the globe. Professor James Ambrose Fleming of University College, London, appointed Scientific Adviser of the Marconi Wireless Company in 1899, was entrusted to design the installation. He was a specialist in high-tension alternating currents. Mr. Vyvyan was selected to supervise construction. Newspapers printed meagre reports that an Italian inventor hoped to link two far-distant points without the aid of visible wires.

The word "visible" appearing in the accounts of 1896-99 indicated the incredulity of the general public. The Gay

Nineties were conservative in regard to electrical miracles; people shook their heads in doubt and wonderment.

Poldhu was ready to "go on the air" for tests with the Isle of Wight in January, 1901. About this time it was decided to erect a twin station at South Wellfleet, Cape Cod. Trusses and beams for the towers were manufactured and shipped to the scene while Marconi, the creator, watched his two stations MBD and WCC grow with the mingled sensations that only an inventor knows. This was in the spring of 1901; but events leading up to the sanguine expectations of the Marconi engineers were of the utmost importance. There were several incidents that showed wireless was "going somewhere," and others were in the race for fame with Marconi.

The Channel steamer *Princess Clementine*, on January 1, 1901, flashed that the barque *Medora* of Stockholm was aground on Ratel Bank; wireless again performed as Marconi said it would. A tug summoned by wireless pulled the craft off and towed it to port.

When the S.S. *Lucania* left Liverpool on August 3, 1901, equipped with wireless, the spirit of Marconi followed it, and on the evening of the sixth day he was delighted to learn that the operator had communicated with Nantucket Lightship at a distance of seventy miles.

Professor Reginald A. Fessenden, who was experimenting with a chemical detector, had applied (Sept. 28, 1901) for a United States patent on "improvements in apparatus for wireless transmission of electro-magnetic waves, said improvements relating more specially to transmission and reproduction of words or other audible sounds." He proposed to build a high-frequency alternator to generate the waves instead of a spark apparatus.

Valdemar Poulsen and William Duddell were conducting

successful tests with an electric arc transmitter, which they believed would be a boon to long-distance communication, making the signals steadier and more dependable.

The fame of wireless was spreading. The first German wireless station which had opened on Borkum Island (Feb. 18, 1900) had been constructed by the Marconi Company. Ten days later the S.S. *Kaiser Wilhelm der Grosse* equipped with wireless left port as the pioneer seagoing passenger vessel to carry such service for its voyagers. Borkum Island heard the signals from the ship sixty miles away! Incidentally, the German Norddeutscher Lloyd was the first shipping company to adopt the Marconi service. Belgium's pioneer wireless station had been completed at Lapanne (Nov. 2, 1900).

Marconi, on April 26, 1900, had protected his interests by filing application for a patent on his "tuned or syntonic and multiplex telegraphy on a single aerial." It was the famous patent No. 7777 and over it a long, defensive struggle was destined to ensue. It would have to stand all tests of the courts if Marconi was to be established as the master of wireless!

The importance of this patent was that it covered the use of tuned closed circuits with tuned open circuits in both the transmitter and receiver. It embraced the entire principle of tuning. Marconi, to prove the fundamental significance and practicality of the idea, demonstrated multiplex wireless in 1900 by connecting two or more receivers to one antenna, and when they were tuned to different wave lengths they worked. He demonstrated multiplex transmission in 1901 across 156 miles between St. Catherine's, Isle of Wight and the Lizard. And so the "four sevens" patent became historic; it revealed the genius of Marconi.

In recounting the event, Professor Ambrose Fleming of

University College, London, in a letter published in the London *Times,* said: [1]

> Two operators at St. Catherine's, Isle of Wight, were instructed to send simultaneously two different wireless messages to Poole, Dorset, and without delay or mistake the two were correctly recorded and printed down at the same time in Morse signals on the tapes of the two corresponding receivers at Poole.
>
> In this first demonstration each receiver was connected to its own independent aerial wire, hung from the same mast. But greater wonders followed. Mr. Marconi placed the receivers at Poole one on the top of the other, and connected them both to one and the same wire, about forty feet in length attached to the mast.
>
> I then asked to have two messages sent at the same moment by the operator at St. Catherine's, one in English and one in French. Without failure, each receiver at Poole rolled out its paper tape, the message in English perfect on one and that in French on the other.
>
> When it is realized that these visible dots and dashes are the result of trains of intermingled electric waves rushing with the speed of light across the intervening thirty miles, caught on one and the same short aerial wire and disentangled and sorted out automatically by the two machines into intelligible messages in different languages, the wonder of it all cannot but strike the mind.
>
> . . . So perfect is the independence that nothing done on one circuit now affects the other, unless desired.

Yes, this thing called wireless was so simple, but even so how could a layman catch the idea. The engineers liked this simile of a stone tossed into a placid pond: A series of ripples is created which spread out in ever-widening circles; any small bits of wood floating on the surface are bobbed up and down by each successive ripple. The stone is the "transmitter"; the pond is the "ether"; the wood is the "receiver."

But think how complicated the ripples if ten stones or even two were thrown in at once. To detect each ripple

[1] October 4, 1900.

Poldhu's first circular aerial on the southwest tip of England, the site from which the pioneer transoceanic signal took wing for a flight to Newfoundland where Marconi plucked it from space.

This simple apparatus thrilled the mauve decade and startled the world, when Marconi used it to flash some of the first wireless signals at Bologna. Note the copper-plate aerial at the top. G. S. Kemp is at the key.

clearly, that was the trick—and Marconi could do it; he separated each one by tuning.

.   .   .   .   .   .

A queer-looking structure, never before seen on the English landscape or anywhere else for that matter, was attracting attention on the forbidding rocks that jut out into the Atlantic at Poldhu. It was Marconi's latest idea of what an aerial system should comprise. There was to be a ring of twenty wooden masts, each about 200 feet high, arranged in a semicircle 200 feet in diameter, covering about an acre. It was designed as the "frame" of a conical aerial consisting of 400 wires.

By the end of August, 1901, the masts were nearly completed, but a cyclone swept the English coast on September 17; the big masts blew down like so many toothpicks after it had taken eleven months to erect them. Disappointment swept through the Marconi ranks. The engineers said it meant postponement of three months or more to remove the wreckage and build anew.

The "sister" towers on Cape Cod suffered a similar disaster a few weeks later.

Marconi was too anxious, too unconquerable a soul to permit fallen masts to get the best of him. He decided it might be possible to utilize a simpler aerial. So two poles, instead of twenty, each 150 feet high, were erected. A triangular stay was stretched between the masts and from it were suspended fifty-five copper wires. They were about a yard apart at the top and converged at the bottom, forming a fan-shaped aerial.

Everything was ready for a preliminary test.

The fiery spark crashed across the gap electrifying the makeshift web of wire and the bleak November air.

A wireless outpost at Crookhaven, Ireland, 225 miles

away, heard the signals with such intensity that the engineers felt certain the power was sufficient to drive a message across the Atlantic—ten times as far as Poldhu to Crookhaven!

Marconi was sure it would. He decided to conduct the first test in Newfoundland—the nearest point in America to the Old World.

Bound on a historic journey, he sailed on November 26 from Liverpool on the liner *Sardinian*, accompanied by two assistants, G. S. Kemp [2] and P. W. Paget.

They had odd baggage for three men. Small captive balloons and a number of large kites were in the luggage. They knew the inclement weather in Canada at this season of the year and the shortness of the time at their disposal made it impossible to erect high masts to hold aloft antenna wires. But the kites and balloons might do the trick, thereby saving time and expense and possibly make history.

Undramatically, in fact, unnoticed, the trio of pioneers landed at St. John's on Friday, December 6, and the following day, before beginning operations they visited the Governor, Sir Cavendish Boyle, Premier, Sir Robert Bond, and other members of the Ministry, who promised heartiest cooperation. They cheerfully placed the resources of every department of the government at Marconi's disposal to facilitate his work.

"After taking a look at various sites," said Marconi, "which might prove suitable, I considered the best one was on Signal Hill, a lofty eminence overlooking the port and forming a natural bulwark which protects it from the fury of the Atlantic winds. On top of this hill is a small plateau some two acres in area, which seemed very suitable for manipulation of the balloons and kites. On a crag on this

[2] Mr. Kemp was one of Marconi's most valued electricians and his diary of wireless was a great asset to Marconi when in court fighting patent litigation and infringements.

plateau rose the new Cabot Memorial Tower, erected in commemoration of the famous Italian explorer John Cabot, and designed as a signal station. Close to it there was the old military barracks, then used as a hospital. It was in the forum of this building that we set up the apparatus and made preparations for the great experiment.

"On Monday, December 9, we began work. On Tuesday we flew a kite with 600 feet of aerial as a preliminary test, and on Wednesday we inflated one of the balloons, which made its first ascent during the morning. It was about fourteen feet in diameter and contained about 1,000 cubic feet of hydrogen gas, quite sufficient to hold up the aerial, which consisted of wire weighing about ten pounds. After a short while, however, the blustery wind ripped the balloon away from the wire. The balloon sailed out over the sea. We concluded, perhaps the kites would be better, and on Thursday morning, in spite of a gusty gale we managed to fly a kite up 400 feet.

"The critical moment had come, for which the way had been prepared by six years of hard and unremitting work, despite the usual criticisms directed at anything new. I was about to test the truth of my belief.

"In view of the importance of all that was at stake, I had decided not to trust entirely to the usual arrangement of having the coherer signals record automatically on a paper tape through a relay and Morse instrument, but to use instead a telephone connected to a self-restoring coherer. The human ear being much more sensitive than the recorder it would be more likely to hear the signal.

"Before leaving England I had given detailed instructions for transmission of a certain signal, the Morse telegraphic 'S'—three dots—at a fixed time each day beginning as soon as word was received that everything at St. John's was in readiness. If the invention could receive on the kite-wire in

Newfoundland some of the electric waves produced, I knew the solution of the problem of transoceanic wireless telegraphy was at hand.

"I cabled Poldhu to begin sending at 3 o'clock in the afternoon, English time, continuing until 6 o'clock; that is, from 11:30 to 2:30 o'clock in St. John's."

As the hands of the clock moved toward noon on Thursday (December 12, 1901), Marconi sat waiting with the telephone receiver held to his ear. It was an intense hour of expectation. Arranged on the table were the delicate instruments ready for a decisive test. There was no calibrated dial tuner to facilitate adjusting the circuit to a specific wave length. In fact, the wave of Poldhu was not measured. There was no device to measure it. Professor Fleming thought there should be some method of measuring wave length but he had yet to invent his cymometer or wave-meter.

The length of Poldhu's wave was a guess. There was nothing precise or scientific about tuning. But based on the fact that the aerial was 200 feet high and that it was linked with a series coil or "jigger," Professor Fleming estimated the wave length was not less than about 3,000 feet or 960 meters.

Marconi had to hunt for the wave.

A wire ran out through the window of Cabot Tower, thence to a pole and upward to the kite which could be seen swaying overhead. It was a raw day. A cold sea thundered at the base of the 300-foot cliff. Oceanward through the mist rose dimly the rude outlines of Cape Spear, the easternmost point of the North American continent.

Beyond rolled the unbroken ocean, nearly 2,000 miles to the coast of the British Isles; wireless might leap that in one ninety-third of a second! Across the harbor the city of St. John's lay on the hillside. No one had taken enough interest in the experiment to go up through the snow to Signal Hill. Even the ubiquitous reporter was absent.

In Cabot Tower, the veteran signalman stood in the look-out's nest scanning the horizon for ships, little dreaming that mysterious waves might be coming out of the sky from England.

Wireless was ready for the crucial test. Its destiny was at stake. So was Marconi's. Everything that could be done had been done. The receiving outfit was as sensitive as Marconi could make it; he had faith that these instruments would pick up the faintest trace of a signal.

Marconi listened and listened. Not a sound was heard for half an hour. He inspected the instruments. They looked perfect. Had something gone wrong at Poldhu? Had some mysterious force led the signals astray? Was the curvature of the globe a barrier? All these things flashed through his mind, coupled with the fact that it was almost fantastic to believe an unseen wave of intelligence could cross through the ocean air and strike such a slender target as a copper wire. It seemed incredible. It would be so easy for the message to travel off in some undesired direction.

Marconi knew, however, if the signal went east, north or south it would also go west and to that wire antenna dangling from the kite.

Without warning there was a sharp click in the earphones. What caused it? Was some stray static playing a prank? Indeed not! Marconi had at last found the right tuning adjustment to put him in touch with Poldhu!

"Suddenly, at about 12:30 o'clock, unmistakably three scant little clicks in the telephone receiver, corresponding to three dots in the Morse code, sounded several times in my ear as I listened intently," said Marconi, in recounting the day. "But I would not be satisfied without corroboration.

" 'Can you hear anything, Kemp?' I said, handing the receiver to him.

"Kemp heard the same thing I did, and I knew then that I had been absolutely right in my anticipation," recalled Marconi. "Electric waves which were being sent out from Poldhu had traversed the Atlantic serenely ignoring the curvature of the earth, which so many doubters considered would be a fatal obstacle. I knew then that the day on which I should be able to send full messages without wires or cables across the Atlantic was not very far away. Distance had been overcome, and further development of the sending and receiving instruments was all that was required."

Wireless had flashed across the Atlantic's sky like "some meteor that the sun exhales."

Again and again Marconi and Kemp listened to be sure there was no mistake. Paget was called in. He listened but heard nothing; he was slightly deaf. What Marconi and Kemp heard must have been Poldhu. There was no other wireless station in the world to send that pre-arranged signal. And a marvel was that it was noon time; it would have been so much easier to perform the feat at night when darkness aids the flight of long-wave wireless. Marconi was not aware of that.

It was mid-afternoon. The kite gyrated wildly in the gale that swept in from the sea. The antenna failed to maintain the maximum altitude and the fluctuating height naturally influenced reception. The wind tugged and tugged at the kite, finally at 2:20 o'clock the antenna was lifted within range of the repetitious dots. And that gave further verification.

At dusk the inventor and his companions went down the hill toward the city sparkling with lights. He made no statement to the press. In fact, he felt rather depressed because he had not intercepted a continuous stream of signals. Possibly the stress of the preceding days had something to do with his disheartened feeling.

It is said that a secret is no longer a secret if more than one person holds it, but that night three men kept a secret from the world. And what they harbored was front-page news—news that would find a place in history books.

They went to sleep dreaming of what they had heard and in hope that a new day would put the stamp of success on their work by further verification. It almost seemed too true for them to believe their own ears. They would listen again for the three elusive dots.

They were up on the hill early the next morning, anxious to lend an ear to space at noon, for that was the appointed time for Poldhu to broadcast.

The signals came on schedule but were not quite as distinct as the day before. The changing weather on a 2,000 mile front could make a radical difference in behavior of the waves. There was no doubt, however, that wireless had spanned the Atlantic. Nevertheless, the modest inventor hesitated to make his achievement public, lest it seem too extraordinary for belief.

Finally, after withholding the news for two days, certainly evidence of his conservatism and self-restraint, Marconi issued a statement to the press, and on that Sabbath morning the world knew but doubted.

Under a one-column headline, "Wireless Signals Across the Atlantic—Marconi says he has received them from England," *The New York Times*, on December 15, featured the following story:

St. John's, N. F., Dec. 14.—Guglielmo Marconi announced tonight the most wonderful scientific development of recent times. He stated that he had received electric signals across the Atlantic ocean from his station in Cornwall.

Signor Marconi explains that before leaving England he made his plans for trying to accomplish this result, for, while his primary object was to communicate with Atlantic liners in mid-ocean, he also hoped to receive wireless messages across the Atlantic. . . . Though satisfied of the genuineness of the signals and that he has succeeded in his attempts to establish communication across the Atlantic without the use of wires, he emphasizes the fact that the system is yet only in an embryonic stage.

He says, however, that the possibilities of its ultimate development are demonstrated by the success of the present experiment with incomplete and imperfect apparatus, as the signals can only be received by the most sensitively adjusted apparatus, and he is working under great difficulties owing to the conditions prevailing here. . . . He will return to England next week and will remain in England until the coronation of King Edward next summer, and he hopes to send the news across the Atlantic by the wireless method, so as to prove the capability of the system for such purposes.

". . . To Mr. Hertz, of course, belongs the distinction of having discovered the electric waves, and by his experiments he proved that electricity in its progress through space, follows the law of optics," said Signor Marconi. "Many others have made experiments in the same direction as I, but so far no one has obtained such results at anything approaching the distances I have done with these Hertzian waves. Fog has no effect upon the signals, nor has even the most solid substance. The waves can penetrate walls, and rocks without being materially affected.

"It is possible to send many messages in different directions at the same time but care must be taken to tune the transmitters and receivers to the same frequency or 'note.' I mean they must be in sympathy. And this tuning is effected by varying the capacity and self-induction of certain conductors which are joined to the transmitting and receiving instruments, so that the message intended for a particular receiver is thus rendered quite undecipherable on another. . . . Wireless telegraphy is a possibility anywhere, and it will, I think, soon be a reality in many places."

The scientific world was mindful that Marconi had never released a statement in public until absolutely certain of the facts. He never had to withdraw a notice as to his progress. As soon as the significance of the event was realized star reporters and special magazine writers rushed northward from New York to get the story from the lips of the inventor.

Three pioneers of wireless who posed for this picture in 1901, historic in the annals of communication, for on December 12th they picked up the first transatlantic signal—George S. Kemp, Guglielmo Marconi and G. W. Paget.

He told them it cost $200,000 to get the three dots across the Atlantic!

Newspapers went back into their files to find out more about the evolution of this wireless which seemed to come as a bolt from the blue. *The New York Times* pointed out that Nikola Tesla some years previous in discussing his theories and discoveries hinted at possibilities of telegraphing through the air and earth.[3] Mr. Tesla was quoted:

In pursuing this line of work I have had the good fortune to discover some facts which are certainly novel, and which I am glad to say, have been recognized by scientific men both here and abroad. I think the probable result of these investigations will be the production of a more efficient source of light, thus supplementing the wasteful process of light productions.

My experiments have been almost entirely confined to alternating currents of high potential. An alternating current is a current changed periodically in direction; and the word potential expresses the force and energy with which these currents are made to pass. In this particular case the force is very great. The fact that a current vibrates back and forth rapidly in this way tends to set up or create waves in the ether, which is a hypothetical thing that was invented to explain the phenomena of light.

One result of my investigation, the possibility of which has been proved by experiment, is the transmission of energy through the air. I advanced that theory some time ago. . . . The plan I have suggested is to disturb by powerful machinery the electricity of the earth thus setting it in vibration. Proper appliances will be constructed to take up the energy transmitted by these vibrations, transforming them into a suitable form of power to be made available for the practical wants of life.

The outlook for wireless telegraphy is problematical. But one thing is certain, we shall be able to send very important short messages from centre to centre.

To Marconi there was nothing problematical about the future; he had spanned the Atlantic. He had upset the calculations of mathematicians. He began to talk about commercial service. Professor Fleming told him that the dif-

[3] December 15, 1901.

fraction or bending of the waves around the earth would be increased by increasing the wave length. He urged Marconi to lengthen the wave, and he would design an instrument to measure them, even if they were 20,000 feet from crest to crest.[4]

Lexicologists got busy; they asserted "wireless telegraphy" was a term satisfactory to no one, and pointed to the fact that the U. S. Army Signal Corps had rejected it. After long and profound meditation, the word "aerogram" was suggested for the message; "aerographer" for the operator; and "aerography," instead of wireless—but wireless it would remain.

[4] Fleming invented cymometer or wavemeter in October 1904.

IX

THE HERO OF THE HOUR

IT was easy to understand the public reaction. One had only to look back to 1858, when the first cable actually delivered a message. Many had to hear the signals themselves before they would believe. Others were not convinced even by affidavits of those who made it possible. If the popular imagination could not be fired with a direct link between the hemispheres how could wireless, an invisible thread of communication, incite faith and dispel all doubt in a short time, despite the fact that Edison, Bell, Morse and other notables of science had taught the world to be chary of disbelief?

Congratulations poured in on Marconi. He dined with Sir Cavendish Boyle, Governor of Newfoundland, prior to departure for Cape Spear to select a site for the erection of a pole 200 feet high, which he believed would give the best results possible under existing conditions.

A report from St. John's, on December 15, 1901, stated: "On Tuesday the inventor proposes to have Governor Boyle, Premier Bond and other Colonial dignitaries examine his tests so that they may satisfy themselves of the absolute genuineness of the proceedings. There is much speculation here as to the practical possibilities of wireless telegraphy. Signor Marconi is satisfied from his previous experiments that great surprises are in store for the world. He has the warmest support in this colony, where he is generally admired owing to his achievements at so young an age."

Marconi returned to St. John's from Cape Spear on De-

cember 16 and was served with legal documents from the
solicitors of the Anglo-American Telegraph Company. The
papers notified him that the company possessed a monopoly
of the telegraph business within Newfoundland and its dependencies, and demanded that he cease his experiments and
remove his apparatus forthwith else the company would
apply to the Supreme Court for an injunction restraining
further trials.

All was not sunshine. At Cape Spear the inventor experienced poor luck. The weather was rendered extremely unpleasant by fog, wind and a rainstorm, making it impossible
for Marconi to decide upon a site for a new station. And
while his hopes were being dashed by inclement atmospherics, he received a report, which afterwards proved to be
incorrect, that Edison discredited the announcement of signals having been received from Cornwall. He replied that
the signals were received by himself; they were absolutely
genuine.

"I fully believe that Marconi succeeded in signaling between the coasts of Newfoundland and Cornwall, England,
by his system of wireless telegraphy," said Michael I. Pupin,
Professor of Electrical Mechanics at Columbia University.[1]
"According to the newspaper reports I have read, the signals
were very faint but that has little to do with it. The distance, which is about 1,800 miles between these two points,
was overcome, and further development of the sending instruments is all that is required. . . . This new system, if
it is adopted, will not affect the cables as far as I can see at
the present time, for it must be understood that the cables
are being perfected constantly. At the present time there
are fourteen cables between Europe and America. . . . One
point which is of great value and interest to the scientific
world is that Marconi has proved conclusively that the

[1] December 16, 1901.

curvature of the earth is no obstacle to wireless telegraphy. . . . Marconi deserves great credit for pushing this work so persistently and intelligently, and it is only to be regretted that there are so many so-called scientists and electricians who are trying to get around Marconi's patent, and thus deprive him and his people of the credit and benefits of the work to which they are fully entitled."

"If Marconi says that he has communicated across the seas I know of no reason," said Professor A. E. Dolbear of Tufts College, himself a wireless enthusiast, "why I should not fully believe that he had solved the problem."

Editorially, under the caption, "The Epoch-Making Marconi," *The New York Times* on December 17 said:

If Marconi succeeds in his experiments with intercontinental wireless telegraphy his name will stand through the ages among the very first of the world's great inventors.

The thing he is attempting to do would be almost transforming in its effect upon the social life, the business and political relations of the peoples of the earth. The animating spirit of modern invention is to overcome the obstacles of time and space, "to associate all the races of mankind," by bringing them nearer together. Commerce, of course, has done more than any other agency to make that association intimate and lasting.

The electric telegraph, in the form of ocean cables, was a great step in advance. The sending of messages without wires through natural media of communication will be a still longer and more wonderful advance, if it shall prove that the art can be perfected and made practicable up to the measure of present confident predictions.

Everything depends on that. The cables are too slow and too costly for these modern times. Professor Pupin in his comment upon Marconi's experiment says that "nobody doubts at the present time that the cable will soon be made from forty to fifty times as fast as it is at the present day."

If the capacity of ocean cables is not very soon increased by such electrical improvements as he has in mind the inventive genius of this age will be open to accusation of not keeping up, with its urgent requirements. We understand that at twenty-five cents a word the fourteen Atlantic cables now in operation are fully occupied during the business hours of the day. That means that in this matter demand has outrun supply. It would be better for the world if communication between the countries that ocean divides could be much increased in volume through a saving of cost and time.

The initial success of Marconi appeals powerfully to the imagination. It will be the fervent hope of all intelligent men that wireless telegraphy will very soon prove to be not a mere "scientific toy," but a system for daily and common use. The men of science point out the obstacles. They have commonly been deemed insuperable. The first triumph is an augury of future conquests.

T. C. Martin, editor of *The Electrical World,* said:

I believed that Marconi would be successful but did not anticipate it so soon. . . . I am sorry that Mr. Tesla, who has given the matter so much thought and experimentation, and to whose initiative so much of the work is due, should not also have been able to accomplish this wonderful feat.

I have talked with Professor Fessenden, who is now engaged on the subject for the United States Government, and with Dr. Kennelly, at one time an expert for Mr. Edison, and they agreed as to the feasibility and near possibility of the achievement.

Although Mr. Marconi is to be heartily congratulated on his magnificent results the idea is not to be jumped at that cables are any less useful than heretofore. So far as is known, there is no means of preventing successfully the interference of wireless signals, and until they become automatically selective it would mean that only one station on each side of the Atlantic, or even on each side of New York bay, would engage in business. Even should this difficulty be overcome, as it doubtless will be, I find it hard to believe that it will be so entirely removed as to involve the complete supercession of cables.

Leaders in science the world over concurred on the remark:

"Marconi's creation, like that of the poet who gathers the words of other men in a perfect lyric, was none the less brilliant and original.

"The present is an epoch of astounding activity in applied science," said Sir Oliver Lodge. "Progress is a thing of months and weeks, almost days. The long lines of isolated ripples of past discovery seem blending into a mighty wave, on the crest of which one begins to discern some oncoming magnificent generalization.

"The suspense is becoming feverish, at times almost painful.

One feels like a boy who has been long strumming on a silent keyboard of a deserted organ, into the chest of which an unseen power begins to blow a vivifying breath.

"Astonished, he now finds that the touch of the finger elicits a responsive note, and he hesitates, half-delighted, half-affrighted, lest he should be deafened by the chords which it seems he can now almost summon at his will."

Sir Oliver Lodge in his book "Talks About Wireless," commented: [2]

"When Signor Marconi succeeded in sending the letter 'S' by Morse signals from Cornwall to Ireland to Newfoundland, it constituted an epoch in human history, on its physical side, and was an astonishing and remarkable feat."

Later in the same book he remarks:

"It is needless to emphasize the world-wide character of Mr. Marconi's subsequent developments; his discovery of the power of ether waves to curve around the earth to immense distances, his discovery also of the adverse effect of sunshine, and the more recent discovery that short waves can travel efficiently to the Antipodes."

Sir Cavendish Boyle, who had cabled reports on the achievement to King Edward, arranged a luncheon in honor of Marconi. Among those present were Premier Bond, the Cabinet Ministers and the heads of departments. The affair was practically a State function. In expressing his appreciation for the courtesies of the Dominion, Marconi said:

"If my system of wireless telegraphy can be commercially established between the different parts of the earth, in regard to which I may state I have not the slightest doubt, it would bring about an enormous cheapening in the methods of communication at present existing.

"The system of submarine cables of today fulfills the demands of communication to a great extent. But the great cost of the cables themselves, and their heavy working expenses, cause the existing methods to be beyond the reach of

[2] "Talks About Wireless" by Sir Oliver Lodge, Cassel Company, 1925.

a majority of the people inhabiting the various countries of the world. But could this new method be applied, I believe the cost of what we now call cabling to England might be reduced at least twenty fold. The present rate is twenty-five cents a word. I do not see why eventually, with the wireless system this cost should not be reduced to one cent a word or less."

Discussion everywhere centered around wireless versus the cables. A dispatch from London read:

The fall in the securities of cable companies which commenced with the announcement of the success of Marconi's experiments in having signals transmitted across the ocean by his wireless system of telegraphy has been continuous throughout the week.

"Marconi and the Anglo-American," was the title of an editorial in *The New York Times,* on December 19:

The more the incident of the proceedings of the Anglo-American Cable Company against Signor Marconi is considered, the more evident it becomes that the management of that company is in the hands of short-sighted, narrow-minded, unprogressive persons who are much in need of supplementing the Lord's Prayer with a petition to be taught to know their daily bread when they see it.

Pending an adjustment of the "disagreement," Signor Marconi has gone over to Nova Scotia, where he will continue his experiments. If he should find that he can transmit intelligible signals as well from there as from Newfoundland, and that the slightly greater distance does not complicate his system or increase its difficulties in operation whatever advantage has been supposed to reside in the Anglo-American's telegraph monopoly of Newfoundland will be at an end, thus destroying another highly prized asset of the company. . . .

People have begun to think that the eagerness manifested by the cable companies to discredit Marconi and embarrass his experiments warrants a suspicion that the profits of the present tariff are more satisfactory than the representatives of these companies are desirous the public shall believe.

Marconi could have been helped in no better way than by recognizing his system as a dangerous competitor before he had ventured to make that claim for it himself.

On second thought that is the way Marconi reasoned. At first he was amazed at the warning, but as he reflected upon it he wondered, "Is this not evidence of the belief of practical men in the future commercial importance of wireless?"

For the ether to be a formidable competitor of land wires was not so easy since telegraph lines cost approximately $100 a mile, whereas the ocean cables cost $1,000 a mile, and require expensive steamers to repair and maintain them, so figured P. T. McGrath, editor of the *Evening Herald*, St. John's, Newfoundland.[3]

"A transatlantic cable represents an initial outlay of at least three million dollars, besides the cost of its maintenance," explained Mr. McGrath. "A Marconi station can be built for $60,000. Three of these bringing the two worlds into contact, will cost only $180,000, while their maintenance should be insignificant. What his success will mean can best be grasped by considering the extent of the property which would be displaced thereby, although it is only since August 5, 1858, forty-three years ago, that the first Atlantic cable was laid. There are now fourteen along the Atlantic bed, and in the whole world 1,769 telegraph cables of various sizes, with a total length of almost 189,000 nautical miles, enough to girdle the earth seven times.

"These require a great number of ocean-going cable steamers for their laying and repairs, and while the total value of the cables cannot be computed easily, it is known to be a fact that British capitalists have $100,000,000 invested in cable stocks."

As the word spread that Marconi had stopped testing, he was deluged with offers of sites for experimental stations. Alexander Graham Bell, inventor of the telephone, offered him use of his property at Cape Breton. The Finance Minister of Canada extended on behalf of the government every facility for the location of a station in Nova Scotia. Marconi accepted. Before resuming work, however, he decided to return to England to consult business associates, chief among them Jameson Davis. He said he was sailing on De-

[3] *The Century Illustrated Monthly Magazine*, March, 1902.

cember 22 on the steamer *Sardinian* for England, and would return to New York in January.

.   .   .   .   .   .

As the train pulled away from the scene of his triumph in Newfoundland, across the island on the way to Nova Scotia, it seemed that every farmer and fisherman came to the depots to catch a glimpse of the wizard of wireless. He was only twenty-seven years old. The boyish smile and youthful appearance coupled with the magnitude of his achievement won the admiration of the throngs.

Ray Stannard Baker, who interviewed Marconi at St. John's several days after the transatlantic triumph, described him as somewhat above medium height and deliberate in his movements despite a highly strung temperament.[4] He observed Marconi unlike the inventor of tradition. Those who visualized him unshaven, disheveled and unkempt, with trousers unpressed and collar and tie missing after a long siege in the laboratory, never hold such a picture in their minds once they have met the man. He is scrupulously neat in dress and in work. No photograph or painting could portray the peculiar luster in his countenance when he is interested or excited.

Those who have the pleasure of meeting him are immediately impressed that they are in the presence of a man of intense nervous activity and mental absorption. He talks little; is straightforward and unassuming, submitting goodnaturedly, although with evident unwillingness to being lionized. In his public addresses he has been clear and sensible. He is reluctant to write for any publication; nor does he engage in scientific disputes, and even when violently attacked he lets his work prove his point.

One factor that has endeared him to the world is his

[4] *McClure's Magazine*, February, 1902.

acceptance of success with a calmness, almost unconcern; he certainly expected it. Boastfulness is not in his make-up. Opposition is his keenest spur to greater effort.

He speaks English as perfectly as he does Italian. He speaks little French, but with an English accent. Indeed, his blue eyes, light hair and fair complexion give him decidedly the appearance of an Englishman, so that the stranger who meets him would never suspect Italian blood in his veins. One of the first messages conveying news of his success at St. John's went to his mother and father in London where they divided their time with the Marconi estate in Italy.

"There has never been the least doubt that Marconi embarked on experimental research because he loved it," said Mr. Baker. "No amount of honor or money could tempt him from the pursuit of the great things in wireless which he sees before him. Besides being an inventor, he is a shrewd business man with a clear appreciation of the value of his inventions and of their possibilities when generally introduced. What is more he knows how to go about the task of introducing them."

This was the man the Canadians applauded.

.   .   .   .   .   .

After a brief consultation with his English associates, Marconi was back in New York on January 12. Reporters found him at the Hoffman House, and although he said his time was very limited he consented to an interview.

"I will be in New York until Wednesday, when I expect to sail for England on the *Teutonic*," said Marconi. "As soon as I reach the other side I will start to work to get stations in readiness for the transmission of messages, commercial and otherwise, across the Atlantic. There will be two stations on each side; those in Europe being located at Cornwall and Belgium. Those on the American side will be at Nova Scotia and on Cape Cod."

Were your recent tests in Newfoundland satisfactory to you? he was asked.

"Eminently so," was the quick response; "not so much on account of the transmission of the letter 'S' as that is the letter generally used in telegraphic testing, but because the letters were received according to a prearranged plan both as to the number of times they were to be sent and at the speed agreed upon."

His attention was called to the suggestion of anchoring steam vessels at convenient places on the Atlantic, equipped with wireless apparatus, thus enabling messages to be relayed to ships and to the other shore.

"That is ridiculous," he replied. "There is no use for any such system. I have absolutely no sympathy with any such proposition. Messages can be sent across the Atlantic without any intermediate stations."

The American Institute of Electrical Engineers arranged a Marconi celebration in the uniquely decorated Astor Gallery of the Waldorf-Astoria.[5] On the wall back of the guest's table was a black tablet framed in smilax and studded with electric lights that spelled "Marconi." At the eastern end of the gallery, above the 300 diners, was a tablet on which, traced in electric lights, was the word "Poldhu," and on the western end was the word, "St. John's." These tablets were linked by a silken cable festooned along the wall of the gallery, and on the cable tiny electric lamps were distributed to make at intervals the letter "S" in the Morse code.

The guest table was ablaze with tiny electric lights peeping from banks of smilax and surmounted by bouquets of American beauty roses. On the menu cards was a half-tone

[5] January 13, 1902.

picture of the inventor in the center of a scene representing the transmission of the first wireless message across the ocean. The galleries were jammed with spectators.

The cue for the first applause of the evening was the entrance of a long procession of waiters bearing aloft the ices which were surmounted by telegraph poles, steamships and sailing vessels fitted with wireless. The telegraph poles were made of solid ice.

"Frozen out," was the prophetic cry of the diners as they saw the crystal poles—did they signalize the end of the telegraph? Marconi arose and clapped his hands in glee. Then the signal "S" began to flash from the tablet, "Poldhu," as Dr. Charles Proteus Steinmetz, president of the Institute, called the diners to order, and turned the meeting over to T. C. Martin, toastmaster for the occasion.

A letter was read from Thomas Alva Edison: "I am sorry not to be present to pay my respects to Marconi. I would like to meet that young man who has had the monumental audacity to attempt and succeed in jumping an electric wave across the Atlantic."

"I was talking with Mr. Edison within the last ten days," reported Mr. Martin, "and he said that he thought that some time there might be daily signals across the Atlantic without wires, but that he did not know when, and being preoccupied he did not think he would have time to do it himself [laughter]. He said to me, 'Martin, I'm glad he did it. That fellow's work puts him in my class. It's a good thing we caught him young.' [Laughter.]"

There were more cheers when the toastmaster turned to a letter from Nikola Tesla, who said that he felt that he "could not rise to the occasion. . . . Marconi is a splendid worker and a deep thinker . . . and may prove one of those whose powers increase and reach out for the good of the race and the honor of his country."

The toastmaster's presentation of Marconi was brief, "For an introduction to such a man, look about you!"

Amid a salvo of applause the young inventor arose, and began to speak in a low but distinct tone without gestures; with a modesty almost amounting to diffidence, he told of the various disappointments leading up to his triumph:

"I can hardly find words to express my gratitude and thanks for the reception I have received here tonight. I thank you very much for the appreciation of the work which I have been fortunate enough to carry out. I feel myself to be highly honored to be entertained by such a great body as the American Institute of Electrical Engineers. I think it is well known all over the world that Americans stand first in applied electrical engineering. I feel myself greatly honored to be in the midst of so many eminent men, whose names are household words in the whole civilized world.

"With your permission I will give you a brief description of what my system has at present accomplished, especially in reference to use on ships, and what I hope it will accomplish in the future.

"Wireless telegraphy is now attracting very great attention all over the world, and its progress is not slow. Five years ago the system with which my name is identified was working over a distance of about two miles, but its range has been rapidly increased until a few months ago it was quite possible to communicate by means of an improved and attuned system over a distance of more than 200 miles. The commercial application of the system has been given serious consideration, and improvements of importance have been made.

"It may interest you to know that the commercial application of the system has been tried in Great Britain, its chief base being in England. There are more than seventy ships carrying permanent installations for wireless telegraphy; of these, thirty-seven are in the British navy, twelve in the Italian navy, and the remainder are on the large liners, such as the Cunard Line, the North German Lloyd, and the Beaver Line. There are more than twenty stations in operation on land in Great Britain, and more are in course of construction.

"I regret very much that it is impossible for me in a brief address to go into the scientific details, and the scientific developments of my system. I would like very much to do so, but I cannot at this time. I think it is right that I should correct some of the popular opinions which prevail as to the subject of wireless telegraphy.

"It seems to be the general opinion, that when a message is sent into space anyone with a necessary apparatus can intercept that message and read it. Of course, this would be very awkward and would hurt the system from a commercial standpoint. No one would wish to have his private affairs made public in that way. For instance, stock quotations or other matters of secret could be found out. By experiments and improvements which have been made, messages can be read only when the receiver and transmitter are attuned.

"The perfected system is not at present in use on the ships. It has been deemed necessary that each ship should be equipped with apparatus which will permit of its reading a message from any other ship, because of the possibility of aid being required. Therefore, all ships are attuned so that one ship can call up any other ship, but it is practicable to have all the apparatus so attuned that the messages transmitted can in no way be received by any other apparatus except that attuned to receive the message."

Marconi then reviewed his early experiments in England

and expressed appreciation for the aid rendered to him by the British Government.

"Also I have been very greatly encouraged by the Government of Canada," he continued, "and the sympathy they have given has encouraged me in my work. I think it will be admitted that one of the greatest features of civilization in all the world is the facility with which people can communicate with each other living long distances apart. My hope is that in no great distant future I shall bring my system to the point of perfection of allowing friends and relatives to communicate with each other across the ocean at small expense.

"At present by the existing cable system the sending of messages across the seas is put out of reach of people of moderate circumstances. The cost of laying the cables is so large that cable companies have to charge a high price for the service. My system will cheapen the cost very greatly.

"I have built very largely on the work of others, and before concluding I would like to mention a few names. I may miss a few of them, but I would like to mention Clerk Maxwell, Lord Kelvin, Professor Henry and Professor Hertz. I do not know if you are aware that the message received at St. John's was heard through a telephone receiver and in connection with the telephone the name of Professor Alexander Graham Bell is inseparable.

"I hope that I may bring this work to a successful completion. As a stranger here I thank you very much for your kind expressions and for your hospitality—I drink to the health of the American Institute of Electrical Engineers!"

Marconi lifted a glass from the table, holding it high above his head, lowered it to his lips and began to drink before the diners grasped the situation. Quickly all picked up glasses and drank in silence a toast—in a few seconds

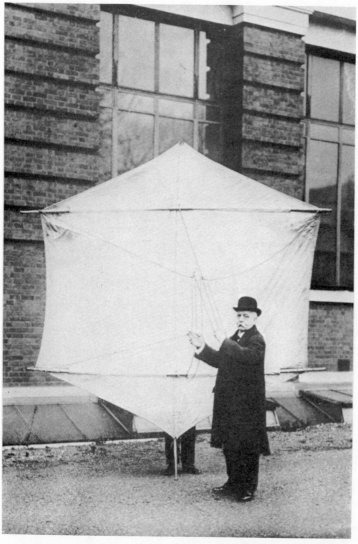

Famous among kites—G. S. Kemp, Marconi pioneer, displays the one that carried the wire antenna aloft to intercept the first letter "S" that fluttered across the sea from Poldhu to Newfoundland.

cheers resounded through the banquet hall while Guglielmo Marconi bowed acknowledgment to the plaudits. There was no doubt that Americans believed in him and in his achievements.

Two days later a glowing tribute to the character and conservatism of the young man was printed by *The New York Times:* [6]

Signor Marconi is not a stranger to the representative men of his profession in the United States, but it may be truthfully said that he leaves our shores with the respect and good wishes of every electrical engineer and the confidence of everyone financially interested in the telegraph business.

At the banquet given in his honor Monday evening by the American Institute of Electrical Engineers he made his first specific statement of the results claimed by him as already achieved and of his hopes as to the future of his work. This statement was so modest, so free from every trace of exaggeration for business purposes, so generously just in its recognition of the obligation to the pioneers in experimentation along the lines he has followed, so frank in acknowledging the claims of the living as well as the dead, and withal so conservative in its predicting of what may follow the work he now has in hand, that everyone present realized that to Marconi was not only due the honor of his discoveries in the field of mechanics, but the still higher honor which belongs to one who can subordinate all professional jealousies and rivalries to the truth.

From the wreath woven for his own brow he borrowed enough to make wreaths for his predecessors and colleagues in the study of electrical waves—Clerk Maxwell, Lord Kelvin, Professor Henry, Dr. Hertz, Alexander Graham Bell and others—and by what he took from it his own was rather enriched than impoverished.

It cannot have escaped the notice of those for whom the subject of wireless telegraphy has even a news interest, that to establish the fact that the feat of transmitting intelligible signals in prearranged order and frequency of occurrence no other evidence was needed than Signor Marconi's unsupported and unverified statement. Immediately on receipt of telegraphic intelligence from Newfoundland that this feat had been accomplished and representative engineers of the world were interviewed, and with-

[6] January 15, 1902.

out exception their response was: "If Marconi says it is true, I believe it."

There have been few great facts in science thus accepted with unquestioning confidence on the authority of one known to be anything but disinterested. In Marconi's case all that he claimed was conceded even before the details were known. No higher tribute could have been paid by the world of science to an inventor than was paid to Marconi by this unquestioning acceptance of the announcement that he had succeeded in accomplishing the seemingly impossible.

Concerning the commercial value of Marconi's work, his own claims are all that can safely be made at the moment. He hopes to give his system commercial value: if he does it will undoubtedly facilitate and cheapen electrical communication. He makes no boasts, and indulges in no extravagant promises. He does not understand the art of promotion, perhaps, but he has established a character for truthfulness and conservatism, and when he makes the announcement that his system can compete successfully with cables and land wires for business, we venture to say that he will have no need of the services of a promoter to capitalize his invention.

·   ·   ·   ·   ·   ·

When the steamer *Philadelphia* pulled away from the wharf on January 22, again Marconi was at sea, this time with plenty to read and to think about, for he had been the recipient of a large mail. There were epistles of congratulations from all walks of life; royalty, statesmen, inventors and scientists. Some wanted advice. Others asked favors. Within a week he had received offers to write more articles, to lecture and to visit more places than he could in several years.

All the world suddenly became interested in this hero of the hour from picturesque Bologna—and well it might be for he was just beginning!

On the way to England he had opportunity to collect his thoughts and to study the results of the Newfoundland tests. He had been led to believe by his early experiments that long distances could be covered only from high masts and long suspended wires. The transoceanic results, however, seemed to substantiate a theory that the waves somehow follow around the earth conforming to its curve. He was convinced that one of the secrets of long-distance transmission was the use of a more powerful current at the transmitter, and he planned to verify this idea in the next trials between the continents.

The manner in which the wireless waves apparently curved around the globe set many scientists thinking. Old theories seemed to be in error. Oliver Heaviside, an English physicist and telephone engineer, who had watched the Marconi experiments with interest, had published a book on "Electromagnetic Theory," in 1893. He was not so sure that the signals clung to the curvature of the sphere as a fly crawls around an orange. He had a theory that a halo-like layer of ionized air high above the surface of the globe acted as a "mirror" reflecting the messages back to the earth.

Professor Arthur Kennelly of Harvard University agreed with Heaviside, so the "mirror" that billows up and down at high altitudes like the big top of a circus in a gale, was named the Heaviside-Kennelly layer or surface.

Marconi found that even those who believed in him still wondered if there was room for more than one or two powerful stations in the world. If a dozen or so began sending at once, how could any one be understood?

Tuning! That was the secret.

But what does that mean? Well, a Marconi engineer explained, if the transmitter is radiating 600,000 vibrations a second, the receiver in tune with it will take only 600,000 vibrations. The action is much the same as that of the familiar tuning fork which responds only to another tuning fork having exactly the same "tune" or number of vibrations a second. That is where wireless acquired the term tuning, the importance of which could not be overestimated, for it untangled the nerves of the wireless system.

Visionary writers predicted, "the spy of the future must be an electrical expert who slips in somehow and steals the secrets of the enemy's tunes." They foresaw all ships provided with instruments tuned alike, so that they could communicate freely with one another, and have no fear that the enemy could read the message. They visualized telegraph companies each with its own tuned instruments, and each government with special tunes. Predictions were made that the time would come when banking and business houses or even families and friends would each have their own wireless system with individual secret tunes. For example, it was pointed out that since there are millions of different vibrations, there would be no lack of tunes. The British navy might be tuned to receive only messages of 500,000 vibrations to the second; the German navy 1,000,000 vibrations; the United States navy, 900,000 and so on indefinitely. This was the forecast in 1902.

Tuning was a great boon to wireless progress but it was no panacea for secrecy. What it did was literally to divide "the ether" into thousands of narrow channels so a multitude of stations could operate simultaneously without interference. It was soon discovered, however, that unless the messages were coded or scrambled in some unique way there was nothing to prevent a million listeners from tuning in on the electromagetic vibrations of any navy, government or business enterprise, providing, of course, that they all had receiving outfits the dials of which could be turned from tune to tune or wave to wave.

The public watching this wireless mysticism in the heavens between the continents, unlike a theatre audience gathered to be entertained by a magician, wondered if the transoceanic trick were really possible or just what sleight-of-hand had fooled them.

If Marconi could capture an elusive signal why not have some sort of machine automatically record the dots and dashes? That would be proof unassisted by the human element. Marconi would do it; he accepted the challenge.

X

ON BOARD THE *PHILADELPHIA*

FRONT pages of newspapers dated February 22, 1902 featured news of storms on land and sea. Where was the *Kronprinz Wilhelm?* That was the big mystery story of the day. Somewhere on the Atlantic tossed by a violent gale was Prince Henry on board the *Kronprinz Wilhelm* long overdue in New York.

The Marconi operator of the Cunard liner *Etruria* at her pier in the North River tried in vain to communicate with the German ship, while agents of the North German Lloyd expressed utmost confidence in the big liner. . . . On the same night, lashed by a fierce wind, the 71st Armory in New York was burned to the ground and seventeen perished in the Park Avenue Hotel blaze. . . . A gale was raging along the Irish coast preventing the *Lucania* from landing passengers and mail at Queenstown, forcing her to proceed to Liverpool. . . . The White Star liner *Teutonic* docked a day late in New York after a "boisterous and hazardous voyage." . . . The storm routed all New York street cleaners and the headlines exclaimed "not a man braves the wind or rain." . . . Telegraph and telephone service was stopped by "the unabated fury, the worst storm in at least a dozen years."

Amid all this hurly-burly in the world's news the steamer *Philadelphia* slipped quietly away from Cherbourg at midnight on February 22, 1902. The inventor of wireless was on board en route to Canada to sign the final draft of an agreement for erection of a powerful transmitter at Glace Bay, Nova Scotia. There was too much to be done for a man of Marconi's inventive temperament to lounge idly about the decks. He had a habit of making the most of his time. Life for him proceeded, never paused. Storms ahead did not worry him; in them might lurk an opportunity for his machine!

When he walked up the gangplank of the *Philadelphia* a wireless receiving set went with him, also a recording instrument that printed blue-colored dots and dashes on a paper tape. This was to be no voyage of vacation for Marconi. With him on the ship were: H. S. Saunders of the Marconi Wireless Telegraph Company, of London; two engineers, R. N. Vyvyan and J. D. Taylor; two operators, Messrs. Stacey and Franklin; and Marconi's secretary.

Few among the passengers were aware that this young man of twenty-seven years had the power in several small boxes to talk back and forth with people on the shore, far beyond the horizon, while the ship was rolling and tossing on its way to America. No time was lost in completing the shipboard wireless installation; it was quickly "on the air."

Several test messages were sent and received until the 250-mile preliminary experimental limit was passed. Chief Officer C. Marsden was in the wireless cabin when a message was keyed, the *Philadelphia* then being about 500 miles from England. He could scarcely believe it, nevertheless, he had seen the miracle performed. Excited he rushed about the ship to tell his fellow officers. But the seafaring men only laughed. Some of them knew what Marconi hoped to do but they doubted he could do it.

The *Philadelphia* had a prearranged schedule with Poldhu, so at the appointed time the next day the skeptical sailors crowded around Marconi's room. There sat the young Italian with his eyes on the clock and the wireless instruments. He lifted a little brake on a roll of tape and the white strip began to move. Tap, tap, tap clicked the inker's metallic finger as it registered what the invisible waves were saying, in fact, it was expressing the thoughts of men 1,000 miles away.

Shortly after midnight on the 24th, scores of signals were intercepted across 1,032 miles. Just before dawn on the 25th, the ship was 1,551 miles from Poldhu and the tape recorded perfectly. No telephone receiver was used. The tape and the telegraph printer told the story in writing.

Now, there was no human agency to think or imagine; nothing to fool the ear or cause it to err. Some one remarked that when a machine does a thing humans believe; but as long as a man stands between, humans are likely to doubt.

Captain A. R. Mills, veteran of numerous transatlantic trips, was puzzled. He didn't know what to make of it. To think that he could communicate with people on the shore more than 1,000 miles distant—well, that was almost too much for an "old salt" to comprehend.

"Let me show you how accurately these instruments operate," volunteered Marconi, turning to the Captain when the ship was in mid-ocean. "Now watch and I will release the brake on the reel of tape just a few seconds before the appointed time, and we shall see when the signals begin, and whether they arrive right on the schedule."

Ten seconds prior to the zero hour Marconi lifted the latch and the tape wiggled along; the coherer ticked and the inker clicked against the paper tape. Calmly Marconi took the message off the instrument and read it aloud: "Stiff southwest breeze. Fairly heavy swell."

"Is that proof enough?" smiled the man who performed the magic.

Captain Mills was smiling too. Enthusiastically, he patted his distinguished passenger on the back and vigorously shook his hand, then took the message and signed it and the first officer too endorsed it with his signature.

"Now let us see if these instruments will get anything during the five minutes' rest period of the Poldhu operators," said Marconi. "You know some of the scientists contend the receiver may be affected by atmospheric electricity. It is possible, too, that some of the other ocean liners equipped with wireless may be operating within range of this ship. If they are, we shall not know it, for these instruments are tuned to receive messages from the Cornwall station only. But some people say I cannot tune the messages."

Again the Captain and the inventor waited. The tape was allowed to unroll during the Poldhu rest period. Then suddenly, and as strangely as before the telegraphic inker tapped, leaving a line of blue marks. The operators were back on the job and Marconi halfway across the ocean heard the click every time they pressed the key that released a dot or a dash of energy. Day after day the signals continued and the last were picked up when the *Philadelphia* was 2,099 miles from Lands End. The Poldhu to Newfoundland record had been broken and the inventor had printed proof of his achievement.

There were yards of "telegraph" tape dotted and dashed with thousands of signals to bear witness. By way of voucher, the ship's Captain and Chief Officer signed and certified the messages which they saw jotted down by the instruments. This evidence included the dispatches received up to 1551.5 miles and signals which had traveled 2,099 miles.

Reporters were on the dock to meet Marconi when the *Philadelphia* arrived in New York on March 1, and he met them again later in the day at the Hoffman House for an interview in which questions flew thick and fast. Here was front-page news.

The newspaper headlines of March 2 featured: "Marconi's Triumph in Mid-ocean." And the reporters had noted that Marconi, although he said he was not at all surprised at the results, was, nevertheless, a very happy young man.

Proudly he showed them a chart of the Atlantic compiled by Captain Mills, tracing the route of the *Philadelphia* and the points at which messages were received from Poldhu were indicated by little red stars. The chart was autographed by the Captain and First Officer with this notation:

Messages received on board steamship *Philadelphia* from Marconi station at Poldhu (Cornwall) as follows: No. 1—250.5 miles; No. 2—464.5 miles; No. 3—1,032.3 miles; No. 4—1,163.5 miles; No. 5—1,551.5 miles.

Signals 2,099 miles from Poldhu when we were in Latitude 42.01 N., and Longitude 47.23 W.

"Will they now say I was mistaken in Newfoundland?" asked Marconi with a look of defiance.

The Poldhu transmitter was practically the same as used in the Newfoundland test, a Marconi engineer explained. The dynamos generated from six to forty horsepower creating a voltage of 20,000, and this was stepped up to 250,000 volts of high tension energy. When the operator pressed the long-handled key, a snake-like spark a foot long and as thick as a blacksmith's wrist sprang across the gap. The very room, decorated with danger signs, seemed to quiver and crackle with power. But despite all the power only an infinitesimal amount of the radiated energy struck the *Philadelphia's* antenna. That was what made the trick of reception so wonderful; it was making something invisible and inaudible talk after the mysterious whisper of science was plucked from space.

"Before I sailed from England," Marconi continued, "instructions were given to the operators at Poldhu to send signals at stated intervals during the week of our voyage. They were to operate two hours out of every twelve, or one hour out of every six, sending messages and test signals in periods of ten minutes, alternating with intervals of five-minute rests.

"This merely confirms what I have previously done in Newfoundland. There is no longer any question about the ability of wireless telegraphy to transmit messages across the Atlantic. As to distance over which messages can be sent, I will say that it is a matter depending solely on the strength of the apparatus used.

"As for the curvature of the earth affecting the currents, as the cable people thought it would, that has been proved untrue. That objection on their part, though, I think, was rather imaginary, than a real one. The wish was probably father to the thought."

Do you think a message could be transmitted around the world from the same place, the sending apparatus facing in one direction and the receiving apparatus in the other? a reporter inquired.

"Well, it's possible," was the reply, "but I do not think it is what you would call a paying investment."

When asked what he thought the speed of wireless, Marconi replied, "I have made no calculations as to that, but assume it travels at the same speed as light, 186,000 miles a second."

Jubilantly, Mr. Saunders of the Marconi Company declared the *Philadelphia* voyage "a grand triumph for Marconi wireless."

"It confirms," he said, "all that Mr. Marconi has claimed for it and more, too. We are prepared to meet any one who may dispute our claims on this trip, and confront them with incontrovertible proof of what has been done."

Marconi was asked what Lord Londonderry, the Postmaster General of Great Britain meant by saying that the operation of the Marconi Company might interfere with the experiments of the British Admiralty.

"Well," he replied, "the British ships are using my instruments. The Government is paying $25,000 per annum for the use of the apparatus on a very few vessels. If the powers should decide to make me take away my stations and would pay, as they would have to, for the privilege of making my experiments themselves, then I would think I had made a good bargain. The sum they are now paying shows the basis on what they would pay to do what I am doing.

"The Admiralty's instruments are of the old style and were put in before I solved the problem of attuning to prevent intercommunication. So you see, we might interfere with the Government, but they cannot interfere with us.

"England is not the country in which I hope to accomplish much," he continued. "They are a little old-fashioned over there, you know. Some of the people do not even want the wireless system tested. They say it is too much trouble. Furthermore, England is not the proper field in which to make great strides in testing the land advantages of the system, which is as adaptable to inland and short-distance service as it is to transoceanic service."

How about that station in South Africa? a reporter asked as a parting shot as the interview ended.

"Let's finish the Atlantic first," was Marconi's answer, given with a smile.

It was evident in the press over the next few days that Marconi by his use of the Atlantic as a laboratory, had "challenged attention to the rapid movement of wireless in the direction of complete commercial utility"; signals across 2,099 miles left little room for skepticism.

There was agreement on all sides among scientists and laymen, that "the waves of etheric disturbance launched into space from the transmitting mechanism may be compared to a giant voice crying in the wilderness, and needing only an ear sufficiently sensitive to hear it at any distance to which the ever-widening circles of its undulations may reach."

The problem of wireless now resolved itself into making the "voice" loud enough to traverse the Atlantic, and the ear sensitive enough to catch its message—but that riddle no longer belonged to the discoverer; it was on the work-bench of the mechanician and electrician.

The evolution of wireless was seen working radical changes in international business relations and closer political alliances, and the newspapers vouchsafed that "what Marconi has already done will be of lasting benefit," or in the words of the *Electrical Review*, "His work is great in achieved results and greater in its potentialities of new usefulness." Mariners and newsdom were delighted that soon the Nantucket Shoals Lightship would be reporting news of incoming craft fully ten hours earlier than formerly possible, and in storms and fog as well as clear weather.

Those who saw the dots and dashes streaked across the tape from the *Philadelphia*, read more than the actual messages; even greater significance was found in reading "between the lines." There were rumors of lower cable rates, but in the same breath it was predicted that such a move was sure to spell ruin for the undersea lines. However, this figuring on disaster was not sustained by arithmetic, according to those who believed the cable tariffs had been held up too long because of freedom from competition.

"It will be without precedent in the history of progress," said *The New York Times*, "if this step (lower rates), which the cables now affect to regard as disastrous, does not so increase the volume of business to be handled that instead of hurting them competition will result to their immediate and permanent advantage."

There was yet much to be done; but the lessons learned

on board the *Philadelphia* were most valuable sign posts to new advances.

"It was during the trials on the *Philadelphia* that I discovered a marked and detrimental effect of daylight on wireless transmission, and the greater ease with which messages could be sent over long distances at night," said Marconi.[1] "I was of the opinion that weak signals during the daytime might have been caused by the loss of energy at the transmitter due to the diselectrification of the highly charged elevated aerial under the influence of sunlight.

"I am now inclined to believe that the absorption of the electric waves during the daytime is due to the ionization of the gaseous molecules of the air effected by ultra-violet light. As the ultra-violet rays, which emanate from the sun, are largely absorbed in the upper atmosphere, it is probable that the portion of the earth's atmosphere which is facing the sun will contain more ions or electrons than that portion which is in darkness. Therefore, as Professor J. J. Thomson of the Royal Institution has shown, this illuminated and ionized air will absorb some of the energy of the electric waves. The fact remains that clear sunlight and blue skies, though transparent, act as a kind of fog to powerful Hertzian waves."

Now, the question was, how to penetrate the "sunlight fog," but the Marconi men were fully confident that they would succeed completely in putting an end to the age-old isolation and dangerous solitude of the sea. Already they had whirled an invisible electric halo around King Neptune.

Because of Marconi's scientific proof that "there are more things in heaven and earth than are dreamt in our philosophy," man was fast beginning to think in terms of the globe; oceans and continents were shrinking. Wireless was prepar-

[1] Paper read by Marconi before Royal Institution, London, on June 12, 1902.

ing to tap an inexhaustible traffic between the Old and New Worlds, for "all that a man hath will he give for his life, and pretty near all that a man could afford has hitherto been asked for the privilege of lengthening life by saving time which composes it." Wireless by its annihilation of distance saves delay; it saves time.

XI

MARCONI AT GLACE BAY AND CAPE COD

DESPITE the copious evidence that wireless had conquered the Atlantic from continent to continent and from shore to ship, there were some who grasped for the last straws of skepticism by pointing out that the historic signals had traveled from east to west as the sun, but would they go in the opposite direction?

Marconi said, yes.

He would prove that the whirl of the earthly sphere had little or no influence on the waves. Glace Bay, Nova Scotia, was selected as the site for a transmitter to demonstrate that wireless could travel east as well as west.

While installation work was in progress at Glace Bay, Marconi patented a new receiving set. The coherer was still used but other parts of the circuit were greatly improved. For example, he used earphones, a tuning transformer and variable condensers to vary the capacity of both the primary and secondary circuits of the tuner. This made tuning more selective; stations could be separated more easily to avoid overlapping.

Mindful that the coherer was the weak link in the circuit he turned to develop a detector based on a discovery of Sir Ernest Rutherford in 1895. He had observed that a small, permanently magnetized needle, when suspended at the end of an electromagnet, was deflected by the rise and fall of the current in the coils of the electromagnet. In this principle Marconi saw an opportunity to sensitize his receiving set and he utilized it in designing a magnetic detector. He used a pair of horseshoe permanent magnets, slowly revolved over an electromagnet, the coils of which were connected to earphones. Fluctuations in the current caused by the incoming signals were audible in the headphones.

Since the engineers supervising the erection of the station at Glace Bay were not ready for Marconi to appear on the scene, he took advantage of the time by accepting an offer of the Italian Government to loan him the cruiser *Carlo Alberto* to facilitate long-distance tests of the magnetic detector, which had been officially introduced on June 25, 1902. On the ship a young lieutenant was specially detached, the Marquis Luigi Solari, who assisted Marconi, eventually to associate himself with the inventor and follow him throughout the romance of his career.

During the summer months with the inventor on board, the ship cruised across the North Sea to Kronstadt; to Kiel and along the Scandinavian coast, then to Portugal and southward to Africa, and back to Italian waters. While the cruiser was at Cape Skagen, the novel detector throbbed with signals from Poldhu, 800 miles distant, and at Kronstadt, 1,600 miles away. In fact, the Poldhu signals were never missing at night, but the daylight range was never more than 500 miles.

The *Carlo Alberto* turned westward with its sensitive "ear" when reports from Canada indicated the stentorian spark of a second-hand 75-kilowatt alternator at Glace Bay was ready for Marconi to be tested. He arrived at Sydney, Cape Breton, on October 31.

The first transmissions at Glace Bay were disappointing and Marconi was forced to make numerous modifications. The work was difficult because there was no instrument to measure the length of the waves. Out of the frustration, however, daily the engineers learned something new about wireless.

The first attempt to reach Poldhu from Glace Bay was made on November 19, 1902, but the operators in England failed to hear even the faintest tick; on the 28th unreadable dots and dashes were intercepted. Changes were made in the equipment and on December 5 the signals were deciphered across the ocean.

"Let us see if we can raise Cornwall," said Marconi, as he reached to the pump-handle lever of the sending key, fully three feet long. "Better put your hands over your ears," he warned, just before he pressed the key for the preliminary test.

The noise was deafening; like a machine gun being fired so rapidly that the sound was almost continuous. Long sparks jumped from the knobs of the immense Leyden jars that filled the center of the room, and illuminated the surroundings like lightning.

Crash! Crash! Crash! Four or five times Marconi flashed the signal, three short, sharp, staccato dots—"S" in the Morse code. The silence was tomblike when the noise stopped. He turned from the sending key and picked up a telephone receiver mounted on a headpiece. There he stood patiently, with both ears covered by the headphones, listening for signals while others in the room watched the unwinding tape.

"Here they are," he cried a few minutes later, smiling as the tape confirmed his statement. The inker's needle pressed upon the paper strip for an instant, lifted, pressed again, once more lifted and again transcribed a dot. Then a pause, then a dash, then another dot. That meant "SN," which in the language of the telegrapher means, "I understand."

"The wireless works very much better at night than by day," said the inventor as he tore off strips of the tape as souvenirs for his visitors. "This is the first really clear signal we have had from the other side in the daytime."

Leaving the station Marconi led the way down the bluff that gives the name of "Table Head" to this outlying corner of North America. As the party stood on the bank of the precipice, facing eastward, 2,150 unobstructed miles of ocean lay between them and the English coast. The smoke of a steamer, hull-down below the horizon, was the only thing visible except the sky and restless water.

"A freighter, probably sailing the Great Circle route to a British port," was Marconi's comment. "It was not much beyond where she is now that the *La Bourgogne* sank, with a loss of almost all her passengers, less than five years ago. Had she been equipped with wireless, aid could have been summoned from Sydney, from Newfoundland or from other ships, close to the Grand Banks at the time. The day will come when every ship will carry wireless and every port will have a wireless station. When that time comes there will be no more catastrophes as the wreck of the *La Bourgogne*. If my invention never accomplishes anything else than to save the passengers and crew of one ship it will amply pay me for all the money I have spent on it."

It was December 17, 1902. Two weeks had passed since the inventor of wireless celebrated the first anniversary of the transatlantic triumph. A busy year had fled, and it was time for another feat—the inaugural west-east broadcast.

Sir George R. Parkin, a professor at Upper Canada College and correspondent of the London *Times*, was at Glace Bay. Marconi had invited him as the guest of honor, privileged to send the first message, one of congratulations to England and to Italy. Several naval officers delegated by the Italian Government were also there to watch the tests.

Sir George boarded a train for New York as soon as the opening ceremony was over. Enroute he wrote a complete story of the event. He took his article to the office of *The New York Times*, where two typewritten copies were made, one to be mailed to London, and the other to be published in New York simultaneously with its publication in London.

The "release" of the story from London was anxiously awaited, but weeks passed and it did not come. At last *The New York Times* received, from the dead letter office in Washington, the article which had been mailed to London. Bearing the return address of *The New York Times* on the envelope, it had been sent back because Sir George had underpaid the postage by five cents. With a penalty of the same amount, that made ten cents due on the letter in London, and at that time the London *Times* had an iron-bound rule that all underpaid postage matter should be refused.

Finally the story was printed, and, the newspaper files yellowed and made brittle by age have preserved Sir George's account of Glace Bay:

"A little after midnight our whole party sat down to a light supper. Behind the cheerful table talk of the young men on the staff, one could feel the tension of an unusual anxiety as the moment approached for which they had worked, and to which they had looked forward so long. It was about ten minutes to one when we left the cottage to proceed to the operating room. I believe I was the first outsider allowed to inspect the building and machinery.

"It was a beautiful night—the moon shone brightly on the snow-covered ground. A wind, which all day had driven heavy breakers on the shore, had died away. The air was cold and clear. All the conditions seemed favorable.

"Inside the building, and among its somewhat complicated appliances, the untechnical observer's first impression was that he was among men who understood their work. The machinery was carefully inspected, some adjustments made, and various orders carried out with trained alertness. All put cotton wool in their ears to lessen the force of the electric concussion, which was not unlike the successive explosions of a Maxim gun. As the current was one of most dangerous strength those not engaged in the operations were assigned to places free from risk.

"It had been agreed that at the last moment before transmission, I should make some verbal change in the message agreed on, for the purpose of identification. This was now done and the message thus changed was handed to the inventor, who placed it on the table where his eye could follow it readily. A brief order for the lights over the battery to be put out, another for the current to be turned on, and the operating work began.

"I was struck by the instant change from nervousness to complete confidence which passed over Mr. Marconi's face the moment his hand was on the transmitting apparatus—in this case, a long, wooden lever or key.

"He explained that it would first be necessary to transmit the letter 'S' in order to fix the attention of the operators at Poldhu, and enable them to adjust their instruments. This continued for a minute or more and then, with one hand on the paper from which he read and with the other on the instrument, the inventor began to send across the Atlantic a continuous sentence.

"Outside there was no sign, of course, on the transverse wire from which the electric wave was projected of what was going on, but inside the operating room the words seemed to be spelled out in short flashes of lightning. It was done slowly, since there was no wish on this occasion to test speed. But as it was done, one remembered with a feeling of awe, what he had been told—that only the ninetieth part of a second elapses from the moment when he sees the flash till the time when the record is made at Poldhu.

"What gives it direction? 'We send it into space,' Mr. Marconi had remarked during the afternoon, 'and it must find its way to a point in Cornwall.' Mountains in the path of the current do not affect it the inventor told us, and when we remember that between the point of departure and the point of reception the curvature of the earth represents a mass of land and water more than a hundred miles high, this may be understood better.

"The first west-east message had been sent across the Atlantic. What that means to mankind no one can even guess," said Sir George. "The path to complete success may be long and difficult. Between George Stephenson's Puffing Billy and the great mogul engine which swings the limited express across the American continent, there lies three-quarters of a century of endeavor, experiment and invention. In the great original idea lay the essential thing which has revolutionized the world and the conditions of human intercourse."

After that memorable night the atmosphere did not favor wireless for several days, and some difficulties developed in the alternator so it was not until December 21 that a message from Marconi to the King of Italy, and a greeting to England's King, were intercepted on the other side of the sea.

.   .   .   .   .   .

Sandy Cape Cod was the scene of the next big act in the drama of wireless.

While Glace Bay far to the northward was winning new laurels for Marconi, lattice-like towers had been rising above the sand dunes overlooking the Atlantic, sixteen miles from the tip of Cape Cod's hook. This was South Wellfleet, Massachusetts, known by its call letters CC.[1] Built to communicate with England it was the first high-power station in the

---

[1] Station CC opened by Marconi Wireless Telegraph Company of America, January 19, 1903. Call changed to MCC in 1910 and to WCC in 1913, the apparatus of which was dismantled in 1918, hopelessly out of date.

United States. About three weeks after Glace Bay went on the air Marconi left the northland to play the leading role in wireless on the Cape.

A winter's night at South Wellfleet with a storm raging is thrilling indeed, according to veteran wireless men of that region. They hear the wind whistle through the aerial wires with terrific force, producing unearthly sounds without number; and the boom of the surf on the beach is like that of a cannon.

It was just such a January scene that greeted Marconi when he arrived at the Massachusetts outpost, where clamming and fishing are the chief pursuits of South Wellfleet's winter inhabitants.

The station stood some distance from the town, and was reached by a path which at first rambled through the woods; then across an open field which sloped upward to a sandy hill. On the top of the rise four red, lattice-work towers were seen, described as "the legs of a huge footstool turned bottom side up." A long 20-wire flat-top aerial started from flag-pole masts and ran to the main towers, filling the entire plane between the tips of the 210-foot structures. Then the wires zigzagged downward, weaving back and forth between the front "legs" and the back, tapering gradually until the strands were braided a few feet above the station building. This aerial was designed to make the signals go furthest in an easterly direction. Europe was the goal.

When the crest of the hill was reached the sea came into view for the station stood on a sand dune, eighty odd feet above the beach. Seen from this point, it was apparent that the towers were at the mercy of the gales from every side. It was a desolate-looking spot.

Inside the building the instrument room was the main point of interest. More than half of its area was devoted to a bank of condensers affiliated with the 25-kilowatt spark transmitter. There was a non-synchronous rotary spark gap nearly three feet in diameter and it roared formidably. In the background stood the relay key, which was rather unusual, because it broke the secondary circuit of the power transformer instead of the primary circuit in order to put less strain on the generating apparatus and permit faster and cleaner sending. That was a new idea.

A strong blast of compressed air prevented excessive arcing, across the points of the rotary gap. There was also an air blast on each side of the key and sometimes it carried the flame from the 50-kilowatt secondary current six or eight inches away from the contact points. That's why a long-lever handle of wood was used.

In later years when 10:15 P.M. came around, a solid low-pitched note was heard calling "QST de WCC press to ships fitted with Marconi or Debeg apparatus and subscribing to the Marconi press service. . . ." Perhaps the S.S. *Campania* was listening because it had instituted the first wireless newspaper printed at sea for its passengers.

It was good smooth sending—about eighteen words a minute—formed by a machine which operated the transmitting key in accordance with perforations in a long paper tape. Many an operator in the eastern part of the United States learned his wireless letters at "Grandma Wellfleet's" knee, and will probably never forget the low-pitched note which seemed to fairly pound its way through space like the thud of a hammer.

At South Wellfleet was a newspaperman, Frank Parker Stockbridge, detailed by Samuel S. Chamberlain, managing editor of the *New York Journal,* to send one of the first wireless messages across the Atlantic from Cape Cod. His was an interesting story of what transpired at WCC on the opening night.

"There was a wait of a week or more at Wellfleet for Marconi to get the apparatus adjusted for transatlantic work," said Stockbridge. "One evening, after supper, Marconi telephoned me at the hotel: 'Can you come over right away?' It was a particularly dark night and the wind was blowing across the Cape at about forty miles an hour.

" 'We shall get it across tonight,' said Marconi. 'The instruments are well adjusted and we got a signal across to the other side a little while ago. We have been receiving their signals for two or three days. I think that some time between now and midnight I shall be able to get that message across for you.'

"It did not take us long to draft a dispatch addressed to the editor of the London *Times* congratulating him and the English people on this new bond of communication between the great English-speaking nations, and signed William R. Hearst. It was arranged that I should be in the postoffice all the rest of the evening, where Marconi promised to call me as soon as he had the news I was waiting for. It seemed like hours before the telephone rang. Marconi was on the wire, jubilant and excited.

" 'I have just got your message across,' he said. 'The President wanted to send a message to King Edward. We sent that, and Mr. Hearst's message, and picked up the return signal verifying reception on the other side.' "

President Roosevelt's greeting read:

His Majesty, Edward VII, London, England.
    In taking advantage of the wonderful triumph of scientific research and ingenuity which has been achieved in perfecting a system of wireless telegraphy, I extend on behalf of the American people most cordial greetings and good wishes to you and all the people of the British Empire.
                                        Theodore Roosevelt.
    South Wellfleet, Mass., Jan. 19, 1903.

The monarch answered:

The President, White House, Wash., America.

I thank you most sincerely for the kind message which I have just received from you through Marconi's transatlantic wireless telegraph. I sincerely reciprocate in the name of the people of the British Empire the cordial greetings and friendly sentiment expressed by you on behalf of the American nation, and I heartily wish you and your country every possible prosperity.

Edward R. and I.

Sandringham, Jan. 19, 1903.

The Roosevelt message to King Edward was broadcast from Cape Cod between 9 and 11 P.M., and Glace Bay repeated it for reception at Poldhu between 11 P.M., and midnight. It was received direct from Cape Cod and was, therefore, the first wireless message to be received in England direct from the United States, according to R. N. Vyvyan, the engineer in charge. Other messages were exchanged until January 22, when Marconi sailed for England and home.

Bologna's welcome was a civic affair long to be remembered by Marconi and the townsfolk. The young scientist was accorded a public reception that crowded the Littoriale Gymnasium to its doors with the elite of the city.

It was a proud moment for his father and mother. Anna Marconi, in character with her native Ireland, smiled happily. Giuseppe Marconi, native of emotional Italy, wept for joy as he saw his youngest son feted by the town he loved.

Seated between father and mother, Bologna's honored guest was complimented and praised by city officials and scientists from the university, until embarrassment almost forced him to beat a retreat. He tried to speak but his voice shook and his trembling fingers threatened to drop the upraised wine glass. Great as Marconi had become in the realm of scientific achievement, he had devoted little time to the artistry of oratory.

But his modesty and bashfulness pleased the people of

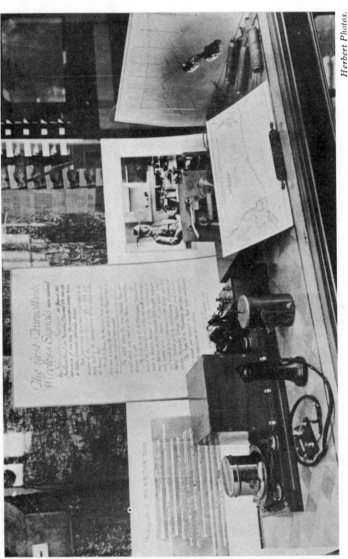

Historic evidence—receiver used by Marconi to detect the first transatlantic signal; illustration shows the inventor with the apparatus in the barracks on Signal Hill.

Bologna far more than sparkling eloquence could have done. They read in his blushes and halting speech the welcome fact that success had failed to spoil him.

Professor Righi's speech was a feature of the reception. "Perhaps no one can appreciate better than I his exceptional inventive power and his unusual intellectual gifts," said the aged scientist. "It is to the credit of Marconi that he has proved how much those are in error who regard with disdainful or indifferent eyes the work carried on in the silence of the laboratory by modest students of science."

In Rome a greater and more solemn reception took place; the Eternal City was en fête for Marconi and he was granted the freedom of the metropolis.

.   .   .   .   .   .

Only five years had passed since the general public first heard of Marconi. He was now one of the most "interviewed" of public men.[2] Reporters hunted him; and when they drove him to cover they haunted him. Scarcely a day passed that he was not questioned as to his work or begged to give some exclusive bit of information. He had been photographed from all possible angles; he had been interviewed at all possible times, and sometimes at impossible times.

Marconi was beginning to learn that fame is its own punishment; and that he must submit to the delicate torments of the inquisition instituted by the modern press. Observers considered it no wonder he left the impression of being intensely wearied by interviewers. At best they noted he was but pleasantly unhappy with them. In this respect he might be called "the Lindbergh of wireless."

The *Scientific American* correspondent caught an excel-

[2] "An Impression of Marconi," *Scientific American*, February 7, 1903.

lent impression of this man from Italy; an impression that would apply as truly descriptive in 1937 as in 1903:

When you meet him for the first time you know that he is not a cordial man; and yet you feel that he will not rebuff you, that he will probably do for you what he can. His manner is that of chilly reserve. In the press he is referred to as "the young Anglo-Italian" who has done some startling things which are not very clearly explained. . . . A cool, calculating man of the North is this so-called Anglo-Italian.

For a successful inventor Marconi appears the least joyous of men. His features are melancholy in expression. They are those of a man fast approaching forty—not those of a man of twenty-eight. His face is impassive, his eye almost cold. When he smiles he half shuts his eyes, wrinkles the muscles of his cheek and draws up the corners of his mouth. It is not a pleasant smile.

If you visit Marconi with the expectation that he will do most of the talking you will find that you are grievously mistaken. You must do the talking yourself. To be sure, he answers questions frankly and fully; but he will not converse voluntarily. You discover quickly enough that his reticence is the reticence of modesty. When he discusses the Marconi system of wireless telegraphy, he refers to it as "our" system, not as "my" system. He praises where praise is due, recognizing fully that it is not given to any one man to learn all the secrets of science, and that great results are obtained usually by the cooperation of many minds working to a common end.

He acknowledges fully and openly how important to himself has been the work of his predecessors, and even that of some of his contemporaries. "The success of the experiments with which I have been engaged is the logical results of myself and my assistants in the last few years, and of scientific investigations of the latter part of the century," he himself says. "Revolutionize" is a word not included in the vocabulary which he uses to describe the possibilities of his invention. He frankly admits that it is not his purpose to render submarine cables useless; he is satisfied if he can successfully compete with them; or if he can only make them cut down their present rates.

And yet, he talks of his system with a certain air of easy confidence, which leads you to infer that if any man will ever succeed in outdoing the submarine cables, it is Guglielmo Marconi. It is not often that he prophesies; and when he does you feel that he knows; or as he himself puts it, "It is not my policy to make a statement before I am absolutely sure of the facts."

Although he is modest he does not wrong himself by belittling his own work. He talks of his magnetic receiver almost objectively, as if it were the production of some other inventor's mind, which is all the more noteworthy because the instrument in question is, probably, the most valuable contribution to wireless telegraphic apparatus made since the invention of the coherer. He admits his receiver's great speed and its general merit, and expresses his opinion of its recent remarkable performance at Cape Cod in terms of mild approval, which are, however, not utterly devoid of a tinge of pleasure. It is difficult to picture Marconi waxing enthusiastic even over a very great achievement. It is significant that the newspaper men who saw him after his wonderful feat at Cape Cod merely reported him to be in exceptionally good humor.

He has had unusual obstacles to contend with in the development of his ideas. There have been technical difficulties, of which he is now fortunately able to speak as things of the past. The reason for these difficulties he describes in a simple way without a trace of the pride that he probably feels in having overcome them: "Any other machine enables the inventor to shut himself up in a room and announce results when it is wise for him to do so. Wireless telegraphy is different, especially in the way that we labor. It is not a case of one machine here and one in England; but of half a machine here, and another half in England. And each of these machines must be adjusted, the one to the other." . . .

As he himself recognizes the merit of the labors of those who went before him, it is fitting that others should recognize the fact that his organizing talent has brought together a hundred contributory speculations and detached discoveries into harmonious relations, and has given us a system of wireless telegraphy, still susceptible of improvement in many respects, no doubt, but practical in the attainment of results scarcely deemed possible by present agencies.

.   .   .   .

Wireless was growing in leaps and bounds from one point on the earth to another. It was no myth. The years 1900 to 1905 brought spectacular advances.

The Red Star Liner *Kroonland* proceeding westward after leaving the Channel encountered a terrific gale.[3] A big

[3] December 4, 1903.

comber struck the rudder and completely disabled the steering gear. Within half an hour the *Kroonland's* operator, Ludwig Arnson, established communication with H.M.S. *Kent* which stood by while messages were sent to Cape Clear, 130 miles distant. The *Kroonland* was towed to Queenstown and on the way sent reassuring bulletins and specifications for a new rudder. This was the first American ship to send the wireless distress call—CQD.

About this time Professor Reginald Fessenden offered a radically new liquid detector known as "the electrolytic." Into a solution 20 percent sulphuric or nitric acid dipped a silver-coated platinum wire about the thickness of a horsehair. It was not particularly popular with operators, however, because the acid often spilled or leaked, and, furthermore, they had continually to melt the end of the wire to obtain a good contact, thereby restoring maximum sensitivity.

General Henry H. C. Dunwoody of the U. S. Army and G. W. Pickard developed a simpler and more efficient form of detector—the crystal. The simplicity of this unit opened the gateway of experimentation to many a boy interested in wireless. A small piece of galena held tightly in a metal cup or clip did the trick. A thin wire popularly known as "the catwhisker" tickled the surface of the mineral. There were some spots on the crystal more sensitive to wireless than others.

The main disadvantage, of course, was that the delicate wire was easily jarred off the sensitive point, and it might slip off while a message was being received. On shipboard the vibrations and rolling of the craft made it more exasperating for the operator. In search of a more stable device it was discovered that carborundum gripped in a metal cup would suffice if a piece of carbon pressed firmly against the surface. Once adjusted it was not easily jarred, and it be-

came popular on ships as a supplement to the magnetic detector. Wireless was through with the coherer. An insig-
nificant-looking piece of galena, iron pyrites, carborundum,
galena or even a piece of coal could detect signals originat-
ing many miles away, and these detectors could be made for
a few cents.

England as a maritime center had become the nucleus of
wireless activity. Nevertheless, with so many foreign vessels
being equipped several incidents occurred to disclose some
sort of government regulation and cooperation between nations necessary to establish definite standards for general
communication.

Germany took the initiative and as a result the first
International Radiotelegraphic Conference was held in Berlin, opening on August 4, 1903. The leading powers sent
representatives and in general agreed to certain proposals,
but Great Britain and Italy did not fully approve the recom-
mendations. It was explained that they both had wireless
rules in effect which were partly in conflict with the proposed
regulations; they could not amend or abrogate conveniently
the rules already in force.

However, there is an old story in wireless circles that goes
back beyond the days of wireless regulations. It seems that
Prince Henry, brother of Kaiser Wilhelm of Germany, en
route from Hamburg to New York, while off the English
coast flashed a wireless order to Marconi stations to relay
his personal messages. The Marconi men inquired if he was
in need of assistance, otherwise, they were under no contract
or international obligation to handle his traffic for his ship
was equipped with German-made instruments. The Prince
angrily reported the incident to the Kaiser, who immediately
through diplomatic channels proposed an international wireless conclave to formulate regulations to control communication.

The Marconi interests, however, contended that the real purpose of the conference was to open the way for promotion of German wireless. Marconi officials insisted that their stations on land and sea would always be at the disposal of vessels in distress, but the Marconi system was entitled to the commercial rights to be derived from the service it had initiated.

The Germans, nevertheless, feared a Marconi monopoly despite the fact that it might be the legitimate monopoly of an inventor. Competition, the Germans asserted, would reduce wireless rates and improve the service for all countries, specially those still without wireless service. The German view of the situation was considered to be more industrial than humanitarian, according to the Italians.

Further light is cast upon the attitude of Germany toward the Marconi Company, and the bitter feeling of Marconi, by an episode related by R. N. Vyvyan, one of Marconi's early engineering assistants.[4] He recalled how Marconi had been invited to Rome as guest of the Italian Government, and the German Emperor, who had arrived the previous day, was also a guest of the King at the Quirinal. At dinner that night, the Kaiser, in a discussion of wireless, turned to Marconi and said,

"Signor Marconi, you must not think I have any animosity against yourself but the policy of your company I object to."

"Your Imperial Majesty," replied Marconi, "I should be overwhelmed if I thought you had any personal animosity against myself but the policy of my company is decided by myself."

It is of interest to recall that prior to enactment of the British Wireless Act in 1904 no license was required to erect wireless stations in the United Kingdom for communication

---

[4] "Wireless Over 30 Years," 1933.

with points outside territorial waters. The Marconi Company had installed stations, and when the Wireless Act came into force the transmitters constituted a legitimate and lawfully established vested industry, which the British Government had justly so considered.

It was folly to believe, however, that wireless had reached perfection; that its chief function was in marine communication and across the Atlantic. Evidence was plentiful that the Marconi invention was but a seedling; it might never cease to grow.

Progress called for new devices, and science would supply them to nurture what Marconi had conceived and started. Wireless was a "gold field" for experimenters. Young and old, amateurs and electrical engineers working in woodsheds and attics, and in finely equipped laboratories rushed in after Marconi had staked his claims. In such a fertile field of science no one knew from what quarters revolutionary and novel inventions might spring.

Marconi, the Italian business man's son, had done his part and now John Ambrose Fleming, the son of a minister, the Rev. James Fleming of England, introduced the valve detector, the forerunner of a wondrous vacuum tube, foreordained to revolutionize all branches of the science.

Fleming had worked for three years at Cambridge under Professor James Clerk Maxwell, therefore, as an extraordinarily keen student he was duly prepared and well qualified to know what wireless needed to forge ahead. It was this same Fleming who assisted Marconi at Poldhu. He called his new device "a two-element thermionic valve detector," and patented it under No. 24850. This invention of 1904 vintage would win him the honor of knighthood (in 1929) for his "valuable service in science and industry." The courts would uphold his patent and praise its "very meritorious service and practical usefulness."

Wireless in 1904 was one of the marvels of the St. Louis World's Fair. It seemed everybody had heard of Marconi by this time. The public was more than anxious to see the apparatus, and to hear the crack of the mystic spark.

The year 1905 was a turning point in more ways than one for Marconi. It was a year of invention. The rumbles of a patent war were more disturbing. Later, in looking back, Marconi remarked:

"In 1905 my experience led me to patent and introduce the horizontal directional aerial, which at once brought about the most marked improvement in the strength of signals. It is from this point and by this new discovery that real progress in long-distance work is dated."

XII

WEDDING BELLS—AND WIRELESS

THE jingle of wedding bells and the strains of "Lohengrin" supplemented the sputtering tattoo of dots and dashes for Marconi, who at the age of thirty-one, following in the footsteps of his father, selected a bride from the Emerald Isle. On March 16, 1905, at St. George's Church in Hanover Square, London, he married the Hon. Beatrice O'Brien, a daughter of Lord Inchiquin. Sailing on the *Campania* bound for New York the Marconis went to Canada to see the new wireless station at Glace Bay.

From this marriage, which did not prove happy, there were three children: Degna, born in September, 1908; Giulio, on May 21, 1910, and Gioia, on April 10, 1916.

.   .   .   .   .   .

The Atlantic cable had just celebrated its jubilee year—1904. The question still persisted, "Will Marconi supplant the cables?" The Newfoundland legislature in 1854 had given the submarine telegraph cable across the Atlantic exclusive landing and working rights in Newfoundland for fifty years. This clause insuring monopoly was credited with making the enterprise possible, because Newfoundland was but 1,650 miles from the Irish coast, and obviously the organization with exclusive rights, possessed a great advantage over any competitor. But now there was wireless; and it had made immense strides since the first letter "S" found its way across the Atlantic to startle the cable men.

Marconi, in 1905, could foresee the day when 200 words would be flashed across the ocean in a minute, and "the general use of wireless instead of the mails for a large portion of the personal correspondence that now passes between America and Europe, is a certain development of the future."

There were some who classed the hope of the wireless men to compete with the cables as "one of the fairy-tales of science," and in tribute to Cyrus W. Field they added, "we could better spare a whole fleet of ocean greyhounds than lose the electric cable links in the chain of international communication."

Electricity was called a handmaiden of civilization, and the cables "the silent messengers of civilized intercourse sent racing along the ocean bed." It was recalled that prior to 1866 America and Europe were at least a fortnight apart; the cables linked the hemispheres, but so did wireless, for Marconi had proved that the invisible waves could do it too, and in the twinkle of an eye. The two worlds had been linked telegraphically by the words, "Glory to God in the highest," spelled by dots and dashes that sped along the gloomy caverns of the deep. The London *Times* commented that "the wildest exaggerations of an Arabian tale have been outdone by this simple achievement of modern times." Yet wireless was simpler and less costly.

Nevertheless, the cable continued to add to its mileage. For example, even in 1901 the big English cable to Australia, which was 15,000 miles long in its several sections, cost $1,800 a mile. By 1905 the cable's efficiency was greatly enhanced and it could work at the rate of eighty words a minute, and if pushed could handle 200 words a minute. Wireless would have to learn this trick of high speed to compete with such service. The cable had a "duplex" system; wireless had not. But some day it might.

No one thought in 1905 that within thirty years an inter-

national audience would eavesdrop on a presidential inaugural in the United States and hear the very voices of Calvin
Coolidge, Herbert Hoover, Franklin D. Roosevelt and those
to follow, take the oath of office on the portico of the
national Capitol.

The cables had never done that, but the cable experts
pointed with pride to the fact that the quickest message ever
sent was the one announcing President McKinley's re-
election. It went around the world in forty-nine minutes,
on a line that had been cleared of all traffic for two hours,
waiting for the flash. From Washington the message sped
to New York, Nova Scotia, Newfoundland, Ireland, Gibraltar, Malta, Alexandria, Suez, Aden, Bombay, Madras,
Penang, Singapore, Hong Kong, Manila and back to the
United States on the Pacific cable.

No, wireless telegraphy was not as yet regarded as a serious competitor of such a mighty system of globe-encircling
communication. In fact, it was remarked that petroleum did
not destroy the use of gas, nor electricity the employment of
either; nor did wireless portend the doom of the cables.
Marconi wireless, it was said, "is only in the experimental
stages, and it is not unreasonable to expect a prolonged
hiatus before it banishes the living wires as outworn
devices."

.   .   .   .   .   .

Wireless progress on the heels of 1905 was rapid; startling in many ways. Lee de Forest added the grid or third
element to Fleming's valve, greatly improving its efficiency.
What a future that little glass bulb had in store for it! Such
a simple, innocent-looking device yet it would some day
antiquate the old spark, the cumbersome, high frequency
alternators, and the glaring electrical arcs, when man un-
raveled the electronic secrets. It would cause all space to

scintillate with human thoughts and music, and even pictures!

Fessenden was doing some remarkable radiophone work with a high frequency alternator at Brant Rock, Mass. Hundreds of patents pertaining to wireless would be chalked up under his name before his death (1932).

Marconi was called upon to defend his ethereal rights. The courts, it was apparent, were to be the scene of many legal battles. It was in 1905 that the Marconi Company instituted suit against the De Forest Wireless Telegraph Company. In pronouncing the decision in Marconi's favor, Judge William K. Townsend of the United States Circuit Court took pains to dispel all doubt as to whether or not Guglielmo Marconi was actually the founder of wireless telegraphy. In what was referred to as "a magnificent flowery peroration, quite appropriately Latin in feeling," his Honor pictured Marconi as "a fearless forerunner of science."

While Marconi was winning decisions in court that fortified his claims, the utility of his invention was expanding. The business world was fast becoming alert to the fact that wireless had many uses outside of the mariners' circle.

Why not a press service across the Atlantic? Newspapers were clamoring for it. Competition with the cable might be a good thing. Rates might be lowered. Furthermore, if the undersea lines were ever ripped apart wireless would keep the stream of traffic flowing. Wireless speeded news while it was fresh.

To demonstrate the natural alliance of news and wireless, in the spring of 1903 an attempt was made to flash dispatches from America to the London *Times*. It was considered to be quite a feat that 267 words of wirelessed news were published during the latter days of March and the early part of April. With the approach of summer, however, reception became less reliable so the *Times'* service was temporarily discontinued. But the cue had been given to Marconi that the printing presses were more anxious than ever for him to increase the power of wireless so that it might dependably reach out to the far corners of the earth to flash news that might be inked in a hurry.

Marconi sensed the demand. So numerous had been the improvements evolved during the tests at Poldhu and Cape Breton that those plants were, even at this early date, completely antiquated. Rather than attempt to apply the new ideas to the old installations Marconi decided to build a long-distance station in Ireland, and move from Glace Bay to a different site in the vicinity where land was available for larger aerials. Greater power would be the feature of these stations.

Clifden, Ireland, was chosen as the site of a 300-kilowatt plant, incorporating radically new ideas, including a novel aerial system, and the large condensers were made of metal plates suspended in air instead of the customary glass plate capacities. There was a unique rotary spark gap designed to produce a whistle-like note more distinguishable at the receiver, especially through static and other signals.

Preparations were complete on October 15, 1907 for a limited press and commercial service. Wireless was ready to join the Old and New Worlds in transoceanic public service—at ten cents a word and five cents a word for press.

It was 11:39 o'clock in the morning (in Ireland) on October 17 that W. S. Entwistle, the engineer in charge at Clifden, issued orders to send and receive the first public messages over the new circuit. Contact with Glace Bay was quickly established. Preliminary tests indicated conditions ideal for transmission and reception on both sides of the Atlantic.

The operator at the Irish end was handed a sheaf of messages and the one on top went westward first. It was from Privy Councillor Lord Avebury to *The New York Times:*

I trust that the introduction of wireless will more closely unite the people of the United States and Great Britain, who seem to form one nation, though under two Governments, and whose interests are really identical.—Avebury.

This message was followed by one from the *Times'* correspondent in Nova Scotia:

Glace Bay, N. S., Oct. 17.
Mr. Marconi says: "Congratulate *New York Times* on having received first westward press message!"

Then came in full the original message filed by the *Times'* correspondent in London, from which the above short dispatch was condensed to meet the fifty-word limit imposed by the Marconi Company upon the first message transmitted. The full text read:

This message marks the opening of the transatlantic wireless service. It is now eleven years since William Marconi, in May, 1896, announced in New York that he had discovered the secret by which messages might be flashed through space without the assistance of wires or cables such as were used in the ordinary methods of telegraphy at that time.

Mr. Marconi's statements were received with skepticism, and his prediction of the wonders which he felt confident could be worked by means of his application of the Hertzian waves was openly disputed even by electricians, who ought from their knowledge of the feats achieved by electric sparks to have recognized that the limits of its potentialities had not been reached.

Mr. Marconi, as this message testifies, has not accomplished all that he expresses confidence in being able to do. This message, which I have handed in at the London office of the Marconi Wireless Telegraph Company for transmission to New York by the Marconi system speaks for itself.

There is pleasure in transmitting by wireless telegraphy the following messages from representative Englishmen which have been furnished by the signatories for publication in *The New*

York Times in connection with one of the most remarkable achievements of modern science.

The Duke of Argyll's message was:
"The air message is an emblem of the kinship of two peoples who love freedom."

Sir George Taubman Goldie sent:
"May this latest triumph of science consolidate the essential unity of the English speaking nations, the forerunner of the unity of mankind."

Field Marshal Viscount Wolseley's message read:
"I rejoice that a new link between the United States and the mother country has been created. May it strengthen the union between all English speaking races."

Alfred Austin, Poet Laureate, flashed:
"Let the Stars and Stripes and the Union Jack still float most high together."

The message of Sir Norman Lockyer, scientist, said:
"All honor to the country where, beyond all others, the Central Government, the State Legislatures, and private citizens foster education and research as the true, and indeed the only, foundation of a nation's greatness. Such a nation will be the one to profit most from the future victories of science which are certain to beggar the achievements of the present as wireless telegraphy pales the achievements of the past."

Georges Clemenceau, Prime Minister of France, forwarded this message:
"In the inauguration of the marvelous means of communication put at their disposition from this time forward the two great Republics could not but find it a happy occasion to congratulate themselves and to express the most cordial wishes for the maintenance of peace in the work for the happiness of the people in the joint responsibility."

The first newspaper dispatch received at London, read:
"*The New York Times* sends greetings to the *London Daily Mail* with congratulations to Marconi on the inauguration of his wireless system."

The next message went to Lord Kelvin, 15 Eaton Place, London:
"Very happy to be able to send you and Lady Kelvin most

cordial greetings transmitted through ether from Canada to Ireland.—Marconi."

Lord Kelvin's reply from Largs, Scotland, read:
"Marconi, Glace Bay: Heartiest thanks for your kind telegram and congratulations on your practical use of ether.—Kelvin."

The Dublin Stock Exchange congratulated the New York Stock Exchange on the successful inauguration of a quick, inexpensive wireless system between America and Great Britain.

The Governor General of Canada sent greetings to King Edward.

This had been a busy day. Up to 7:30 P.M., 10,000 words had been exchanged and many messages were on file at both ends of the circuit. Marconi remained on the job all day at Glace Bay lending a helping hand whenever needed.

"Only those who worked with Marconi throughout these four years realize the wonderful courage he showed under frequent disappointments, the extraordinary fertility of his mind in inventing new methods to displace others found faulty," said R. N. Vyvyan, the engineer in charge,[1] "and his willingness to work, often for sixteen hours at a time when any interesting development was being tested. At the same time the Directors of the Marconi Company showed wonderful confidence in Marconi, and courage in continuing to vote the large sums necessary from year to year until success was finally achieved."

There was no evidence in the outdoor scene at Glace Bay to indicate that this event marked a new era in transatlantic telegraphy, except that from the tops of the four towers floated the flags of Italy, the United States, Great Britain and Canada.

All hands could be seen in the operating room and engine room, each attending to his appointed task, hurrying here and there in its execution, while Chief Engineer Vyvyan kept

[1] "Wireless Over Thirty Years," R. N. Vyvyan.

a watchful eye over everything. At his signal the machinery was set in motion, switches were manipulated, and all was ready for transmission of the first messages.

The operator then pressed a key. There was a flash of light accompanied by a sharp musical report, quickly followed by others, which formed themselves into the characters of the Morse code, and one realized that a message was speeding to its destination on the other side of the Atlantic.

Then the switches were thrown out and the receiving operator, wearing a telephone headgear, was observed busily engaged in taking down the business then being transmitted to Ireland from Canada. The simplicity of the operation was astounding when one considered the wonder of the feat.

It was a proud day for Marconi, and late that night he said:

I am entirely satisfied. Everything worked splendidly. We are going to operate a limited service for awhile, but we have already handled from 5,000 to 10,000 words on account of it being a special day. A large number of the congratulatory and press dispatches were exchanged between London and New York. We did not transmit commercial or private messages as a rule today, as we made it sort of press day.

It cannot be called an inaugural. We had our real opening two years ago when telegrams were passed between the President and King. We have not, therefore, addressed anything to crowned heads, but we are just quietly starting to do a regular business between Europe and America in continuation of the old service. Sir Wilfred Laurier sent two messages this morning. He called wireless "one more triumph for Empire and science." I am, indeed, pleased with the result.

Among the 10,000 words that crossed the sea were these:

London, via Marconi Wireless.
Glace Bay, N. S., Oct. 17, 1907.
Mr. Peter Cooper Hewitt, 51 Madison Ave., New York, N. Y.
I think that all of us who have dabbled in science sufficiently and who understand the difficulties that one has to encounter even

with the ponderable should take off our hats to Mr. Marconi and congratulate him upon his almost unbelievable success in dealing with the imponderable. All honor to Marconi! Perhaps the next step will be to harness the whole energy of Niagara to make an attempt to communicate with the planet Mars.

Hiram Maxim.

Have you chosen a name for wireless messages?

"No, not yet," said the inventor, "Marconigram seems to stick on the tongue, but so far we have no other."

Peter Cooper Hewitt had an electrical studio in the old Madison Square Garden Building. Equipped with a Marconi magnetic detector, he was among the first New Yorkers who endeavored to pick up messages from England. In a glass box-like enclosure glowed a blue light. Heavy magnets were balanced against the bottom of the glass and overhead were strings of wires several of which led to the top of the historic tower near the gilded Diana.

When he donned the nickel headband holding two receivers that capped his ears Hewitt could tune the set and hear Cape Cod but nothing from Glace Bay or Ireland. He thrilled guests by letting them hear Galilee, New Jersey, talking with a vessel on the way to Europe. He could hear No. 42 Broadway calling Nova Scotia. He could eavesdrop on tugs in the harbor, steamers in Long Island Sound and ships off Nantucket Lightship.

"A great achievement for Marconi," remarked Mr. Hewitt in commenting on the opening of commercial transoceanic service. "He has crowned his ambition. Marconi's untiring work and endeavors perfected wireless telegraphy so that it became available for ships, and now his work is crowned with success by the establishment of transatlantic communication, which if considered from the information possessed by scientists ten years ago, is a most marvelous achievement. It is one that will prove of far greater utility than communication between ships which he has already established.

"In this great epoch of wireless, brought about by Marconi's untiring skill and development, it must not be forgotten that Hertz's appreciation and physical rendering of Maxwell's theorem rendered it possible.

"This morning I met Professor Fessenden, an indefatigable worker in the completion of wireless possibilities, and he told me that he had picked up messages from England at his Brant Rock, Massachusetts, station. If the messages from the other side have been received by wireless as near New York as the Massachusetts coast, there is an extreme probability that they will in a short time be intercepted here and handled in a way that will meet the demands of the times in inter-continental communication."

Marconi was not long in extending his service. On February 8, 1908 ordinary commercial traffic was instituted between London and Montreal through land wire connections between those cities and the Clifden-Glace Bay transmitters. Incidentally, the transoceanic service by the Marconi system has never been discontinued from that date, except in 1909 when the Glace Bay station was destroyed by fire. A new plant was installed. By the end of February 1908, about 119,945 words of press and commercial dispatches had been broadcast across the sea. The Clifden service was later transferred to Carnarvon, Wales.

"In seven years the useful range of wireless has increased from 200 to 2,500 miles," said Marconi.[2] "In view of that fact, he will be a bold prophet who will venture to affirm what may not be done in seven years more. I do not claim that wireless telegraphy is infallible. . . . No telegraph system is secret. The contents of every telegram are known to

[2] Lecture on "Wireless Telegraphy," March 20, 1908, before Royal Institution, London.

every operator who handles it. . . . I am very confident that it is only a question of time, and not a very long time, before wireless over great distances, possibly around the world, will become an indispensable aid to commerce and civilization.

"Whether the new telegraphy will or will not injure or displace the cables is still a matter of conjecture, but in my opinion it rests a good deal on what the cables can do in the way of cheaper rates. Whatever may be the view as to its shortcomings and defects, there can be no doubt that wireless across the ocean has come to stay and will continue to advance."

The British Post Office, in 1909, expressed a desire to purchase the shore stations of the Marconi Company, which were employed for communication with ships, and an agreement was entered into whereby on September 29, 1909, the nine coastal transmitters were to be sold. The consideration paid was $75,000 or an average of $8,330 per station. The owners of the Poulsen station were allowed to continue the use of it for commercial purposes for some two or three years after the Post Office had become possessed of the Marconi stations.

The scientific rather than the business or industrial promotion of wireless held the greater fascination for Marconi, and while commercial deals were in progress he, nevertheless, continued experimenting. He returned to Rome on December 29, 1911 from the sands of Tripoli where he had been conducting some strange experiments.

"We were surprised and gratified to find that wireless messages could be sent with absolute security over the desert without the usual masts," he reported. "Instead of on poles, wire is laid on the sand, in the direction in which the message is to be sent. It goes, and is received without any interruption, exactly the same as though the usual system were employed.

"The sand is an absolute non-conductor, so electric waves

are not disturbed in any way. The sand being dry, neither rain nor tempest can affect the waves. The advantages of this are so evident it seems almost ridiculous to enumerate them."

The dispatch concluded: "Marconi never remains long in Rome and after the foregoing conversation left at once for the North Sea."

XIII

TESTED BY DISASTER AT SEA

AN invention, no matter how expedient it appears in theory or prophecy, is frequently tested in the crucible of disaster before mankind thoroughly comprehends and appreciates its value.

Some day a big ship might founder. That would be a crucial test for the Marconi contraptions. It would etch the glory of wireless on the dark background of calamity at sea. But it would be "a disaster darker even than Martinique" for the inventor if ever an ocean liner, equipped with wireless, went to a watery grave with human souls washed off its decks.

Some day, it seemed, this terrible test of wireless was sure to come, for ever since ships plied the seven seas collisions and wrecks, storms and mystery, permeated through the stories of sailors. In the throes of catastrophe men had gone down to the sea in ships never to be heard from again after they waved farewell; never a trace of what happened or where. They vanished as the grim reaper swept across the waves, sending the helpless to a sepulcher in the sea.

But now, wireless could call for assistance. It could warn of hurricanes and icebergs, and possibly ward off the blow. It could guide vessels through fog when screeching sirens and swath-like beams from lighthouses failed to penetrate. The utility of wireless at sea became evident in more ways than the mere handling of friendly bon voyage messages, news bulletins or business dispatches.

Wireless had proved itself under favorable conditions across the Channel and across the Atlantic, but what would it do in time of emergency in the dead of night at sea, with all lights out and frantic people screaming for help far off any shore?

First of all a distress signal known instantly by all, no matter what their tongue, must be in readiness for such a day.

The CQD was chosen in 1904; in 1908 it gave way to SOS, quicker to send and more easily recognized—three dots, three dashes and three more dots!

But the dash, dot, dash, dot—dash, dash, dot, dash—dash, dot, dot, of the long CQD remained in force to play an heroic role in disaster and write itself on the pages of marine history, because all nations had not promptly ratified the SOS.

. . . . . .

Fog hung heavy over Sandy Hook on the night of January 23, 1909. Suddenly there was a crunching, ripping noise. The S.S. *Republic,* bound from New York to the sunny Mediterranean, had been moving slowly, feeling her way through the impenetrable darkness, and a little off the beaten path of ocean liners. She had turned a bit north to get a start on the long sweep across the Atlantic.

Out of the night came a dozen quickly repeated blasts of a nervous fog siren, apparently dangerously at hand.

A hazy shape in the mist loomed up, bearing down like some monster of the deep on the luxuriously outfitted *Republic* and 461 human souls. There was no time to reverse engines. Two ships crashed!

The *Republic* lurched over on one side as the sharp prow of the colliding vessel gouged through the iron plates, tore them asunder and opened wide the engine room of the White

Star liner. Then the other vessel pulled away, righted herself and staggered off in the murk.

Captain Inman Sealby called the *Republic's* crew to quarters. The bulkheads were closed, shutting off the engine room from other parts of the ship. Luckily the *Republic* was one of the 180 ships equipped with Marconi apparatus. All hope rested with the wireless!

The S.S. *Florida's* bow, for that was the ship of Lloyd's Italiano Line that rammed the *Republic,* had crumbled and stove in the side of the wireless cabin. It was smashed to splinters, but fate had saved the instruments and had spared the twenty-six-year-old Marconi man, an English lad; John R. Binns, known to his shipmates as Jack, had been asleep in his bunk.

The smash startled him. His first thought when tossed from slumber was that the ship had run aground in the fog. He peered through the wrecked woodwork from his bunk and saw a lifeboat torn from its davits, which his sleepy eyes visualized as a rock. All the lights went out!

Binns climbed out of the cabin and tried to make his way to the captain on the bridge. But the wreckage blocked his path. The ship's dynamos stopped. Binns tried the storage batteries—the emergency current supply for the wireless. The steward came from the pilot house and led Binns through the wreckage so he could report to the skipper that the Marconi equipment was working. Then Binns rushed back to the cabin and called Siasconset on Nantucket Island. A. H. Ginman was the operator on watch there.

The CQD flashed from the masthead. It was the ambulance call.

Ginman heard the spark of the *Republic* say, "We are shipwrecked. Stand by for captain's message."

In reply Siasconset flashed, "All right, OM (Old Man). Where are you?"

Then came the captain's report. Sealby ordered the following message broadcast:

Republic rammed by unknown steamer, twenty-six miles southwest of Nantucket Lightship. Badly in need of immediate assistance, but no danger to life.

It was 5:30 o'clock in the morning on January 23, 1909. A disaster was impending 175 miles east of Ambrose Lightship.

Five minutes after the CQD had sped across the waters in search of assistance, the operator at Siasconset broadcast the assuring news that the U.S. Revenue Cutter *Acushnet* was proceeding from Woods Hole, Mass., to Latitude 40, Longitude 70, where the *Republic* was foundering.

The *Baltic*, the French liner *La Lorraine* from Havre, the *Furnessia* of Glasgow, the Nantucket wireless station, the S.S. *City of Everett*, the United States naval stations at Newport, Woods Hole, and Provincetown, and the *Lucania* from Liverpool, had also picked up the call of distress. The ships turned in their tracks and sped toward the stricken vessel, while the land stations rushed aid from near-by ports.

Never before had wireless such a chance to prove its value at sea. Dawn revealed the peril of the *Republic*.

The *Baltic* was 115 miles east of Sandy Hook, inbound. The *Lorraine*, inbound, was 70 miles east of Sandy Hook. The Cunarder *Lucania* was just east of Nantucket. The torpedo boat *Cushing* was on its way full speed from Newport. The *Acushnet* was less than 100 miles away. The revenue cutter *Mohawk* left New Bedford. The cutter *Seneca* was speeding from New London. All had one purpose—to reach the *Republic* before she sank!

All Sunday the helpless *Republic* drifted as more water poured into her wounds, making her position more perilous as the hours passed. She was settling fast. Captain Sealby radioed:

Come to our leeward to take up our boats. Have *Lorraine* and *Lucania* convoy the *Florida.*

From the bridge of his sinking ship Captain Sealby said:

Passengers of the *Republic,* I want to advise you that the steamer has been injured in collision. We are in no immediate danger, but I want to ask you to stand by me and act with coolness and judgment.

There is, I repeat, no immediate danger, but to be on the safe side it is necessary for you to be transferred to the *Florida* as soon as possible. It will take some time.

I expect that you will be cool and not get excited. Take your time getting into the lifeboats. Remember the women and children go first, and the first cabin next and then the others. The crew will be the last to leave the vessel.

There were shouts of approval and a cheer or two, and then, with a direct objective before them, and the prospect of not standing by helplessly any longer, the passengers hastened in orderly manner to prepare for transfer. The sea was calm. The transfer of the passengers took a trifle more than two hours. The shift was accomplished without a mishap.

Darkness and thick weather set in again. Bombs sounding in the distance revealed that the *Baltic* on its rescue mission was near. The *Republic's* wireless was weakening. The batteries were running down. The *Baltic* said by wireless that only a solitary bomb was left. And the faint rumble following that message left little doubt that the *Baltic* would soon be alongside.

Captain Sealby took direction from which the last bomb sounded, and Binns wirelessed to the *Baltic* how to steer to reach the *Republic.* There were no radio direction finders, else the task in the fog would have been less puzzling—less of a guess.

Soon a fog horn sounded faintly. Binns told the *Baltic* to

proceed carefully as she was apparently close to the port side. A cheer went up from the *Republic's* decks. Off the stern, ablaze with light, was the *Baltic,* which Binns later described as "the most beautiful sight in the world is a ship at sea, especially when that ship is needed to supply a link between life and death."

The *Baltic* was on the scene!

Now the *Florida* with her bow ripped away was in peril herself. The passengers had to transfer again, this time to the rescue ship.

The *Baltic* and the *Florida* lay about two miles apart as ten lifeboats, each capable of carrying ten passengers, in addition to a crew, crossed the intervening water under rays of searchlights. A sea was running and the little boats tossed and pitched as they wended their way back and forth between the two vessels, laden until their gunwales were almost under, then riding back with the lightness of feathers, after depositing their passengers.

The *Republic* and *Florida* passengers totaled 1,650. The *Baltic* carried 90 first-class passengers, 170 second class, 220 steerage, far below capacity, so could easily care for extra passengers saved at sea.

The *Florida* was ready to proceed to New York. But before she left, thirty-eight of the *Republic's* crew, including Binns, went back to the sinking ship to await the tugs. The *Furnessia* stood by to safeguard those who returned to the ship. Slowly and under her own steam the *Florida* pulled away from the scene. Her bow and cutwater were smashed and her two forward holds filled with water. Still the liner floated and, freed of her passengers, now safe on board the *Baltic,* she struggled to reach New York.

The *Florida's* departure was not the last act in the drama. It was but the climax. The shore was anxious for news.

The Marconi man on the *Baltic*, H. G. Tattersall, broadcast with an unsteady hand that revealed fatigue from long hours at the key:

The steamship *Florida* collided with the *Republic* 175 miles east of the Ambrose Lightship at 5:30 A.M., on Saturday (January 23, 1909). The *Republic's* passengers were transferred to the *Florida*. The *Republic* is rapidly sinking. It is doubtful if she will remain afloat much longer. The *Baltic* has taken all the passengers aboard. The *Lucania, Lorraine* and *Furnessia* are standing by to render assistance and to convoy the *Florida* to New York.

It is reported on board that four passengers on the *Republic* have been killed. The weather is threatening and the *Florida* is seriously damaged. We hear that assistance is coming from New York—signed, Marconi operator.

The *Baltic* started for New York shortly after one o'clock on the morning of January 24, as its radio sputtered:

I can send no more. I have been constantly at the key without sleep for fifty-two hours.

And so the rescue ship sailed away to land the survivors who had not many hours before waved good-bye to friends on the wharf in New York, as they shoved off for what they hoped to be a happy Winter cruise along sunny shores, intending to call at the Azores, Madeira, Gibraltar, Genoa, Naples and Alexandria. But fate, fog and King Neptune halted their pleasures in a wintry clime. Wireless saved them!

Guglielmo Marconi was hailed as a benefactor of mankind.

"I am exceedingly gratified and very grateful that wireless telegraphy has been the means of saving so many lives," said Marconi in London. "I am confident its usefulness will go on increasing with the extension of the system by smaller ships as well as by the great liners, because of the ever-increasing range of instruments."

What was happening off Nantucket?

The *Republic* still had the right of way on the wireless. She was in distress.

The fog lifted the next morning. The *Republic* was a pitiful sight in the gray of the morning. Her engine fires were out and her engine room flooded by the waves that washed in through the gaping wound in her side. This once queen of the ocean was at the mercy of winds and waves, drifting —to a watery grave.

Lifting of the mist revealed a fleet of salvage tugs on the scene in hopes of towing the *Republic* to port. But they would have to hurry. The S.S. *New York* had taken a position not far away and the *Furnessia* was still standing by, ready to offer assistance. Life of the 15,400-ton *Republic*, commissioned in 1904 and valued at $1,500,000, was fast ebbing. For several years she had held the record for the fastest passage between Boston and Queenstown. She was luxuriously equipped and had a beautiful dining salon that seated 200 diners. The room was furnished in ornamental wood. The upholstery was of rich texture, and the wood carvings the finest to be found on any ship afloat. Now her one funnel, at a rakish angle, was not befitting the grandeur and pride of an Atlantic Queen.

The cutter *Gresham* arrived, quickly took a tow line aboard and steamed ahead with the *Furnessia*, attached by two lines to the stern of the *Republic* to steer her toward New York. The derelict destroyer *Seneca*, in command of Captain Reynolds, arrived and put a line aboard the *Gresham* so that it, too, could assist in the tow.

But they did not go far. Settling of the *Republic* sent the *Gresham's* crew into fever of activity. Hurried orders rang out from the bridge and boat crews tumbled over the side. They pulled with rapid strokes through a choppy sea to the side of the big passenger ship, the gunwales of which were almost under water. From the end of a rope the *Republic's* crew abandoned ship and jumped into a small boat. The hawser connecting the *Republic* with the *Gresham* was quickly severed with an ax. The *Gresham's* seamen in the lifeboat pulled with full speed toward their own craft to dodge the suction. All lines to the sinking ship were cut. Yards astern, the *Furnessia* men had thrown their line into the sea. And none too quick, because the *Republic* was going, and the water around her surged with bubbles of air. The big steamer's stern plunged downward.

A searchlight's beam gave a last, fleeting glimpse of the bow. Captain Sealby jumped and so did First Officer Williams. The bow rose quivering into the air and then backed ignominiously toward the bottom of the sea. Chaotic waves washed over the spot where but a moment before the *Republic* had floated and struggled to live.

"Down, down, down went the *Republic*," said Captain Sealby in describing his experience, "and soon she was entirely submerged. A moment later I was in the water. I wore my greatcoat, and the air getting under that made it support me, while the binocular, the revolver and the cartridges that were in my pocket acted as ballast. The water around me was seething and roaring, due to suction as she sank. Several times I was carried down, only to be churned back to the surface again. I was wet through and through and my coat became a perilous burden instead of support. I could not get it off. I found a stout piece of lumber and made fast as best I could.

"All this time the searchlights of the *Seneca* and *Gresham* were playing about me. I fumbled in my pocket and got out my pistol. Then I got a cartridge and put it in the cylinder.

I had no idea it would go off, but it did. My strength was fast going. I found a towel in the water and managed to wave it—a few minutes later a lifeboat picked me up. First Officer Williams had been picked up earlier and had directed the hunt for me."

Soon after Captain Sealby had been hauled aboard the *Gresham* he wirelessed:

Republic sunk. All hands saved. Making Gay Head on the *Gresham*.

And while the valiant effort had been made to save the *Republic*, the *Florida*, under Captain Angelo Ruspini, was moving slowly toward New York. On January 26, with thirty feet of her bow cut away and tilted at such a perilous angle that she seemed about to dive into the harbor, she reached New York. At her halyards between the masts were the "not under control" signals, black and grim, while her flags half-masted, told of death on board.

The *Florida* had lost four negro seamen, killed by the impact. And two passengers of the *Republic*, Mrs. Eugene Lynch of Boston, Mass., and T. J. Mooney of Langdon, N. D., in outside cabins had been crushed when the ships collided. They went to watery graves with the *Republic*, forty-five fathoms down.

Striding up and down the pier with a nervousness that revealed lack of sleep, the little, slim, red-whiskered Londoner, Tattersall of the *Baltic*, said, "Was I excited? No; it's the awful nervous strain of striving, always striving to get the right messages, when half a dozen gigantic batteries are jerking flashes to you at the same time, drowning each other out, pounding in your ears, making the night seem to swarm with sparks before your eyes. That's what gets on a man's nerves; that's what makes you next to insane. I hardly knew what to do, with the *Republic* calling me faintly, so faintly that I could not make out whether they were saying: 'We are sinking!' or 'All safe!'—But all the time I kept calling 'Republic! Republic!' and telling them we were coming to their aid."

The gallant Binns was feted on every hand; dinners, theatres, medals and kisses.

"I can't stand any more of this," he told friends after five days of the ordeal. "I never want to see my own picture again. It was nothing. Any fellow could do that much."

And off he fled to his home in England.

.   .   .   .   .   .

The first decade of the twentieth century neared an end, with the infant wireless beginning to utter spoken words instead of a mere jabber of dots and dashes. Wireless was talking and learning to sing!

Dr. Lee de Forest was teaching wireless how to use an electrical tongue and through new instruments he evolved, chiefly the audion (three-element vacuum tube), Enrico Caruso, the distinguished tenor, and a number of other Metropolitan Opera stars, on January 13, 1910, sent their golden voices into space from backstage of the opera's mid-Victorian setting on Broadway. The songs reached the wireless cabin of the steamer *Avon* at sea, and amateur experimenters in Connecticut eavesdropped. A newspaper observed that "it begins to look as if an enterprising inventor had perfected a can opener for use on 'canned' opera."

Jubilantly, De Forest predicted that some day vessels departing from New York would have "Pagliacci," "Cavalleria Rusticana" and other operatic masterpieces every evening until half-way to Europe and then they would be entertained by concerts from London, Paris or Berlin. That seemed fantastic!

By what miracle of science could a symphony of 100 or

more musicians, and a stage crowded with singers, ever be electrified and sent through the air with every tone preserved and reassembled as the original? That could never be! One voice might go by wireless but never a chorus. One violin might play but never a symphony orchestra playing Verdi, Wagner, Beethoven or Puccini.

This thing called the wireless telephone presented weird possibilities. It gave dreamers something to work upon.

"The messages wirelessed ten years ago have not reached some of the nearest stars," said Marconi when asked where the signals might end. "When they arrive there, why should they stop? It is like the attempt to express one-third as a decimal fraction; you can go on forever without coming to any sign of an end.

"What is jolly about science is this: It encourages one to go on dreaming. Science demands a flexible mind. It's no use interrogating the universe with a formula. You've got to observe it, take what it gives you and then reflect upon it with the aid of reason and experience.

"Science keeps one young. I cannot understand the savant who grows bowed and yellow in a workroom. I like to be out in the open looking at the universe, asking it questions, letting the mystery of it soak right into the mind, admiring the wonderful beauty of it all, and then think my way to the truth of things."

Marconi knew that wireless in 1910 needed more driving power in its wings to fly long distances with dependability. It needed strength to combat the elements and bombardments of static flung at it from all directions by magnetic storms. Electricians heard the call of the wireless engineers for more power and this was their answer:

If you can use oscillations of low frequency for wireless then we can make you a powerful dynamo-electric generator that will produce them.

You will no longer have to depend upon the spark gap with its intermittent, spitting explosions. We will give you a powerful high frequency machine that will send out a continuous, smooth train of oscillations and yet will have 100 horsepower to drive the signals as far as you wish.

That was a promise. The wireless men told them to go ahead. But while the big alternators were being built as a means of setting the "ether" in vibration, the spark transmitters were made more powerful.

Arlington, Va., went on the air in 1912. Men listening in at Eiffel Tower picked up the shrill note from along the banks of the Potomac. Great masts went skyward at Nauen, Germany, at Sayville on Long Island and at Tuckerton, N. J. POZ, that was the call of Nauen, and WSL was Sayville. Both were wafting strong signals to and fro across the Atlantic. Did the electrical experts realize that within a year or two, wireless and these big stations would be embroiled in a World War?

While other nations were linking their capitals with distant domains and colonies, Italy, the land that gave wireless to the world, was feebly represented in space. Marconi was anxious to give his native land a globe-girdling voice.

When the summer of 1911 arrived, the inventor was in Italy personally supervising the finishing touches on the most powerful station in the world being erected for the Italian Government at Coltano, near Pisa. The primary aim was for communication with the Italian station at Massowah in the Red Sea, and with the Argentine, because a large proportion of the population of that South American Republic was Italian. A new station was under construction at Buenos Aires, 7,000 miles from Coltano—the other end of the two-way ethereal channel through southern skies.

Coltano's first experimental program was carried out with Clifden, Ireland. The operators at Glace Bay eavesdropped, and the Italian signals reached them so satisfactorily that two-way communication was immediately established between Italy and Nova Scotia. Marconi, mindful of the loyal support and the faith of *The New York Times* in his invention from the beginning, sent the first message direct from Coltano to Glace Bay as follows:

November 19, 1911.
To the Editor of *The New York Times:*
 My best greetings transmitted by wireless telegraph from Italy to America. Pisa, 5:47 P.M.

G. Marconi.

This was a long distance: it exceeded by more than 1,000 miles the Ireland-Nova Scotia route. The signals had traversed over one-fourth the way around the earth. There seemed to be little doubt in the minds of scientists that the day was not far distant when Marconi would envelop the globe with wireless by spinning an invisible peel around the planet in much the same fashion that a skin surrounds an orange.

Several days after the first message winged its way from Italy to the New World, *The New York Times,* on November 21, 1911, called attention to the fact that the waves from Coltano "did better than literally sweep from Greenland's icy mountain to India's coral strand."

Some one with a flair for mathematics estimated, if the waves went out from Italy in all directions over the face of the earth, and were caught as far west as 4,000 miles, the messages might have been intercepted in the east by a wireless tower in the mountains of Tibet.

This is how it was figured:

Pisa is situated at about 44 degrees north latitude, and, counting 60 miles to a degree, 4,000 miles due south of Pisa would be a point in the south Atlantic ocean, about 22 degrees south latitude. Ships off the coast of German Southwest Africa might have picked up the message if they had proper equipment.

Toward the north the signal would have actually reached the north pole and had some 600 miles to spare. It could also have been caught in Brazil.

Taking Pisa as the pole of the sphere of the earth, and a point on the opposite side of the earth as a second sending station, and each sending wireless currents, 16,000 miles of the earth's circumference could be reached.

This would leave an untouched belt about 4,000 miles wide outside the influence of the currents. The area of this untouched belt would be about 100,000,000 square miles.

Taking the total area of the earth as roughly 200,000,000 square miles, the two stations could cover about half the whole surface of the earth. The message that went out from Coltano covered about one-quarter of the area of the globe.

Marconi showed that these mathematical calculations were not far wrong. While his assistants hurled messages across Africa and over the South Atlantic, he intercepted them on the S.S. *Principessa Mafalda* up to 4,000 miles by day and 6,735 miles at night.

If a ship could hear a message that far, it ought to be safe almost anywhere on the seven seas. Fate was soon to test that theory.

Marconi was back on Manhattan Island again on March 16, 1912, to attend a dinner in the Tower Hall of The Times Building, celebrating three months of daily foreign news service by wireless.

Messages of congratulation were received while the dinner was in progress. From England, Earl Grey, former Governor General of Canada, flashed:

London, March 16.—To Marconi and *The New York Times:* Heartily wish you success in your splendid endeavor to facilitate conversation between the English speaking peoples separated from each other by distance only.

Sir Rufus Isaacs, Attorney General of Great Britain, wirelessed:

London, March 17.—Please congratulate Marconi and my brother (Godfrey Isaacs, General Manager Marconi Company) on the successful development of a marvelous enterprise. I wish them all success in New York, and hope that by the time they come back the coal strike will be finished.

Marconi had by this time been caricatured and cartooned as a man with winged feet, sparks snapping out like lightning flashes from his finger tips, so that some actually expected to see such a character—a man from Mars. Some one with a poetic turn of mind, who saw Marconi for the first time, described him as a human being unadorned with zigzag electric horns, and remarked that surely the stars must have conspired to put the vast power of wireless into his hands because here was a wizard who could walk down Broadway, mingle with his fellowmen and never be noticed in the crowd because of any freak characteristics.

"What would you have done if you had been poor?" Marconi was asked.

"I don't believe I would have been an inventor," he replied with a whimsical smile. "I might have been a sailor."

"And you would not have starved for wireless?"

"Oh! never," responded the inventor with a broad smile. "I have too good a digestion."

Pioneers on his engineering staff, however, grin at the thought of food surpassing wireless with this Gulliver of science, whom they referred to among themselves as "G M."

"We would send food in to him when he was working long hours without interruption," said an associate who knew him at the turn of the century. "The tray would come out untouched.

"It was the same with Edison; I knew him, too. But both were human beings. They could not go on forever without sustenance and recreation."

PART III

XIV

S O S—WE'VE STRUCK A BERG!

THE steamship *Titanic,* giantess of the sea and pride of marine architects, sailed on April 10, 1912, from Southampton, England, with more than two thousand people bound on a fatal voyage.

Scarcely had the new Queen of the Atlantic drawn away from her berth when she had a hairbreadth escape from collision with the American Line steamer *New York,* yanked from its moorings by the tremendous suction caused by the big black hulk getting underway. That the narrowly avoided crash was the apocalypse of a collision in which the debonair *Titanic* was to play the role of a pygmy could not have entered the mind of a single passenger. It was a happy crowd that ran to the railing to watch the sailors of the *New York* struggle to regain control of their ship in the whirlpools stirred up by the steel monster of the briny deep, which the sirens in the harbor were serenading.

Then the triton gathered headway, moving slowly while within range of other vessels, gradually increasing speed as she left the land behind, until finally she was racing proudly through the ocean waves with Manhattan Island as the goal.

She boasted wireless instruments of the latest design, but the electric flashes did not have sufficient power for a transatlantic liner to maintain constant communication with shore throughout the voyage, unless the messages were relayed by other vessels. So the world, after reading cable reports of the *Titanic's* gallant departure, settled down to await the news of her triumphant approach to New York.

The press heralded the occasion:

When the *Titanic,* which for at least a year will be the largest vessel in the world, steams into the Hudson this week New Yorkers will see a ship that is more than four city blocks long, and which if stood on end would be 181.7 feet higher than the Metropolitan Tower; 270 feet higher than the Singer Building. The 46,328-ton ship is 882 feet in length.

Proud was the crew and joyous the voyagers, some bound for the New World to establish new homes, business men and honeymooners all enjoying this spirited dash across the Atlantic. Cares and worries of the busy world had been left behind. The exhilarating sea inspired new hopes.

It was Sunday. The *Titanic* was two days from New York. Through the clear sky vibrated messages notifying the audacious Captain Edward J. Smith that the Labrador current was bearing vast masses of ice across the path of his ship. Veteran sailors on other boats cautiously warned him that the *Titanic* was speeding toward floating hulks of ice, earth and rock, some of the mounds towering two hundred feet above the ocean with seven-eighths of their ponderous bulk lurking beneath the waves.

At noon on that Sabbath the ever-alert *Baltic* cautioned the bearded master of the *Titanic* that ice and plenty of it floated within five miles of her lane. The *Baltic* broadcast a second warning at five o'clock. The *Coronian, Parisian* and *New Amsterdam* reported ice fields "extending as far to the northeast as the horizon is visible." The ice was no secret. Mariners expect it in the North Atlantic at that season of the year.

Captain Smith thanked Captain Ranson of the *Baltic* and reported fine weather; the four-funneled *Titanic* was passing through the soft warmth of the Gulf Stream, but after sunset it gave way to bitter cold—and peril. Stars twinkled in the ebony setting of the sky.

So thick was the white menace that the *California* at 6:30 o'clock stopped in the vicinity toward which the *Titanic* was racing; and wirelessed, "passed one large iceberg, two more in sight to the southward." That was at 7:15 o'clock. Captain Lord told the *Titanic* at 10:20 P.M., ship's time, he was "stopped and surrounded by ice." But the *Titanic* plunged ahead twenty-four and one-half miles per hour, while its wireless brusquely replied, "Shut up, I'm busy with Cape Race."

Quartermaster Hitchins, the *Titanic's* steersman, saw thick-ribbed ice when he came up on the bridge at eight o'clock. Lookouts in the crow's nest signaled shortly after 11:30 o'clock, ship's time, that large icebergs loomed ahead. Some of the passengers were overjoyed; they had always wanted to see an iceberg from the time of school days, little realizing the danger of the encounter.

"Hard astarboard, full speed astern!" shouted First Officer W. M. Murdoch. The ship was too fast; her bow swung a bit, but not enough and she struck. It was 11:40 P.M.

Too late! In thirty-six seconds a jagged monster as resistless as steel ripped the starboard bow with a "slight jolt," yet terrific enough to throw the watertight doors out of working order. Water poured into the forward compartments and boiler room through a 300-foot slash under the waterline; the big ship had run into a deathtrap!

The palatial, "unsinkable" *Titanic* was lurching into eternity—two miles deep—in less than three hours she would be gone forever. No one realized it. A few passengers left their staterooms to see what caused the sudden thud. They were assured there was nothing to worry about, so returned to their berths. But not for long; men rapped on the doors and ordered passengers to put on lifebelts. For what? they inquired.

Captain Smith ran to the wireless cabin:

"We've struck an iceberg and I'm having an inspection made to tell what it has done to us. You had better get ready to send out a call for assistance. But don't send it until I tell you."

The youthful wireless operators could not believe a CQD (distress call) would ever leap from the proud *Titanic's* masthead.

But to their surprise, in ten minutes Captain Smith returned and ordered: "Send the call for assistance!"

John George Phillips, the senior operator, asked, "What shall I send?"

"The regulation international call for help," prescribed the Captain. "Just that."

Phillips gripped the key. His wrist moved up and down. The spark crashed across the gap. Uncanny shadows danced on the wall in the light of those electric flashes. The CQD was in the night air winging its way through the darkness with the hope that some one might hear.

"Come at once, we've struck a berg. It's a CQD, OM (Old Man)."

"Send SOS; it's a new signal and it may be your last chance to send it," jokingly suggested Harold Bride, the twenty-two-year-old junior operator.

These wireless men shared the opinion of marine architects; the majestic *Titanic* could not be punctured and be sent to the bottom of the Atlantic by an iceberg—but icebergs are devils of the deep in northern waters.

Phillips interspersed the CQD with SOS.

CQD SOS from MGY (call of the *Titanic*). We've struck a berg. Sinking fast. Come to our assistance. Position, Latitude 41.46 North, Longitude 50.14 West, MGY.

The steamship *Frankfurt* answered. So did the *Carpathia*. Bride rushed down the deck crowded with scrambling men and women to tell the Captain the *Carpathia* was heading for the scene.

Five minutes later the anxious Captain ran to the wireless room. It was the link between life and death. The chronometers registered 11:55 P.M.

"What are you sending?" he inquired quickly.

"CQD," replied Phillips. The wireless was growing weaker. The engine rooms were being flooded.

The mammoth ship began to have a forward list. Everything on board went topsyturvy. Frantic people were rushing about the decks. The water was close to the upper boat deck. The *Titanic's* great sister ship, *Olympic*, heard that she was sinking by the head. It was midnight. Phillips worked the key while Bride threw an overcoat around him and strapped a lifebelt on his back. The last raft had gone. Phillips told the *Olympic* that women were being put off in boats and asked the *Olympic* to have her boats ready to lower. It was 12:36.

The Captain shouted: "Men, you have done your full duty. You can do no more. Abandon your cabin. Now it's every man for himself. You look out for yourselves. I release you. That's the way of it at this kind of a time. Every man for himself."

The boat deck was awash. Phillips continued to send. Water was flowing into the *Titanic's* wireless. Its spark of life was gone. It was 1:27.

Phillips ran aft; the last he was ever seen alive. Bride vanished overboard holding onto an oar lock of a collapsible boat.

The ship's band on the after-deck was playing a ragtime tune.

It was 2:10 in the morning. Green rockets went skyward from the upper deck. Ten minutes later those in the lifeboats saw the green starboard light vanish. The band was playing "Autumn," two lines of which were as a prayer:

> *Hold me up in mighty waters,*
> *Keep my eyes on things above.*

The big boat stood up on end and dove by her nose, like a huge fish harpooned. Smoke and sparks belched from the funnels. There was an explosion underwater; then a second and a third thunder-like sound. To those huddled in the life-boats it all seemed like a horrible dream, as the intense cold that precedes dawn settled across the ice-strewn water.

As the *Titanic* reared for her final plunge, according to a fireman's story, Captain Smith jumped into the sea from the promenade deck with an infant clutched tenderly in his arms. He swam toward a lifeboat and the little child was lifted to safety, but the Captain wearing a life preserver clung there only a moment and slid off. For a second time he clutched the side of the craft, then took off his life preserver, tossed it on the water and vanished with the words, "I will follow the ship."

Had any one heard the distress calls? That was the paramount question.

Yes, the wireless had spread over the sea and had reached the land! But the coast was far beyond the horizon; the *Titanic* was 1,284 miles east of Sandy Hook.

Harold Bride, swimming with all his might to dodge the suction was the only one aware that the *Frankfurt, Olympic, Carpathia* and *Baltic* had actually responded; possibly others had heard, too. He was pulled aboard a collapsible boat— all around men were swimming and sinking. One man in the boat was dead; he was Phillips.

Cape Race had picked up the SOS and quickly notified the Allan liner *Virginia*. Captain Gambell replied he was on the way.

But what was transpiring out there where the *Titanic's* dots and dashes had become blurred, only to be snuffed out abruptly? That was the first inkling of tragedy. Up to that time there had been hope. But the water that silenced the wireless on the upper deck drowned all hope. The mariners hurrying on the errand of mercy intuitively knew what that meant—so did the newspaper men in New York.

Tragic was the story reported by a meagre bulletin in *The New York Times,* April 15, 1912:

> Cape Race, Newfoundland.
> Sunday night, April 14.
> At 10:25 o'clock tonight the White Star Line steamship *Titanic* called CQD to the Marconi wireless station here and reported having struck an iceberg. The steamship said that immediate assistance was needed.

This dispatch was followed in a half hour by another. It was terrible news. The big ship was sinking by the head! Women and children were being lowered over the side in lifeboats!

Impossible! This *Titanic* was unsinkable. So reasoned the morning readers. Nevertheless, those fragmentary wireless messages seemed to have pulsed with fright. The news men could read between the lines. The story was across three columns of the front page!

Here was the most expensive steamship disaster that ever occurred—"a tragedy of the sea so pitiful and so shocking that the memory of it will not be obliterated in the flight of years."

While the presses rolled off the news, the S.S. *Carpathia,* under Captain Arthur Rostron, which had gaily sailed from New York for Gibraltar and Mediterranean ports on April 11, the day after the *Titanic* left England, had turned in her course to make more news; to write the final chapter of a tragedy.

Harold Cottam was the *Carpathia's* wireless man. Close to midnight on April 14, he was sleepy, so decided to go to his berth. He was partly undressed when some twist of fate —a lucky fluke—sent him back to the wireless in hopes of intercepting news items. He called the S.S. *Parisian*. No reply came from the vessel, but Cape Cod's spark was in the air and Cottam delivered two or three messages. Then he called the *Titanic* to inquire if her operators knew Cape Race had messages on file for them. As he tuned for the reply he was startled to hear the CQD. It was 12:20 P.M.

He asked the *Titanic*, "Shall I go to the Captain and tell him to turn back at once?"

"Yes, yes," flashed the answer.

The plea was rushed to Captain Rostron. Immediately the *Carpathia* was turned around, headed for "North 52 West." The *Titanic* was fifty-eight miles away. Extra stokers were called to duty. The order was for every ounce of speed. The crew prepared the lifeboats for instant service.

Cottam told Phillips the *Carpathia* would be on the scene in less than four hours. He heard the *Virginia* report 170 miles from the *Titanic*, and expected to make the run by ten o'clock Monday morning. The *Olympic* was making all haste from Latitude 40.32 North and Longitude 61.18 West. The *Baltic* was 200 miles away and was making a mad dash to close that mileage gap.

"Come quick, our engine room is flooded to the boilers"— that was the last message intercepted by the *Carpathia*. There was not even a spark from the emergency transmitter after that.

The *Carpathia* was nearest. Her lights on the horizon were the first to cast hope on a troubled scene. At 4:10 A.M., the green flare of a *Titanic* lifeboat was sighted and brought alongside. As dawn revealed the tragic spot, other drifting boats and rafts were seen bobbing on the waves. It was a savage spectacle.

The *Titanic* was no more. She had gone down at 2:20 A.M., on April 15 in 2,760 fathoms of icy water, 800 miles off the Grand Banks of Newfoundland. Wireless had saved 712 lives. The dead numbered 1,517—"a needless sacrifice of noble women and brave men as ever clustered about the Judgment Seat in any single moment of passing time."

Quickly the *Carpathia* sailors lowered potato sacks with ropes. The babies were put into these sack-hammocks and were hoisted gently. Then the women were placed on Bosun's chairs to be pulled up the side of the rescue ship. By nine o'clock sixteen lifeboats had been emptied of survivors. That was all.

The *Carpathia* signaled through the brilliantly sunny sky that she had picked up all survivors—that the gay Queen of the Atlantic had been swallowed by the sea in the middle of the night. The *Baltic,* the *Birma* and other ships returned to their regular tracks. The *California* remained on the scene to pick up any survivors who might have been overlooked. There was nothing to indicate the horror of the night except a slight discoloration, a brown stream in the water in which bits of debris, wood and straw floated. But icebergs were all around.

The world clamored for news, but authentic news was lacking. For several days those on shore did not know whether the *Titanic* had gone down. They hoped against hope. Few could believe or conceive an iceberg might rip a hole in $7,500,000 worth of steel and luxury.

Land stations, numerous ships at sea and hundreds of amateurs tried to reach the *Titanic* or ships rushing to her aid. There was a babel of dots and dashes. That great confusion resulted from jamming the air with wireless messages in a frantic effort to get more news is found in a dispatch of that day, which read:

It was practically impossible to get any reliable information by wireless because of the great number of wireless stations breaking into the field, and because of the work of amateur operators. It appears that the disaster to the *Titanic* had no sooner been flashed over the sea than about every wireless instrument along the cost within range began to transmit with no thought of others, and so the net result soon became a hopeless jumble, from which distorted and inaccurate messages were patched up in haphazard fashion and announced to the anxious world.

This tangle was responsible for the messages reporting the *Titanic* was en route to Halifax under her own steam at six o'clock at night, when, as a matter of fact, she had been sixteen hours under the surface of a sullen sea.

This same chaos was held responsible for reports that passengers were being calmly taken off the ship in the afternoon of April 15, although the great hulk had gone to her doom before dawn.

To show how easy it was to misconstrue the early land dispatches, it developed that the reassuring words supposed to have been sent by Phillips to relatives in Surrey, England, were sent, not by Phillips, but by his brother in London, who was reporting what he had heard, "Making slowly for Halifax; practically unsinkable; don't worry." The relatives assumed the message was from Jack Phillips.

The *Carpathia,* covering thirteen knots an hour, was on her way back to New York. She had the right of way on the wireless, and as she approached the coast only certain stations were permitted to operate, in order to avoid interference. All the ears of wireless were trained on her spark. Flimsy was the news she flashed, because personal messages of grief and sorrow were given preference over press dispatches.

Harold Bride, the *Titanic's* second operator, after ten

hours in the *Carpathia's* sickbay, nursing his wrenched and frozen feet, was summoned to relieve Cottam, fatigued from long hours of constant duty. The two operators alternated at the key until the ship, laden with sadness, steamed slowly to her pier in New York.

The dock was like a stage in a theatre hushed by the approach of a climax; like a play in which something mysterious had happened when the stage was suddenly darkened for a moment. Now the terror of the plot was to be disclosed. This was one of the most dramatic scenes ever witnessed in New York harbor; it contained every element of drama—mystery, hope, pathos, excitement, suspense and tragedy. Lowering of the *Carpathia's* gangplank was a cue that the enormity of the tragedy was about to be revealed.

The quietly spoken Guglielmo Marconi dramatically stepped out upon the dock as police cleared the way. He was one of the first to go up the gangplank to interview the wireless men; and to hear their stories first hand. Up to this time he had refrained from all comment. His silence, while waiting for official news, had added to the suspicion that possibly the *Titanic* had been struck a death blow.

The spotlight was on Marconi and on his wireless; he was the wizard who had thrown invisible lifelines out across the sea.

"It is worth while to have lived to have made it possible for these people to have been saved," said Marconi, bowed in grief as he came down the gangplank. "Just now all the world is thinking of this greatest of sea disasters, I feel that I must speak of it, but I do it reluctantly. I know you will understand me if I say that all those who have been working with me, entertain a true feeling of gratitude that wireless telegraphy has again helped to save human lives. I also want to express my thanks to the press for the hearty approval it has given my invention.

"I am proud, but I see many things that will have to be done if wireless is to be of the fullest utility. It will be necessary to compel all ships to carry two operators, so that one may be on duty at all times.

"Some of the ships failed to hear the *Titanic's* call for help because they were receiving news bulletins from Cape Cod. With two operators, one could be working the news, the other—on any ship equipped properly—could be listening for distress signals, which would not interfere with the long distance news messages."

While the Marconi Company was seeking through its president, John W. Griggs, ex-Governor of New Jersey, to put a stop to wireless confusion and misinformation concerning the *Titanic* disaster, Guglielmo Marconi placed the blame for early false reports chiefly upon the press and the amateur wireless operators.

The inventor was in no pleasant frame of mind when his attention was called to the criticism directed against whoever might have been responsible for the supposedly reliable bulletin that the *Titanic* was being slowly towed into Halifax.

"Good gracious, hasn't the wireless done enough in this instance to free it from complaints?" said Marconi. "If you can prove that one of our operators either sent or gave out that message, I'll take off my hat to you. It is you journalists who are responsible for the confused and unreliable rumors about the *Titanic,* not the wireless.

"This sort of thing happened before there was any wireless. Look at the confused and false reports circulated about the Spanish-American war. Yet there was no wireless in operation then. Here is John Smith, who happens to have a wireless outfit of his own. He gets what he thinks is a flash from the *Titanic* or some other ship, and he reads it as best he can. Then he sends word to the newspapers that he has word from the disaster. He gives it out and the papers print it. It may be entirely wrong or it may be only partly correct; but how is any one to know?

"Now it is perfectly simple to understand why there should have been the long wait between the first wireless message telling of the collision and the dispatch telling of the *Titanic's* sinking," said Marconi. "What happened was this: The *Titanic* struck the iceberg. Immediately the ship's wireless sent out the word and it reached land. The wireless kept working until it could not operate any longer; the ship had gone down.

"Then came the long silence. The *Carpathia* reached the scene, but could send no word to shore. Her wireless was too weak. All she could do was to keep on flashing until the *Olympic,* which had also caught the *Titanic's* call, got within range. Then the *Olympic* with her more powerful apparatus relayed to land what the *Carpathia* sent. Hence, until the *Olympic* got near enough to receive the *Carpathia's* waves, there was no means of communicating with land after the *Titanic* sank. Whatever messages came during that interval certainly would not have been very reliable.

"Why, I myself sent a long message to the *Carpathia* and was unable to get a reply," recalled Marconi. "As for the action of the wireless operator who sold his story that had nothing to do with us. After he went ashore the marketable value of what he knew was his own property."

Meagreness of news had caused numerous complaints. But it was pointed out by the press itself, despite its hunger for news, that wireless dispatches from ships are under the control of the Captain; he is and must be supreme at sea. What and how much to send rests upon his judgment and the public will have to be content with ten lines, although its appetite may demand ten columns.

Furthermore, a ship Captain is not usually a good reporter; his training creates the habit of brevity and reserve in utterance. He is a man who deals with essential facts and not vivid narration.

A special committee from the United States Senate investigated the disaster and reported:

Some things are dearer than life itself. The refusal of Phillips and Bride, the wireless operators, to desert their posts of duty even after water had mounted to the upper deck, is an example of faithfulness worthy of highest praise. The final exit of Phillips from the ship and from the world was not so swift as to prevent him from pausing long enough to pass a cup of water to a fainting woman, who fell from her husband's arm into the operator's chair. Phillips was tardily fleeing from the wireless apparatus where he had ticked off the last message from his ship and from his brain.

. . . We went to the side of the hospital ship with purpose and pity, and saw the almost lifeless survivors and their garments of woe, joy and sorrow so intermingled that it was difficult to discern light from shadow. The sad scene was only varied by the cry of the reunited loved ones whose mutual grief was written in the language of creation.

. . . The electric signal of distress was only sent upon its unseen search for help after a delay of nearly twenty minutes, and its spark was arrested by an accident so providential as to excite wonder. In five minutes more the operator of the *Carpathia* who snatched this secret from the air, would have forgotten his complexities in slumber and no note would have been taken of the awful importance of the passing hour.

Captain Smith, a dauntless sailor of forty years, was declared indifferent to danger. That was one of the direct and contributing causes of the catastrophe. He was over-confident, and that made it easy for the angry elements to strip him of command "while his own willingness to die was the expiating evidence of his fitness to live."

On the pages of marine tragedy is written, "devotion to his craft even as it writhed, twisted and struggled for mastery over its foe, calmed the fears of many of the stricken multitude who hung upon his words, lending dignity to a parting scene."

More than a month later 100 miles away, the White Star Liner *Oceanic* picked up the last relic of the ill-fated liner—a collapsible lifeboat with three dead men. They were the last of the latest maritime creation that steamed westward cutting her first pathway through the North Atlantic with scarcely a ripple to retard its progress. But destiny decreed that this leviathan was to plunge straightway to her fate—"christening salvos acclaimed at once her birth and death."

Civilization agreed that Marconi wireless had done all within its power under dire circumstances. But it could not prevent a helmsman from steering into an iceberg. It could not take the place of lifeboats. It could not prevent over-confident sailors from ignoring danger signals.

Old sailors conceded, "not improbable in days gone by the loss of the *Titanic* would have remained forever a mystery of the sea as black as that which shadows the fate of the *Noronic*. No other vessel was in sight, and none would have passed the scene of the tragedy long after all signs of it had disappeared had not the ethereal signal of distress been given and received."

"In the midst of our thankfulness for deliverance, one name mentioned with deepest feeling of gratitude was that of Marconi," said Colonel Archibald Gracie, a survivor. "I wish that he had been there to hear the chorus of gratitude that went out to him for the wonderful invention that spared us many hours, and perhaps days of wandering about the sea in hunger, storm and cold."

The disaster revealed the need of high power marine transmitters to reach both shores from midocean and all boats in the vicinity at sea. Furthermore, it was clear that lifeboats should be equipped with wireless for communication in case the mother ship went down. A radio direction finder was needed upon which rescue ships could rely and go straight to the scene without loss of time. The radio compass might save time and life if the position report from a stricken ship was in error or garbled in transmission. The *Carpathia* found the *Titanic* wreckage thirty-four miles from the position report that was broadcast.

The importance of an international ice patrol in the North Atlantic was foreseen, whereby the greyhounds of the sea might be warned by wireless of white menaces lurking serenely in their path like death with clutching hands.

All these things would come to pass, but too late for the *Titanic* and the souls that were snuffed out when the gleamy hull dipped beneath the waves.

Ever after, in sad remembrance, the ice patrol vessels would go to the *Titanic's* grave on each anniversary in the springtime, offer prayers and scatter garlands of flowers on the waters under which the short-lived Queen of the Sea lies in a sepulcher she never deserved.

Inspired by all Marconi had accomplished, intensified by the light cast upon his invention by this disaster, Dr. Michael I. Pupin remarked: [1]

Marconi could die and wireless development would inevitably and continuously continue. When I say that I am not slurring Marconi. On the contrary I am giving him praise that is almost beyond words. It means that his work lives on and grows whether he lives or not. And that means his work is immortal. It is the greatest thing that can be said of a man's work.

I say that Bismarck was a greater man than Napoleon. He was. His work lived after him. With Napoleon there were brilliant battles, that built up an artificial empire and yet that empire died with Napoleon. It died even before he did. It died when he was removed from Europe. He was the life of his work. His work had no life itself.

But Bismarck! Prince Bismarck built an empire that lived after him; that lives today and grows stronger with every passing year. Bismarck's work is immortal.

[1] The New York *World,* October 6, 1912.

An excellent study of Marconi and one of his favorite pictures.

It is so with Marconi. His genius gave the idea to the world and he taught the world how to build a telegraphic practice upon the basis of this idea. The world will do the rest. Marconi did an immortal job.

And the further perfecting of his idea, the development of it, needs no genius, calls for none, is employing none.

It is being perfected in laboratories throughout the world, and experimentation that will be useful in its progress is done in every message sent from every station.

The men who do this perfecting will be nameless in the history of wireless. They are the silent heroes of the laboratory. Wasn't it so with the incandescent lamp?

Proud was all the world of Marconi; as proud as he was of his wireless.

"If I could select a crown for Mr. Marconi it would be a coronet surmounted by a globe on which would be inlaid in pearls those magnificent, significant letters CQD"—that was the toast to the wizard of wireless.

.   .   .   .   .   .

With the cries of the survivors still ringing in his ears, "Ti dobbiamo la vita!" Marconi with his usual celerity immediately began, as did other experimenters challenged by the *Titanic,* to perfect the radio compass and beacon stations so that steamships would have no more fear of fog "than they have of starlight or the morning sun."

"Dread of fog is the last remaining anxiety of seafarers," said Marconi. "Several times I have come into Ambrose Channel when the captains have ordered the anchor chains out because of bad weather. We have the same needless trouble at English ports. I have concluded a series of experiments with the so-called 'wireless-compass,' which I have been thinking about for many years. The last test was a complete success. There are more to be made, of course, but I have the thing so far advanced that it cannot disappoint."

What kind of an instrument is it?

"I prefer to answer that after the papers come from the Patent Office," said the inventor. "I would not like to have the fight about patents to make all over again. There was quite enough trouble over that the last time, thank you."

And Marconi smiled. Instead of describing his instrument, he took a piece of paper and illustrated with a pencil what it was designed to accomplish. The drawing consisted of several wireless "lighthouses" on the shore and a number of ships off shore at scattered locations.

"Now, we will suppose that all these lighthouses and these ships are sending wireless flashes in a dense fog or a terrific storm," he explained. "You know the confusion the skipper is in today. He can pick up the messages, but he can get no sense of direction from which the waves come. We plan to supply the missing element. By means of a wireless wave, which will be used exclusively for this kind of work, we are going to give him his sense of direction.

"It is merely a matter of triangulation. The operator tunes in the wireless lighthouse at his right and then the one at his left. That gives him two bearings on the shore. He triangulates and where the two bearing lines cross that is his exact location."

And the fog horns? Will the dreadful tooting that ruins the peace of ocean travel in bad weather be abolished?

"Very largely," replied Marconi. "Why not? Why should the skipper have to blow when he knows just where other vessels lie? He has wireless bearings on them through his direction finder. By watching changes in the bearing he can observe the path of other ships. But, that is going far ahead. There must be regulation of wireless and assurance that all vessels carry equipment before that feature comes up.

"Wireless, however, should not be regulated to death, as it easily could be. But, it simply must be governed in some manner, and the one body fit to do the regulating would be an international board. It's a bigger job than any one nation could handle. All must be considered and must join in the proceedings."

For weeks after the *Titanic* wreck honors and editorial tributes were heaped upon Marconi. All the world had been taught the supreme importance of wireless.

The Grand Cross of the Order of Alfonso XII was presented to him on May 21, 1912, for already Spain, the land of Queen Isabella, which had extended the helping hand to Columbus, was linked directly with America by this Italian's endeavor. It was on February 1, 1912, that King Alfonso had sent a message of greeting to *The New York Times* on the occasion of the opening of the wireless station at Aranjuez, near Madrid.

So useful had wireless become to the *Times* that it boasted, "the first and only newspaper to use the transatlantic wireless telegraph, by which it receives daily more than 2,000 words from Europe." The dispatches were marked, "By Marconi Wireless Telegraph."

America was anxious to know more about wireless so the New York Electrical Society invited Marconi as a lecturer on April 17, 1912.

The *Titanic* disaster was the main headline in all newspapers. Marconi praised as the savior of 712 lives was in the forefront of the news as never before. It seemed that all New York wanted to see him before he returned to Europe, and, incidentally, he had booked passage for the first eastward trip of the *Titanic,* a voyage banned by fate.

The Engineering Societies auditorium was jammed to capacity. When the inventor appeared at the side of the platform the crowd in the balcony saw him first, and the cheering began. It spread to the main floor and was continuous as Marconi bowed many times.

John Bottomley, chairman of the Lecture Committee, opened the meeting by reading a telegram:

I regret my inability to be present at your lecture, but hasten to congratulate you upon the success of your beautiful invention —the wireless telegraph—and in the splendid work your system has done in saving human life in disasters at sea.

The cheering broke out again as the signature was read— "Thomas Alva Edison."

The lecture was largely technical and was illustrated with lantern slides of wireless stations all over the world.

"I am glad to know," said Marconi, "that the American Government is promulgating rules and regulations to thwart interference with wireless messages. Still we don't want too much interference. We don't want the waves of ether enveloped in red tape. For commercial purposes, however, we must have isolation of messages if the science is expected to be developed.

"The chief benefit of wireless is to aid ships in distress and it is one of the greatest gratifications in my life to know that in time of need the wireless has not yet failed in a single instance. It has come to be considered indispensable."

Professor Michael I. Pupin, faithful friend of Marconi, was next on the program. He said:

Marconi is the most modest man that I know. Tonight we heard him give credit to his predecessors, Henry, Faraday, Maxwell and Hertz; and yet the invention of wireless telegraphy belongs solely and absolutely to him. The others had nothing whatever to do with it, and yet Marconi would give them credit. They were all experimenting in other lines.

When Marconi grounded the transmitter and then grounded the receiver and let the spark go, then the world had wireless telegraphy, and no one had ever done that before.

If we must call our aerial waves by some name let us not call them Hertzian waves but Marconi waves. They are his.

The only fault I find with Dr. Marconi is that he worries his brain with the troubles of the investors in his patent. That is a foolish thing for any inventor to do.

The ovation left little doubt that the New Yorkers had enjoyed their glimpse of the Italian, who as an inventor had violated tradition by avoiding a life of hardship and privation. He had not served an apprenticeship in the school of poverty as have so many other famous men.

Although modesty is a marked characteristic, Marconi likes fame. He said so quite frankly. As a boy he dreamed of glory, for he talked with relatives of the time when his system would be used all around the world.

When *Titanic* survivors presented him with a gold tablet on which he was pictured as Apollo scattering sparks to the winds, he assured them he would always cherish the token because it was dear to him and because it made him very good-looking.

And the *Titanic:*

> *In a solitude of the sea,*
> *Deep from human vanity,*
> *And the pride of life that planned her,*
> *stilly couches she.*
>
> *Dim moon-eyed fishes near,*
> *The daintily gilded gear,*
> *Gaze, querying, "What does all this*
> *sumptuousness down here?"*

THOMAS HARDY.

XV

"POLITICS" AND AN ACCIDENT

The whirlpool of an unpleasant "political" incident threatened to draw the inventor into the vortex of a controversy in 1912. For the first time in history the word, Marconi, was in danger of being used for purposes other than the name of a great inventor.

"Marconi" was converted into verbs and adjectives becoming synonymous in the minds of some people with a political scandal and a deal in shares of stock. One of the paramount inventions of the age was on the verge of being dropped into a political boiling pot when the scandal raised by the Tories in England for party purposes echoed far and wide. Tongues wagged freely.

The *Titanic* had excited extraordinary interest in wireless. Over night the prospects of the English Marconi Company brightened, and at the same time the organization was called upon to assist in placing additional capital of the American Marconi Company. The star of destiny for wireless shone brightly against the darkness of the ocean tragedy.

"Godfrey Isaacs, managing director of the English Marconi Company, was the king-pin of the organization," said Dr. James C. H. Macbeth, noted cryptographer and one of the early members of the company. "As an extravagant promoter he had an insatiable love for power; he was the salesman of wireless with the business strategy and enthusiasm necessary to promote such a radically new communication system. He reveled in acquiring telephone and electrical instrument companies to link them as subsidiaries of wireless. He was generally faced with litigation, and from that Marconi, who detested routine business and legal conflicts, suffered pangs. Yet he entrusted the business end of wireless and its promotion to Mr. Isaacs, who presided at the company's meetings and usually at public functions. Speechmaking and writing were sacrifices for Marconi; in either he was concise."

Godfrey Isaacs was the man who accompanied Marconi and associates to the United States to make a deal with the defunct United Wireless Company, the capital of which was $10,000,000. The English Marconi Company guaranteed $7,000,000 of which Godfrey Isaacs made himself personally responsible for placing 500,000 shares. Of these, 250,-000 were sold to Heybourn & Croft, brokers, at 1/4 percent premium; 50,000 at 1/8 percent premium, and 50,000 at 1 7/16 percent premium.

On return to London, Godfrey Isaacs offered some of the shares to his brothers. Harry Isaacs took 50,000 shares on April 9, 1912. Sir Rufus Daniel Isaacs,[1] Attorney General, later Lord Reading, the Lord Chief Justice and Viceroy of India, declined, but on April 12, 1912, was persuaded to take 10,000 shares from his brother Harry at the market price of £2. Guglielmo Marconi held 10,000 shares; the Marconi directors and employees 31,500, while the American group took 150,000 shares.

Sir Rufus parted with 2,000 shares to two of his colleagues in the Government, namely, Lloyd George, Chancellor of the Exchequer, who took 1,000 shares, and the Master of Elibank, who also acquired 1,000 shares, but, according to later testimony, neither paid for them at the time.

[1] Rufus Daniel Isaacs, the Marquess of Reading, died December 30, 1935, age 75.

When the stock of the American company was put on the market the opening quotation was $16 a share. The price rushed up to $20, but by the time the quotation reached that figure it was four o'clock, and the Americans were able to come in and sell out at a handsome profit. This, it was alleged, broke the market and the price steadily declined to $5 a share.

The "scandal" was based on the fact that the English Marconi Company, in March 1910, applied to the British Colonial Office to install wireless stations in various parts of the Empire. The request was referred to the Cable Landing Rights Committee in the jurisdiction of which the matter rested. On May 19, 1911, the committee suggested that such wireless stations should be owned by the State. It was recommended that negotiations be conducted with the Marconi Company. The report was then studied by the Committee of Imperial Defence which unanimously favored the plan to link the Empire by a wireless chain.

Herbert Samuel, Postmaster General, opened negotiations. The Marconi Company submitted its tender on February 13, 1912. The Government accepted it on March 7 and on July 9 the formal contract was signed. However, ratification by Parliament was essential, and it was presented to the House of Commons on August 7. Opposition developed and the action was postponed until the autumn session. It was asserted that the contract had been signed in haste, despite the fact that Herbert Samuel was fortified by the various committees giving him "an encouraging accumulation of assent."

Some members of Parliament considered the terms unduly favorable to the Marconi Company. Newspaper attacks began, but were called, "well-intentioned but ill-informed." In some way the dealings in American Marconis by the Ministers became known, and were confused with the English Company's stock, and connected with the Government's contract with the Marconi Company. By the time Parliament reassembled serious allegations were in the air.

The remark was made that, "Mother Marconi has been a prolific parent and her chickens are spread all over the globe; they have assumed a half-dozen nationalities. . . . The Marconi Ring apparently hoped to make as much out of wireless as Mr. Andrew Carnegie got out of the steel tariff."

The hearing of the case was expected to lay bare the inner history of the Marconi organization and the details of what was called "the greatest gamble in the history of the London Stock Exchange." The fact that several cabinet members were involved in the allegations, made the "scandal" the foremost political issue of the day.

Godfrey Locker-Lampson, Unionist Member of Parliament for Salisbury, and Peter Wright, both shareholders in the English Marconi Company, issued a writ against Godfrey Isaacs, Harry Isaacs, and the directors and brokers of the company, demanding an account of the 500,000 shares of the American Marconi Company, part of which Godfrey Isaacs placed in England.

Investors complained that they lost from $5,000,000 to $7,500,000 by the organization of a pool, the formation and operation of which they contended was illegal. They sought to force the Marconi directors to return to them the difference between the par value of the shares and the highest market price at which they were sold. Incidentally, the English Marconi shares had risen from £2 in August 1911, to over £4 in March 1912, when acceptance of the Marconi contract with the British Government became generally known, and to over £9 by the end of April.

One important question to be decided was whether Godfrey Isaacs had acquired the 500,000 shares of American stock for his own account or for the English Marconi Company.

Allegations continued furiously as a bitter political controversy, until finally a move was made in Parliament for the appointment of a Select Committee to investigate the entire affair; to solve what was called, "The Great Marconi Mystery, which would tax the pen of Conan Doyle, assisted by the brains of Sherlock Holmes to do anything approaching justice to it."

Marconi was placed on the stand. He replied vigorously to the various charges and innuendoes both technical and commercial.

Godfrey Isaacs, he declared, had been subjected to a great number of most ungenerous insinuations, which never could have been made by any one personally acquainted with him, and which could not be and were not believed by any one who knew him or who had worked with him.

"The first British ship on which wireless telegraphy was installed was the royal yacht, *Osborne,* in August 1898," recalled Marconi in a voice that gave evidence of his Italian emotion and the fighting spirit of his Irish blood. "It has been stated by several of the Admiralty witnesses at this inquiry, and before the Select Committee of 1907 that the Admiralty is now using a system of its own, or at least, what could be considered a development of the Marconi system.

"I am at loss to understand on what grounds this statement can be made. I have on many occasions in different parts of the world intercepted the signals transmitted from many of His Majesty's ships, and, in my judgment, there is nothing to suggest that these signals were transmitted by means in any way differing from that of our principal system, and, finally I would state that in September 1911, one of my engineers was invited to inspect the wireless apparatus on one of His Majesty's ships. I accompanied him, and I declare that the system installed upon that ship was the Marconi system pure and simple.

"Certain testimony given before this committee has caused me some surprise—the so-called expert testimony," said Marconi. "I have now at Clifden a system utilizing continuous waves and employing no spark whatever in the transmission of messages. Still, it is a Marconi system. But it has often been stated that the Marconi system was first and always a spark system. This is not so.

"I wish to state most emphatically that I have never at any time speculated in any of the shares of my companies. I have always supported them whenever money has been required, and frequently to very large sums. I have occasionally sold shares, not in consequence of markets or circumstances connected with the company's business, but only when I have required moneys for business in which I am interested other than that of the Marconi companies. During the whole of the period of the boom in shares in the parent company or the American company, or any other of the companies with which I am associated, I have never bought or sold a share.

"I have never taken part in any syndicate, nor have I ever heard of any syndicate, nor do I believe any syndicate ever existed, in connection with any of the shares of any of the Marconi companies. Neither I nor my company has in any way been responsible for the fluctuations of the prices in the market, but I believe that these prices have varied entirely according to the natural supply and demand, in the same way as prices of any security upon the Stock Exchange will fluctuate.

"I do not wish to conclude without expressing my resentment at the reflections which have been made upon my company and upon me for having innocently entered into a contract with His Majesty's Government. I resent the inquiry into and publication given to the affairs of my company, which have no relation whatsoever to the contract entered into with His Majesty's Government, and I would in this respect particularly express my regret that the services which my company and I have for so many years rendered to the Post Office, the Admiralty, the merchant marine, and in fact the whole nation, should not have been deemed worthy of higher consideration."

A dignified rebuke was administered by Marconi to his critics in reply to the witless observations of Lord Robert Cecil. He said,

Because I had an arrangement with the Government, all kinds of things have been said; that His Majesty's Government has done wrong by entering into this arrangement, and that my system is not what it was believed to be. I think you will quite understand that I very much resent all the caustic comments on my name.

You see placards, "Marconi Scandals," "Marconi Scenes," and I strongly object to my name being a byword in politics and a peg on which to hang all sorts of scandalous accusations in which it is not suggested by anyone that I am in any way concerned.

Lord Robert Cecil replied, "Unfortunately your name is the name of the company. I hear no suggestion made against you, Mr. Marconi, at all."

Marconi then gave the committee a list of honors conferred upon him:

I have received the following rewards:—The Fahie Premium from the English Institution of Electrical Engineers; a silver medal from the Royal Society of Arts; a gold medal from the Italian Scientific Society of Rome and a gold medal from the Italian Institution of Electrical Engineers, and gold medals from institutions and societies of the towns of Bologna, Florence, Venice, New York, Madrid, Lisbon and others.

I have also received the award of the Royal Society of Rome, consisting of a diploma and £400 and the award of the Royal Academy of Science of Turin consisting of a diploma and £700.

I was awarded the Nobel Prize for Physics in 1909, which comprised a gold medal, a diploma and the sum of about £4,000.

I hold the degrees of Doctor of Engineering, conferred by the Engineering College of Bologna University, the honorary degree of Doctor of Science of Oxford University, and the LL.D. of the Universities of Glasgow, Aberdeen, Liverpool and Pennsylvania. I am a member of a Royal Commission of the Board of Trade in London.

Prime Minister Asquith took the stand and spoke as "never before" with earnestness and power. He brushed aside with a gesture of contempt the charges of corruption but held there had been breaches of propriety; he berated that section of the press which fanned the flames of calumny and referred to anti-Semitism as "the disgraceful appeals that have been made to racial and religious animosities."

Sir Albert Spicer, as chairman, presented his draft report on May 28, 1913. The committee was unable to find unanimity but all agreed in acquitting the Ministers involved of all corruption charges.

The report found no foundation for any charge made against the Ministers in connection with the negotiation of the contract or of dealings in the shares of the English Marconi Company. Furthermore, it was stated that those who brought the charges had no reason to believe they were true, and, therefore, were guilty of "a slander of a particularly vile character, which could not be too strongly condemned." The committee's report further pointed out that the Ministers had every reason to believe that the American Marconi Company had no interest in the British Marconi Company's agreement with the British Government.

The English Company, however, was a large shareholder in the American organization, and, therefore directly interested in its profits, but the latter had no interest in the English Company and could not benefit, except in prestige, from the contract with the Post Office.

The Select Committee concluded:

> So far as we have been able to ascertain, no minister, official or member of Parliament had been influenced in the discharge of his public duties by reason of any interest he may have had in any of the Marconi or other undertakings connected with wireless telegraphy, or has utilized information coming to him from official sources for the purpose of investment or speculation in any such undertakings.

The "great sensation" ended in a fizzle, and the most deplorable aspect was the cruel association in the popular mind of Mr. Marconi with a political scandal, when not the slightest hint of calumny was ever directed against him. He was cleared of all stigma; no general blame was attached to him. There was no stain on his honor, nor was his name besmirched in the controversy that raged for months with its reckless political bombardments and backfires. In fact, shortly afterwards, King George V conferred personally upon him the honor of knighthood by nominating him an Honorary Knight Grand Cross of the Royal Victorian Order (G.C.V.O.)—a very rare distinction.

When cross-examined on the acquisition of the American Marconi shares Rufus Isaacs had testified that his personal loss in the entire transaction was approximately £1,280; that he possessed no more inside information than any of the persons who entered the market in which floated 1,400,-000 shares. He said, "I had no full inside knowledge. . . . The only extra knowledge I had was that my brother was telling me his views of the prospects which I relied upon."

Resolutely lucid, Rufus Isaacs had made a profound impression upon the Parliamentary Committee, in what was described as "a speech of manliness." With clear-cut, scholarly and ascetic features he rose to speak and was received with prolonged cheering by the Ministerialists; he looked worn and wrought but confronted the House with courage as he began to speak in a low-toned, earnest voice like that of a priest:

In my view no one can protect himself against the suspicion of the evilly disposed. . . . It never occurred to me during the whole course of those transactions that any human being could suspect me of corruption because I purchased American Marconi shares some six weeks after the announcement was made of the acceptance of the tender of the British Marconi Company by the British Government; if I had had all the facts present to my mind at the time I entered into that transaction, if I had known then all that I know now, if all had been disclosed to me which subsequent events have revealed, if I had realized that men could be so suspicious of any action of mine, if I had thought that such misrepresentation could possibly exist, I state quite plainly that I would not have entered into this transaction.

I need scarcely tell the House that I have given this matter very careful consideration before I made this statement, and I say solemnly and sincerely it was a mistake to purchase those shares.

"I acted thoughtlessly, carelessly, mistakenly," said Lloyd George, theatrical and emotional as always; "but I acted openly, innocently, honestly." He added, however, that perhaps the transactions in the American Marconis were not wise, judicious or discreet, still there was a vast difference between indiscretion in private investment and circumstances that would warrant a solemn vote of censure by the House of Commons.

Commenting on the "scandal," the London *Chronicle* said:

Some of the meaner critics attacked Mr. Marconi as a "foreigner," and more belittled his genius or derided his invention. That his mother is an Irish lady, that he loves British institutions, speaks English like a native, and is married to an Irish lady are facts which do not count with malicious critics who emphasize the "Guglielmo" in his name. And yet Marconi has been a purer British patriot than all his critics combined.

It is time that this country wiped away the stain that has been put upon him and gave to the discoverer of an invention that has not only revolutionized the fabric of society, established a new and cheaper means of communication, saved much valuable property and hundreds of lives, the honor that is due him. It would be only just that the nation should do so, even if his inventions were superseded tomorrow.

Marconi is a benefactor of humanity. . . . Marconigrams have been of incalculable value to civilization.

Today one cannot circumvent the globe without being in touch with one or more wireless stations standing like sentinels over some rocky, sea-girt shore. The isolation of the vessel in mid-ocean is a thing of the past; the passenger is no longer cut off from civilization and commerce by an ocean voyage; the daily newspaper filled with Marconigrams has become as indispensable to the passenger on the great liner as the newspaper of the town is to the land-dweller. And it is all owing to the young inventor of Italian birth—but of thoroughly British predilections—who pointed the trident of Britannia with electric fire.

Marconi has not yet completed the dedication of his services to Great Britain. The scheme for the establishment of a chain of wireless stations round the Empire cannot be carried out, however the undertaking is attempted, without the use of Marconi's invention. . . . By this process we are within a short distance of having a regular flow of words entirely on British territory, controlled by the self-governing Colonies concerned, and supported both between ourselves and the Pacific.

The inventor who has made all this possible has not received the full measure of credit for his services to commerce, any more than he has received adequate reward for his services to humanity.

The London *Daily Telegraph* called it "farcical proceedings," and continued:

To him at least a word of apology is due. We are sure the British public regrets the manner in which his name has been dragged through the mire of personal allegations and partisan recriminations.

The *Daily Mail* added: Our considered opinion is that the Ministers concerned in the Marconi affair cannot be deemed guilty of anything worse than grave imprudence and lack of delicacy, followed and complicated by almost incredible stupidity.

The London *Times* said: Nothing which came out in the course of the evidence affords the slightest ground for believing that the Marconi contract was not concluded with a single eye to the public interest. There is no question whatever of "corruption" in the sense that the Ministers made a bad bargain in their public capacity for the sake of private advantage.

It was generally recognized that the inquiry had been a case of "Much Ado About Nothing." The *Saturday Review* remarked, "Searching elusive needles in problematical bundles of hay is not good business."

Insinuations had been whispered along with gossip and rumors. Cecil Chesterton's "Eye Witness" had bluntly stated: "Isaacs' brother is chairman of the Marconi Company. It has, therefore, been secretly arranged between Isaacs and Samuel that the British people shall give the Marconi Company a very large sum of money through the agency of the said Samuel and for the benefit of the said Isaacs."

Rufus Isaacs and Herbert Samuel considered taking legal action but decided not to, upon the advice of Prime Minister H. H. Asquith, who suggested the move for legal redress would only serve to gain notoriety for the "Eye Witness," the report of which he termed "scurrilous rubbish."

Le Matin of Paris, on February 14, 1913, repeated the allegations against the English Ministers, but four days later printed a full apology on the basis that official documents did not support the insinuations.

Rufus Isaacs and Herbert Samuel decided it was high time to bring libel action; the case came up on March 19. The sweeping allegations of Cecil Chesterton failed to stand the test of inquiry.

Godfrey Isaacs sued Cecil Chesterton and the verdict on June 8, 1913, was for Isaacs, the jury finding Chesterton guilty of the charge of criminally libeling Isaacs. The judge said after the verdict that Chesterton's state of mind toward his victim was one of "invincible ignorance."

Vindication of Godfrey Isaacs in "the outrageous campaign of calumny," as the Chesterton case was called, led the London *Daily News* to say:

"Invincible ignorance there was in the crusade of criticism which was without parallel alike for its venom and perversion of facts; but it is not ignorance of innocent purpose; it is willful ignorance, inspired by deliberate ulterior motives. Those motives are two-fold, anti-Semitism and antagonism to the government."

"Wireless was an ideal whip for the imagination of the public once that imagination had been kindled," remarked an American who pioneered in the business end of communication. "Naturally, the possibilities attracted some gamblers and speculators. That is why wireless, long before there was any continuity in its activities, was tossed about in a stock game. That so-called 'scandal' in England, however, was purely political.

"Throughout the entire early days of the invention Marconi clung faithfully to the legitimate side of wireless. Never did he deviate from the scientific aspects of his invention. The business organization and speculation never interested him; in fact, it annoyed him. He was not a good business man. The very fact that the speculators ignored him, although he was the central figure, shows, I think, that the business-end of wireless had not the slightest attraction for him or he for the speculators.

"The promoters claimed wild things for wireless. They predicted even to the astonishment of Marconi, who, by the way, never exaggerates. Of course, many of their dreams eventually came true, but long after they had predicted, and oddly enough, long after their imaginative souls had passed from the earth and from their realms of ticker tape. I knew Godfrey Isaacs intimately. I believe he was an honorable man. He was a live-wire promoter and in that role probably expected wireless to develop more rapidly than it did.

"Marconi told me that if it had not been for the support he received from the Italian Government he could never have kept going on what the English Marconi Company paid him as a salary. Italy paid him twice as much. I doubt that he ever made money in stock deals. The shares that belonged to him rightfully through the organization of the company, he probably held for many years. He was no trader."

Behind the haze of the English "scandal," across the ocean wireless was progressing rapidly under the spur of American enterprise. Godfrey Isaacs had dipped into a reservoir of opportunity when he turned his ambitions toward the United States. Uncle Sam's domain was "wireless minded." The telegraph companies entered an agreement to deliver the wireless traffic to its destination once it was plucked from space at the shore line. The Marconi Wireless Telegraph Company of America on June 7, 1912, signed contracts for the purchase of 550 acres near Belmar, New Jersey, as a site for a $600,000 transatlantic station.

.   .   .   .   .   .

By this time the ocean was "an old story" to Marconi; he had crossed the Atlantic more than fifty times without accident of any sort. His invention had added truth to the expression, "man is safer at sea than on the land." But the dangers lurking on the terra firma overtook him on September 25, 1912, when the motor car in which he was traveling from Spezia to Genoa collided with a car carrying several Venetian ladies.

Marconi was at the wheel of his car making good speed in order to climb a high curving road through the mountains. A quarter of a mile from Casa de Vara outside of Spezia the other car coming down the hill whirled around

a sharp curve, and the two cars crashed. Rescuers found
Marconi stunned and clinging to the wheel. He was bleed-
ing from a gash in the forehead. Occupants of the other car,
including Commendatore Beltrami and his wife, escaped
with a shaking. A naval ambulance from Spezia rushed to
the scene. The accident happened at 12:30 P.M.

No time was lost in getting Marconi to the Naval Hospital in Spezia. All the naval and military surgeons available quickly gathered at the bedside. His right eyeball,
right temple and cheek were badly bruised. The eye was
cut by a splinter of glass piercing the eyeball. Italy was
shocked at the news; messages of sympathy came from all
parts of the world.

Marconi had been a guest at the Royal Hunting Lodge
at San Rossore, and a report of the accident was telegraphed to King Victor Emmanuel, who was one of the first
to send inquiries regarding the inventor's condition. The
monarch wired to Spezia wishing Marconi a speedy recovery, and requested hospital authorities to telegraph news of
the patient's progress twice daily. He dispatched Marquis
Sant'Elia, Master of Ceremonies at the Court, to see that
everything possible was done for Marconi, and to express
fervent wishes for speedy recovery. On October 12, the
King and Queen called at the hospital.

Signor Beltrami, although injured, was deeply grieved over
the affair, and said, "I would have preferred to die or to
have both legs cut off rather than even without blame to
have caused an accident whereof the victim was Mr. Marconi, whom I fervently admire."

The badly wounded eye continued to become worse. The
severe contusions and swelling prevented a thorough exam-
ination for several days, when it was discovered that the
optic nerve had been affected. Marconi suffered neuralgic
pains and the visual power of both eyes showed rapid

diminution. Dr. Baiardi, well-known surgeon of Turin, was summoned. He decided that to save one eye it would be necessary to sacrifice the other. He called Dr. Fuchs of Vienna, one of Europe's most noted eye specialists, into consultation. It was decided the wounded eye should be removed without delay. Marconi, informed of the critical situation, remarked, "Well, I hope my lady friends will love me just the same." He insisted on walking to the operating room unaided.

On October 17, 1912, Marconi lost his right eye. Following the operation this bulletin was issued:

Professor Fuchs of Vienna University and Professor Baiardi of Turin were called in today for consultation and having recognized the necessity of performing the operation of enucleation of the eyeball in order to avoid sympathetic ophthalmia, carried out the operation successfully. The condition of the patient is good and his morale excellent.

Marconi asked to be alone; he wanted to sleep.

Italy was sad, but there was a tinge of joy and of hope in the medical experts' assurance that Marconi's life and sight would be spared. Soon he was seen motoring with his head bandaged, and on November 1 at the Ophthalmic Hospital in Turin Dr. Rubbi of Venice fitted him with an artificial eye, with such perfection that one could scarcely observe it, even when face to face.

Dr. Baiardi refused compensation saying that he had been sufficiently rewarded by the honor of serving the glory of Italian science. Marconi later visited the hospital and left a donation as an expression of his gratitude.

Confinement made the inventor restless; he was anxious to get back to his wireless.

XVI

A STIRRING SPECTACLE

It was a cruel fate that decided three fearful marine disasters had to test the merits of the Marconi invention. First
one ship rammed by another not so far from the shore; second, a great liner in collision with an iceberg far off the
northern coasts; third, a fire in mid-ocean in which a ship
was turned into a floating, tossing hell with a frantic crew
on board. It was from this terrifying scene that the steamer
Volturno broadcast an urgent SOS on October 11, 1913,
right from the middle of the ocean.

Like a miracle wireless turned ten ships flying the flags
of six nations from their beaten paths, and they rushed from
all directions to the stricken vessel which had turned into a
veritable volcano as the flames intensified by explosions
belched from the portholes and hatches.

Six hundred and fifty-seven terrified human beings huddled on the deck hoping and praying that from below the
horizon rescuers would rush to them through the fury of an
autumn storm and gale. To them Marconi loomed as a
savior. His wireless held out hope for life as death stalked
over a mad white-capped sea, seemingly determined to
swallow this ship bound to New York from Rotterdam.

The S.S. *Carmania's* junior operator was listening-in that
morning. Shortly after eight o'clock he picked up three
dots, three dashes and three more dots. That combination
sends a chill through any wireless man. He ran to the chief
operator, who was in his berth after a night on duty at the
key, exclaiming:

"There is some fellow who says his ship is on fire. You had better get on to him and see what he wants."

The senior operator in his nightclothes ran to the wireless cabin. The earphones were pulsing with the cryptic SOS. He heard the *Seydlitz* answer and then asked her to stand by while he received the *Volturno's* position. He rushed the message to the bridge. The steward woke Captain J. C. Barr, who went on deck immediately.

Barr ordered the *Carmania's* speed increased and she turned her nose into a terrific storm "mad as the sea and wind when both contend."

Great waves tumbled across her bow and swept the decks from end to end. She trembled under the onslaught of the waves and the utmost speed of her engines.

Many of the *Carmania* passengers were at breakfast. Their first intimation that anything unusual had happened was the sudden and continuous breaking of the green seas on the decks. The wild plunging of the vessel indicated that the *Carmania's* course had been changed, and that she had turned on an errand of mercy—summoned by wireless.

Soon after noon a curl of smoke was seen on the horizon. The *Carmania* with double-manned stokeholds and steaming twenty knots was the first to arrive through the foam of the surging sea. She was a glorious sight to those caught as the prey of flames. But the violence of the storm kept her from the blazing crater—an unapproachable hulk. It was two o'clock in the afternoon.

The *Seydlitz* hove in sight at 3:30 o'clock. The *Grosser Kurfuerst* and others came in quick succession.

No greater triumph of Marconi wireless was ever portrayed than in the dawn of the next day when the flags of six nations, the United States, England, Belgium, Russia, France, and Germany waved from the masts of a cordon of ships called by wireless to 48.25 N. Lat., and 34.33 W. Long.

There was the *Carmania,* the *Grosser Kurfuerst, La Touraine, Minneapolis, Rappahannock, Narragansett, Devonian, Kroonland, Czar* and the *Seydlitz.* Many of them had rushed up during the night with their waving searchlights and blinking lights adding cheer to a frightful situation.

Each ship told the same story of the spectacle of horror she met when answering the far-flung SOS. Through the gloom and fog of the dying day they saw a vivid crimson shape, waxing and waning in irregular pulsations, and through the glare sharply outlined against the cloud-shrouded background they saw the pitiful figures of the ship's company huddled together on the stern. As they watched they saw the glowing mass leap to a scarlet apex and then die down. An instant later they heard a roar that defined the sudden flare to have been an explosion. The ship was blazing from funnel to forecastle.

A terrific storm was raging. No small boat could live in that chaotic sea. The rescue ships with hundreds of passengers on board were helpless to assist the emigrant vessel wrapped in flames fanned by such a gale. There were plenty of volunteers ready to go over the side to the rescue but the weather defied them. The terror-stricken passengers could be seen on the poop deck while officers and crew made every effort to stop the advancing fire.

The *Carmania* and others on the scene hoped to complete the rescue before nightfall. But the mountainous seas made it impossible as the helpless spectators watched the doomed ship in silent agony.

Grim was the scene in the twilight of that day. Panic-stricken emigrants leaped into the sea to a certain death, but it seemed the only escape from the fire. Those along the rails of the rescue ships saw lifeboats collapse against the

Volturno's veering sides and spill their human freight. Searchlights revealed the tiny specks of humanity struggling in the icy water. Darkness and the whistling gale added to the terror of the heartrending scene as the floating furnace with heavy blasts of pungent smoke illuminated by the flames revealed the *Volturno* was still afloat. The sky was lit with a lurid glare.

The *Grosser Kurfuerst* at 9 P.M., lowered the first boat manned by broad-shouldered Teutons who had spent their lives at sea. Perilously the little craft bobbed up and down in the troughs of the sea. Only the great searchlights of the *Carmania* kept it in view now and then. The German sailors came back at 11 o'clock with twenty-one persons rescued. The boat went back with a fresh crew and returned at 2:30 A.M., with eleven survivors.

Then the *Volturno* wirelessed, "Do not send any more boats until daylight."

Desperately, Captain Inch, in a final appeal before flames licked up the wireless cabin, and sent the aerial crashing to the deck, flashed:

"Cannot something be done to help us? We must abandon ship. Our plates are buckling. Stand in close. I may have to jump for it."

As soon as Captain Barr of the *Carmania* had realized the situation he ordered his Marconi operator to get in touch with an oil steamer he had talked with earlier in the day. It could not be so far away as distance at sea is measured. An abundant supply of oil seemed the only means of subduing the violence of the waves to facilitate rescue operations.

The *Carmania's* spark located the oiler *Narragansett,* whose Captain flashed this jocular reply through the midnight air:

"I'll be up with the milk at six in the morning."

True to his word he arrived at five o'clock with two hoses ready and began drenching the water with oil.

And at dawn the wind abated. It was a stirring spectacle when the parade of liners put off their boats, which danced over the shimmering oil-filmed waters to the work of rescue. They saved 521. Had all remained aboard the burning vessel all would have been saved. The panic that made 136 leap overboard and take to the boats too soon led them to destruction.

The last to leave the doomed ship was the heroic Captain Inch; with him was his dog and the ship's papers. The sailors of the *Kroonland* took them off at eight o'clock that morning.

"There were a series of explosions," said Captain Inch. "The third was terrific. It wrecked the saloon deck and the walls fell in. I had asked the senior Marconi man Pennington to call for help. He informed me that he'd got a reply from the *Carmania*, which wanted to know our position. I said, 'You make the call again and I'll bring the position to you.' While the boats were being put out I took the ship's position to the Marconi house."

The *Volturno* was left a derelict. The British cruiser *Donegal* was dispatched from the west coast of Scotland to destroy the hulk.

The account of the senior operator of the *Volturno* emphasized that the lessons learned from the *Republic* and *Titanic* had not been in vain. The second operator had rendered invaluable aid during the trying hours. The value of emergency batteries was proved. When the main source of current supply from the ship's dynamo was destroyed the extra batteries enabled the Volturno to use its wireless eight hours longer than would have been possible had not the suggestions made after the *Republic* disaster been followed.

And the *Volturno* proved that ships should carry three operators so that at no time would the wireless receiver be without a human ear. Furthermore, lifeboats should be equipped with emergency wireless outfits or automatic senders so the rescue ships could trace them in the dark with the radio compass should they become lost. The value of a radio direction finder on larger ships was evidenced by the fact that the *Grosser Kurfuerst* found the *Volturno* drifting twenty-four miles from the position that was broadcast.

Inspired by the rescue of the passengers and crew from the *Volturno*, the London *Daily Telegraph* on October 15, 1913, said editorially:

But for the invention of Marconi, we should be mourning today a holocaust of the seas of unparalleled horror, the overwhelming by fire in mid-Atlantic of six or seven hundred men, women and children.

There is nothing, perhaps, less noble in the record of our times than the indifference with which the patient research in the service of humanity is rewarded. The practical scientist who bridged the oceans and contracted continents within the span of electric impulse, never received from any state a fitting recognition of his triumph.

He has, it is true, like the inventor of a knife-cleaning machine or of a roadsweeper, received patent rights, which he can exploit commercially. The country where he was born has conferred on him some slight titular honor. English and Scottish universities have admitted him to honorary degrees. But for the rest of the country of his adoption and of his mother's birth, the country on which he has showered such untold benefits has been content to single him out as an unwilling participant in an unsavory scandal.

This is the recognition which England has given to the man who above all others has done the most to rob the sea of its terrors.

Surely the time and occasion have arrived when the State may well revive, if that be necessary, its standard of honor, and grant to the wizard who enabled such a triumph to be achieved in the name of humanity some fitting token of England's gratitude for the great permanent addition he has made to what may be described as our armory of mercy.

Marconi had seen his invention serve mankind, to save hundreds of lives at sea and countless minutes for the business world.

As 1913 closed its pages, he reflected:

I have examined and am responsible for the designs and apparatus installed on more than 1,000 ships. I have arranged all the details of the wireless plants of four stations of 2,000 or more miles range, namely, Clifden, Glace Bay, Coltano and Massana; together with at least twenty other stations in England, America, Italy, Africa and Spain having ranges of 1,000 miles and upward.
I have crossed the Atlantic sixty times in ships fitted with wireless.

An inquiring reporter asked if he was dreaming of new wonders. He replied: [1]

Inventors are too visionary. The reason? It is not far to seek: the inventor is a man of scientific knowledge, of imagination and of enthusiasm.
These three make a good team if they are kept "pulling together"; but every now and then an inventor allows his imagination and enthusiasm to run away with his scientific knowledge.
I try to keep my eyes and ears open.

[1] *The New York Times,* March 24, 1912.

XVII

DEFENDING HISTORIC PATENTS

FEVER of war was in the 1914 air. Marconi, in the United States battling in the courts for his patent rights, learned that the glory road of invention is seldom, if ever, strewn with roses. The climb from the conception of an idea to establishment of priority is a long, tedious journey that tests the mettle of the man, and at times he must wonder if it is all worth the candle. There are many who aim to dim his glory and capture his laurels for themselves. Marconi found the truth in that cynical proverb: "a patent is merely a title to a lawsuit."

The most harrowing part of invention is usually what follows filing of the patent claim. Invention is but the spark that kindles a great fire upon which theorists and imitators seek to offer the inventor to the gods of destruction. The days in the wake of invention are a crucible for the very heart of the man who conceived the idea and carried it to a practical conclusion.

It was not until 1914 that Marconi was declared absolute victor on the patent battlefield. Judge Van Vechten Veeder in a decision in the United States District Court (Eastern District of New York in Brooklyn), paid high tribute to Guglielmo Marconi as the inventor of wireless. He held that all of the patents filed in the United States by Marconi and his associates were valid.

The decision was regarded by the Marconi Company as of the widest importance to the Marconi interests. It put the control of wireless telegraphy in America practically in the company's hands. It declared the National Electric Signaling Company of Pittsburgh, the Marconi Company's only formidable rival in the United States, to be an infringer in vital particulars.

Marconi had attended the hearings before Judge Veeder in June 1913, and upon the witness stand he told the full story of his invention, describing its development from a "toy" that could send sounds across a table at his father's home to an international means of communication capable of sending messages from Ireland to the Argentine.

The suit was brought for damages and an injunction against the National Electric Signaling Company, but it was fought from the first as a test suit to establish the judicial status of the Marconi patents in the United States.

Many authorities were called by the defense to prove that others than Marconi had invented wireless devices, and that inventors, since his system was first put on the market, had the same right to use it as a basis for improvements, in the same way he had to improve upon such devices as he found in existence before his day.

F. W. H. Clay, attorney for the defendants, cross-examined Marconi. The legal questions did not disturb the witness but when the cross-examiner got into the science of wireless, the inventor seemed amused, and once told the attorney smilingly that the question was absurd.

Marconi was asked if he regarded Professor A. E. Kennelly of Harvard University, as an authority on certain phases of wireless.

"He is known as an eminent electrical engineer in America," replied Marconi, avoiding any criticism of him, "and I have no reason to say that he is not an authority on those matters. I do not know that he has studied this subject as deeply as I have along certain lines."

Mr. Clay referred to an article in which Professor Kennelly made statements relating to mathematical problems in wireless science, and he pressed the witness further for his opinion of the author.

"I am afraid that my confidence in Kennelly is shaken by what you have just shown me," replied Marconi. "Whether he is a mathematician or not, like everybody else, he is likely to be wrong."

As Marconi left the courtroom at the end of that day a reporter asked if he was working on any new inventions.

"I am always working," he replied with a smile.

As the trial progressed, witnesses for the defense admitted that the defendant company's apparatus was derived in part from Marconi instruments.

The defense was then centered upon a charge that a decision for the Marconi Company would be in effect the licensing of a monopoly in wireless that would involve even the United States Government's wireless station at Arlington, Virginia, and all other Government installations.

The patents at issue were No. 11,913, issued to William Marconi on July 13, 1897; No. 609,154 issued on August 16, 1898 to Sir Oliver Lodge, and later acquired by Marconi, and No. 763,772 granted on June 28, 1904 to William Marconi. This was the famous "four circuit" tuning patent which covered the basic principles upon which all wireless telegraph systems depended.

Furthermore, this patent was regarded as the most vital of the group, because counterparts of that patent had already been held valid by the courts of Great Britain and France. The decision of Judge Veeder was held by lawyers of the Marconi Company to give the organization control of the international wireless situation.

While the Veeder decision established the validity of the three patents, it held that the National Electric Signaling

Company infringed only the latter two, and not the original Marconi patent, which was issued before improvements made long-distance signaling possible.

Judge Veeder's sweeping decision, which went exhaustively into the history of wireless from the days of Egyptian signal fires down to the Marconi inventions, swept away the defendant company's assertions that others preceded Marconi as inventor of a practical wireless system. This is his summary of what actually had been done:

Maxwell, in 1863, had speculated on the possibility of the production of electric waves which would detach themselves from a source of origin. Hertz, in 1887-88, had proved experimentally that Maxwell's theories were correct. Lodge, in 1889, had repeated Hertz's experiments. Branly, in 1890, had repeated Hertz's experiments and had also discovered that certain substances, in addition to Hertz's ring resonator, were detectors of electric waves. Crookes, in 1892, had forecast the possibilities of wireless telegraphy by the utilization of Hertzian waves.

Lodge, in 1894, had reviewed the experiments of Hertz and Branly and some of his own, touching the form which electric waves took when emanating from their source of origin, and upon substances which would detect these waves. Popoff, in 1895, in similar experiments had noted that he could detect the existence of a distant thunder storm, and expressed the hope that wireless telegraphy could be accomplished by the utilization of Hertzian waves.

But no one had described and demonstrated a system of wireless telegraph apparatus adapted for the transmission and reception of definite, intelligible signals by such means. This was the state of scientific knowledge and practice when in 1896 Marconi applied for his first patent.

"Accordingly I find," said Judge Veeder, "that the evidence establishes Marconi's claim that he was the first to

discover and use any practical means for effective telegraphic transmission and intelligible reception of signals
produced by artificially formed Hertz oscillations."

More than fifty pages of Judge Veeder's decree were devoted to a discussion of the third Marconi patent, which had
been held valid in Europe. Relative to the manner in which
Marconi achieved his final wireless triumph with instruments designed under this patent, Judge Veeder said:

> With this apparatus Marconi communicated across the Atlantic
> in 1901 and the claims in issue constitute the essential features
> of apparatus which has since made possible communication over a
> distance of 6,000 miles. It has been used in more than 1,000
> installations by Marconi, and is admittedly an essential feature
> of the wireless art as at present known and practiced.

Particular stress was laid upon Marconi's discovery of
the vertical aerial wire and the connection of the apparatus
to earth or water, and the advantage gained in adopting
such methods. The opinion which gave Marconi full credit
for the disclosure of the adaptability of such means, stated:

> I think the described characteristics of the grounded vertical
> conductor plainly indicate its utility for a long distance transmis-
> sion, as does also the statement that "the larger the plates of the
> receiver and transmitter and the higher from the earth the plates
> are carried the greater is the distance at which it is possible to
> communicate."

The fact that Lodge made no reference to ground connections in his subsequent lecture on the work of Hertz was
considered as evidence to show that an earlier statement by
him was nothing more than an incidental reference to an
abandoned experiment. The Lodge patent dated August 18,
1898 was discussed in detail, and he was given the credit for
the first realization of the advantage to be derived in the
matter of sharpness of tuning by the use of feebly damped
or more persistent oscillations.

It should not be forgotten, however, that in Marconi's original patent he specified that his elevated capacity areas or plates are "preferably electrically tuned with each other," that is, of similar electrical dimensions.

It cannot be denied, therefore, that Marconi thoroughly understood at the date of issue of his first patent the necessity of tuning the open circuit of his transmitter to the open circuit of the receiver.

Comparing the early work of Hertz in his experimental investigations in respect to tuning with that of Marconi at the time of his discovery of the completed wireless system the opinion of the court stated:

> While Hertz effected whatever tuning was possible in his structure by adjusting the capacity and inductance in the closed receiving circuit, Marconi adjusted the capacity of his open transmitting and receiving circuits.

While Lodge undoubtedly understood the sharp resonance effects to be had in the use of feebly damped oscillations his apparatus left much to be desired in obtaining long-distance communication. Although Lodge in his 1898 patent came forward with a new idea he recognized the impossibility of having a circuit which should be at once a good radiator or absorber and a persistent oscillator. He therefore proposed a compromise.

To quote the court:

> He increased the persistence of vibration of his radiating circuit at the expense of its radiating qualities, and increased the accumulative power of his receiving circuit at the expense of his absorbing qualities.
>
> Effecting this compromise by means of the introduction of an inductance coil in an open circuit, he obtained a train of waves of approximately equal amplitude and thus rendered effective syntony possible. But the syntony thus obtained was utilized for selectivity alone. It was attained at the expense of the radiating and absorbing qualities of the circuit; and Lodge still supposed that for distant signaling the single pulse or whip crack was best.

Dr. Irving Langmuir in his laboratory at Schenectady explains radio research apparatus to the inventor of wireless, during his visit to the United States in 1922.

Where Lodge compromised, Marconi reconciled.

Marconi overcame the difficulties emphasized by Lodge. In his second patent covering improvements upon his own prior apparatus, Marconi solved the puzzle. The improvement consisted in the substitution of a pair of circuits in both transmitter and receiver in place of a single circuit. One was so designed as to radiate or absorb readily, and the other to oscillate persistently and be a good conserver of energy. Finally, the four circuits must be tuned together.

The court distinctly stated that with Marconi's apparatus he was not only able to obtain the persistency of oscillation of the apparatus of Lodge, but also obtained such effects without any sacrifice of radiating qualities, and furthermore allowed an increase in the available amount of energy drawn from the local circuits of the transmitter. With this definite control over radiation effective selectivity was maintained and the distance over which messages could be sent was enormously increased.

The defendants claimed that various inventors had disclosed previously to Marconi his method of "four circuit" tuning. The opinion of the court in each instance disproved and cast aside the allegation. No proof or mention whatsoever was found in the publications or lectures of Fessenden that he recognized the necessity of "four circuit" tuning in a complete wireless system.

Likewise patents of Tesla were brought to the front as being prior disclosures of the Marconi inventions in respect to "four circuit" tuning. The court clearly stated the impossibility of obtaining wireless telegraph communication with apparatus such as Tesla described, for by calculation it was shown that the local oscillatory circuits of the Tesla transmitter were vibrating at a wave length of 1,200 meters while the elevated wire, which he suggested should be somewhere in the vicinity of from six to seven miles in height, would have a wave length from 28,000 to 56,000 meters. The coupling of these two circuits would in no sense bring about a condition of resonance and, therefore, Tesla's conception was declared entirely remote from the subject matter of Marconi's patent.

The defendant argued that Pupin had been instrumental in the discovery of "four circuit" tuning. Ample evidence was introduced to disprove such contentions, closing the matter once and for all. Summing up certain statements by Pupin in 1899 the opinion stated:

It is absolutely incompatible with the supposition that Pupin himself or any one else so far as he knew had solved this problem.

Thus the famous four-circuit tuning patent established Marconi as the master of wireless. The manner in which his work withstood the onslaught in the courts was like a spotlight on his genius and the mind that had a clear conception of wireless from the beginning.

There was not the slightest doubt that to Marconi belonged the diadem of wireless, after Judge Veeder handed down his historic decision on March 17, 1914.

The American press quite generally agreed along this line of thought: "In spite, however, of the fact that litigation over wireless telegraphy will doubtless continue, in one form or another, for years to come, Justice Veeder's decision, confirming as it does others to like effect in England and France, gives Mr. Marconi a strong position from which to conduct his battle.

"It is in harmony too with public sentiment everywhere, for there never has been any question in the general mind as to the originator of wireless, or to whom fame and gratitude should be accorded for the most inestimable benefits which the world has derived and will derive from this remarkable invention."

Almost daily the invention seemed to fulfill predictions. The big station at Nauen, Germany, known by its call letters, POZ, had established communication on March 14, 1914 with Windhoek, Cape of Good Hope, South Africa, 6,000 miles away. In preliminary tests on February 11, the first message between Berlin and New York went to *The New York Times* and carried a greeting to Mayor Mitchel.

Not to be outclassed, Italian warships off the Sicilian coast on March 15, received clear radiophone messages from Clifden, Ireland, 1,750 miles distant and from Rome, 300 miles. The ships, while forty-five miles apart, conversed by the wireless phone for twelve hours without a break.

"The problem of the wireless telephone has been practically solved," said Marconi, who had taken an active part in the tests. "This has been proved by successful experiments on board the Duke of Abruzzi's flagship, the *Regina Elena,* off Augusta, Sicily. . . . If sufficient energy is used radio telephonic communication will be quite possible at the longest distances. My conviction is that the day is not far off when the human voice will cross the Atlantic."

Already possessor of the coveted Nobel Prize, the Medal of the British Council of the Royal Society of Arts was added to Marconi's trophies on June 9, 1914; and he had the Russian Order of St. Anne; the Italian Order of St. Maurice and St. Lazarus; also the Italian Grand Cross of the Crown.

Italy made him a Senatore, i.e., Member of the Upper Legislative Chamber, an honor signifying recognition of a high order of accomplishment in the arts, literature and science. The requisite age is forty, and it is a life appointment. Royal princes are the only members of the Senate who enter automatically. The Senate is dubbed "the Sleepy House" because of the small attendance in ordinary

times and the somnolence frequently displayed in consideration of routine matters.

Whenever a Senatore votes "yes" on a Senatorial appointment it is equivalent to saying to the candidate, "You are
one of Italy's living great men and we welcome you as such."

They are mature men of sober judgment who have
breasted the world and won their way to the top. The
nation awards them for having shed glory upon it.

Marconi was one of them.

He lectured on wireless on March 8, 1914, before a great
crowd at the Augusteo in Rome—the cry everywhere was,
"Marconi—Marconi—Viva Marconi!"

XVIII

MARCONI GOES TO WAR

A DEVASTATING shot was fired on June 28, 1914, in Bosnia. Archduke Francis Ferdinand, heir to the Austrian Empire was slain. A smoldering desire for war was fanned into flames; the battle cries of many nations were wirelessed like wildfire!

There was no time to be lost. Armies were mobilizing along European frontiers. Marconi's invention was rushed into action on land, sea and in the air. Every dot and dash intercepted at listening posts throughout the world pulsed with impending conflict. Every dispatch rang with urgency.

A cryptic flash from the tall German towers at Nauen ordered the S.S. *Kronprinzessin Cecile,* 850 miles off the Irish coast, to dash for a neutral port; she had $10,000,000 in gold on board. She turned like a frightened cat and dashed toward America. Through the morning mist a few days later the big liner nosed her way into the peaceful Bar Harbor—safe for a while from the enemy!

Laboratories hastened to develop new ideas and devices being nurtured in the incubators of electrical experimentation. Never before had there been such a hectic demand for radio telephony, direction finders, vacuum tubes, transmitters and receivers. All were urgently needed in this holocaust. Wireless could cross No Man's Land and the war zone at sea; if intercepted by the foe it would, nevertheless, speed on to deliver its message at the intended mark. It could steal past enemy guns with secrets, which if deciphered might shift battalions and fleets; and change history.

Every kingdom, every Republic needed this wireless of Marconi, because it was invisible, quick as a wink and it traveled far, despite the fact that it could not be depended upon to stay out of enemy territory; but secrets could be couched in code—and so they were.

Here was news, that leaked out later—Marconi was on the S.S. *Lusitania* when chased by a submarine off the Fastnet in April, 1915. And that was the west-bound voyage previous to the trip when the death-dealing torpedo found its mark.

Recalling the incident Marconi explained, "Only a few persons were informed that the periscope of a German submarine had been sighted off the rocky island called the Fastnet by Cape Clear, and that the *Lusitania* with her 22-knot speed, had got clear away before the dreaded commerce destroyer could get near enough to launch a torpedo at her.

"I was surprised to hear that Captain Turner came so close to the Irish coast again on the eastward voyage, but I presume he relied upon the speed of his turbines to elude the submarines. I think the sinking of the *Lusitania* a terrible thing."

Marconi had not been long in New York after the big Cunarder was torpedoed, when the calm of the spring air in his native land was disturbed by the rumble of distant guns. Italy joined the Allies in May, 1915, and declared war on Austria. Marconi volunteered to join the Italian colors.

He was in New York, attending the trial in the United States District Court in Brooklyn, of the suit brought by the Marconi Wireless Telegraph Company of America against the Atlantic Communication Company for alleged infringement of patent rights. The Atlantic Communication Company operated the powerful wireless station at Sayville, Long Island, which was equipped with the Telefunken system, a German apparatus.

Marconi had been the principal witness in the suit of his organization against the company using the Telefunken system and his sudden departure from the United States halted the trial.

In a brief address to Judge Veeder, Marconi said:

"Your Honor, after consultation with the Italian authorities here, I have decided to return to Italy at once. While war between Italy and her foes has not yet been declared, it seems to be only a matter of a few hours. I shall leave for Italy tomorrow and I am therefore impelled to cease my attendance here."

Marconi then bade good-bye to Judge Veeder, who came down from the bench and shook hands with the inventor. After shaking hands with his counsel, Marconi also shook hands with the counsel of the Atlantic Communication Company.

Johann Senneck, a German expert, who had been called from Belgium to testify, remarked to Marconi that they might still part as friends as "the Triple Alliance which binds us, has not yet been dissolved."

"I suppose it will not be improper for me, too, to shake hands, seeing that the Triple Alliance still holds good," said Frederick Fish, one of the counsel for the defendants.

"I shall know more about that when I arrive in Italy," Marconi replied with a broad smile.

Judge Veeder said the trial would be adjourned for two months. If Marconi was unable to attend at that time, a further adjournment would be ordered by the court.

Prior to sailing on the American liner *St. Paul* on May 22, Marconi expressed the belief that the Italian Navy would do fine work in the event it was called into action against a hostile fleet.

"The Italian Navy," he said, "is fit and its officers and men are splendidly trained. Since the war in Europe started several new ships have been commissioned and among them are a number of the dreadnought type. I have recently met many of the officers and have seen a number of the ships myself, and I can say everything that could be done has been done to bring the fleet up to a high state of efficiency. The commanding officer of the fleet is the Duke of the Abruzzi, and Americans know he is a fine and capable type of seaman. Under his direction the fleet has been undergoing a constant training in marksmanship and maneuvering exercises. Never before has the fleet been so ready as now."

Marconi's eye sparkled with emotion. He was off to the war!

What a prize for a German U-boat if it could capture the inventor of wireless!

The voyage was uneventful until European shores were approached, and in those waters all eyes were alert for the tell-tale periscope of an enemy submarine. There was intense excitement among a few on the liner, for, according to a London dispatch the *St. Paul* was chased by a German submarine right up to the bar of the Mersey. The bulletin read: [1]

As we approached the war zone rather elaborate precautions were taken to safeguard Mr. Marconi. His name was not on either the regular passenger list or the purser's list. There was a general tacit agreement among passengers that if the *St. Paul* was stopped by a submarine and Mr. Marconi's person demanded we all would "lie like gentlemen."

Meanwhile Mr. Marconi removed all labels from his luggage, gave his private papers into my care and got into clothes suitable for slipping into a hiding place somewhere down in the bowels of the ship next to the keel, where the chief engineer said the captain himself would be unable to find him.

[1] *The New York Tribune,* June 2, 1915.

We had a concert that night at which Mr. Marconi was to preside. The programs were inadvertently printed with his name as chairman. The captain ordered all programs destroyed. When the concert began the historian, Mr. Trevelyan, took the chair saying, "We were to have had the pleasure of having Mr. Marconi preside, but unfortunately he is not on board."

Sensing the value of radiophone in warfare Uncle Sam lost no time in demonstrating he was fully prepared to take advantage of its possibilities. The naval radio station at Arlington, Virginia, talked by voice with Honolulu 5,000 miles away. Paris, 3,700 miles in the opposite direction eavesdropped on the conversation. It was all made possible by hundreds of vacuum tubes wired in cascade formation.

Inspired by the news when it reached him in Italy, Marconi exclaimed: "There is not a shadow of doubt that wireless telephony across the Atlantic is assured in the future. It does not matter if for the present such a result is possible only under ideal conditions. The very fact that talking over such a distance as Washington to Hawaii has been possible makes it certain that whatever obstacles may exist at present in the way of a fairly perfect service will be removed after further experiments.

"A year or two ago I said that within a few years arrangements would be perfected so that telephonic wireless across the Atlantic would be established. Had it not been for the war, which has projected our activities in other directions, we would soon have a transatlantic wireless telephone.

"After the war a service will be installed. Europe will be within conversational distance of America. It will undoubtedly be possible for New York to call London as easily as Chicago. Atmospheric conditions, of course, must be taken into consideration. At times disturbances will delay connections and otherwise cause trouble. In the event of terrific storms at sea the wireless telephone will work slower.

Constant experiments, however, will do a great deal to remove such difficulties.

"Whether transoceanic telephony will for years to come be anything more than an expensive luxury is another matter," said Marconi. "Millionaires could talk without feeling the pinch. Imperative business conversations might be conducted that way, but I am afraid the general public would find the cost too high. Still, as time goes on, the expense will be reduced, so that the wireless telephone will be a practical means of communication for those having urgent need of it.

"The time will come after the war when a man may take up a telephone receiver in his London home or office, ask the central operator to connect him with New York, and do his talking without any more effort than if he were in conversation over a wire with Paris.

"The wireless telephone messages will be sent through an ordinary telephone station in London, relayed to some coastal wireless station and sent across the Atlantic. The call will be put through to the individual telephone subscriber at the American end without a break. A standard telephone instrument as now used could be employed at each end. The voice will be as clear and distinct as if those talking were not separated by the ocean."

The war postponed the reality of this dream. While the conflict was an obstacle to the oceanic "talk-bridge," it nevertheless, stimulated the research laboratories to perfect devices, which in the future might be extremely useful in linking the Old and New Worlds with spoken words.

The war continued to put added burdens on the minds of scientists as well as militarists.

Marconi was in London on several occasions to arrange for Italian war supplies and to aid the Allies.

When his native land joined the conflict Marconi was

busy scientifically, but his ability and friendship among other nations also made him a tactful diplomat for Italy.

As an officer in the Italian Army he directed a large staff of experts in adapting wireless to warfare. In quest of a secret method of communication he returned to the experiments of his boyhood—the short waves. He evolved new direction finders for spotting enemy sending stations and these same instruments helped Italian ships to get their bearings by wireless from shore stations.

He worked out a system of narrow-casting, using parabolic mirrors to converge the waves in a beam, just as he had tried to do at Salisbury Plain in 1896. Thus he saved generative power and prevented messages from being diffused or broadcast into the enemy camp.

This Italian patriot was no back-of-the-lines soldier.

"I have visited most of the Italian front," he announced while in London, July 22, 1915, buying war material for the army. "From an airplane I saw an artillery battle. It was awe-inspiring. The big shells shook the air like a volcano. Our troops got the best of it. Their spirit is splendid, and their ardor and enthusiasm are beyond praise. It is encouraging for Italians to advance into territory, which was once Italian, became Austrian and is Italian again. The Italian residents who predominate, of course, are delighted. The Austrians, I suppose, are not, but they are treated with consideration. Italy is full of soldiers in training. The entire nation is united and ready to make any sacrifice."

While Marconi and his associates were striving to make wireless more secretive to prevent the enemy from intercepting the waves, he warned that press censorship may be carried too far, even in wartime.

"If only favorable news is published and unfavorable news prohibited," [2] he declared, "the ultimate effect is injurious. It is more than that; it is dangerous for the people resent being misled as to the true state of affairs. They are strong minded and stout hearted enough to face facts, however ominous and disquieting the facts may be. Concealment merely breeds rumors and suspicion. . . . Undue optimism, when proved to be unwarranted, is apt to demoralize the public."

While most of the inventive genius of the world was working day and night to develop new engines and weapons of destruction the inventor of wireless called attention to the fact that all the so-called novelties of carnage, about which there was so much talk, including the submarines, tanks, armored hats, camouflage, hand-bombs, poison gas and flame throwers, were not without a single exception strictly new.

"These war novelties are modern developments of old ideas and devices," declared Marconi. "In the American Civil War, for example, a Confederate submarine sank a Federal vessel. The Greeks used Greek fire in their battles. Poison gas is a more deadly form of the old Chinese stinkpot, which is itself but an application of a natural means of defense possessed by various animals, such as the cuttle-fish and the skunk.

"But aircraft and wireless do constitute new and potent factors in warfare. The Germans dread wireless."

He told the following story to illustrate this point:

While the *Anglo-Californian* was being chased by a U-boat calls for help were answered by several warships entirely out of sight. The conversation that ensued was one of the most extraordinary ever chronicled. To the requests of one war vessel for indications of the attacked ship's course, speed and appearance, the operator replied, "Hurry up, for God's sake. Submarine firing like blazes."

The warship flashed instructions as to the best course to steer, and, even at one stage, by encouragement of her wireless mes-

² *The New York American*, March 10, 1918.

sages was able to prevent the ship from being abandoned by her captain and crew.

Meanwhile the submarine's bombardment grew heavier and heavier. The operator with his instruments already damaged sent another message, "Cannot hear you. Concussion. Am lying on the floor. Broken glass all around me."

The warship replied, "Keep up your courage, old man. Am firing to scare him. Can you report result?"

The submarine was manœuvring abeam to fire a torpedo. Then a faint trail of smoke was sighted on the horizon, which resolved itself into a fast approaching ship. The frightened U-boat dove.

This spectacular getaway recalled an assertion made before the world conflagration began, "if England and Germany ever come to blows, it will be like a battle between a whale and an elephant."

"But in this war," injected Marconi, "we have seen the curious spectacle of the English whale straining every sinew to become a successful elephant, while the German elephant made great efforts to become a successful whale. Happily events have shown that it is apparently easier for a whale to change into an elephant than for an elephant to change into a whale."

The flames of war as they licked around the globe did not prevent wireless from extending its domain, in fact, the conflict encouraged the building of new high-power stations. Up to this time the Orient had not been thoroughly linked into the globe-girdling circuit, but on November 15, 1916, the Japanese Marconi plant at Funabashi, near Yokohama, was opened to send messages to the Marconi antennas at Koko Head, Hawaii. Greetings exchanged between President Wilson and Emperor Yoshihito projected the wireless service two-thirds the way around the earthly sphere.

Marconi stepped out of his role as a wizard of science and went to America in the spring of 1917, as a member of a war mission headed by a cousin of the King of Italy, the Prince of Undine. The United States had declared war against Germany in April and was fighting on the side of Italy against the hordes from beyond the Alps.

The Italian Commission to the United States was dined and fêted at social functions wherever it went to spread the gospel of good will between the Allies and the pledge of victory.

In a devout pilgrimage to the tomb of George Washington at Mount Vernon, Marconi spoke as follows:

"The fellowship of America in the struggle is dear and welcome to all the Allies, but particularly to Italy. Italians and Americans both have had to fight and fight hard for their rights and independence. Millions of Italians have enjoyed the hospitality of America, have contributed by their labor to its development, and have been able to appreciate their freedom.

"All of us who have been constrained to draw the sword, whether in the Old World or the New, are inflexibly resolved that the cause of right shall prevail."

After an extensive trip in a special train through the United States a gala dinner was held in New York in honor of the Commission. A distinguished audience gathered, this time not to hear of wireless exploits, but for firsthand news from the front. War was the big thing of the moment. Every one wanted to know what was being done to stem the onrush of the Kaiser's troops. Marconi was the main speaker, and alert to what was uppermost in the minds of America promised to reveal some new war history. And he did.

"Let me tell you a few facts concerning the inner political history of those fateful days of July, 1914, when the fate of Europe was hanging in a balance," said the man who usually discussed short waves and communication. "Germany did not expect Italy to join her in her savage attack on the liberties of Europe; she did not even care much whether we eventually agreed to remain neutral. Her game was a much deeper and more treacherous one. She wanted us to leave France, our great Latin sister, in doubt as to our intentions.

"On the morning of July 30, 1914, one day before Germany declared war on Russia, and two days before she declared war on France, the Marquis de San Giuliano, who was then our foreign minister, unofficially informed the French ambassador in Rome that Italy would never side with the Central Powers in war of aggression. This information was immediately wired to Paris, but it was not sufficient to make France feel absolutely certain that Italy's attitude was favorable to her, because there was as yet no official declaration of neutrality on our part.

On the 2nd of August 1914, three days before England declared war on Germany, at a Council of Ministers held in Rome, Italy decided formally to declare her neutrality. The news was immediately communicated to our Charge d'Affaires in Paris, the Ambassador being absent. Without a moment's hesitation, at one o'clock in the morning he went to see Mr. Viviani, the French Prime Minister. It was the middle of the night.

"When he was introduced into Mr. Viviani's presence, the latter turned pale and drew back, for he was almost certain that nothing but Italy's decision to join Germany would have brought the Chargé d'Affaires there at that hour. The revulsion of feeling when Mr. Viviani read the telegram was such that he could not hide his emotion. Within half an hour orders had gone forth for the mobilization for service in the north of nearly 1,000,000 men which France would have had to keep on her southern and eastern frontier to guard against a possible attack from Italy.

"The million men helped to stem the advancing tide of the Germans, to win the battle of the Marne, and save France from being crushed by the heel of German militarism.

"Had there been the slightest wavering, the smallest hesitation on the part of Italy, had any Italian politician been found to do one-tenth part of what Bismarck did when he altered the wording of the famous Ems telegram, and thus brought about the Franco-Prussian war, France would not have dared withdraw a single man from the Italian frontier, and the history of the world war might have been written differently."

The mission of the Italian delegates was completed at this dinner. It was time for them to return to Italy. Prior to sailing, Marconi, mindful that the treacherous, war-plagued ocean stretched out ahead of him, remarked in farewell:

I have been in the United States forty times in twenty years. Some of my best friends are here. I belong to many of America's great scientific bodies and I had encouragement and help from the United States in the early days of my work when I very sadly needed it.

Applause after one has gained his victory is all very well and may be extremely pleasant, but what counts most is the cordial helping hand held out when one is struggling and cannot achieve without it. That was extended to me by America as heartily as it was from my own country at a time when there was much galling scepticism in all Europe except Italy.

I have always treasured the generous encouragement and support extended by Americans since my first landing in New York.

The American democracy is the greatest in the world. It has the vast material wealth necessary to the conduct of the greatest campaign (World War) ever made by any nation since the start of the history of the world. It has ideals and fights for them. It has developed inventive genius which has given to humanity many of the greatest scientific and mechanical treasures including steamship, telegraph, telephone, airplane and many of the engines of destruction utilized by both sides in this war.

I shall never forget Mr. Edison's laconic comment when the first weak signal vibrated across the ocean—"If Marconi says it's true, it's true." Nothing ever pleased me as those words.

Marconi mysteriously disappeared. His departure for Italy was shrouded in secrecy. The seas were infested with deadly explosives and submarines lurked like sly monsters of the deep. The war was raging on all fronts. Not even the inventor of wireless, a benefactor of humanity, would be spared a watery grave if one of the sleek torpedoes hit its prey. Every precaution was taken lest a wireless flash went seaward to notify a U-boat to watch for a liner carrying the Italian Commission—for if it did Marconi's own magic might play a part in his destruction.

Asked if there was anything he could say about his own specialty, when he reached London, Marconi smiled, and answered:

There will be a lot of surprises after the war. You know what has been accomplished in aviation because you see the bombs falling about you, but you can't tell what is being done in other branches of science.

The war was far from the final shot.

Long streams of dots and dashes told the story day in, day out. Lengthy casualty lists flowed through the air to sadden North America. Intermingled were claims of battles won. The incessant dots and dashes reported how fate was balancing the scales in the fight to "make the world safe for democracy." It was in the autumn of 1918 that Marconigrams brought long-to-be-remembered news across the Atlantic. It was history. Here is a message that sent a ray of hope whirling around the globe on October 6, 1918:

The note transmitted to President Wilson through agency of Swiss Government is as follows colon quote German Government request President of United States of America to take his hand in restoration of peace comma to inform all belligerent states of this request and to invite them to send plenipotentiaries for the purpose of making negotiations stop it accepts programme presented by President United States of America in message to Congress of eight of January nineteen hundred eighteen and his later declarations comma especially address of twenty seventh of September as foundation for peace negotiations stop in order to prevent further bloodshed German government requests immediate conclusion of general armistice on land water and in the air unquote stop. Berlin (8:58 PM)

Thousands and thousands of words followed this historic message from Nauen's lofty aerial in an effort to re-establish peace; there seemed to be no end to the Morse symbols dispatched over the ocean from Germany and from France. Some were in English, some in German, some in French—and some in secret code destined for the White House.

The wireless men could read between the lines—the fighting was nearly over; on November 11, 1918, they plucked authentic armistice news from the wintry air. But that did not mean that the wireless men could go home. Countless messages had to be tossed back and forth across the sea; there seemed to be no end to the list of casualties. Then the troops began to sail back to America; every soldier had more than one message to send to anxious folks at home. Wireless had never been so busy as in 1919. Words, words, words flowed out from the Peace Conference in Paris. Marconi was there to sign the treaty for Italy with Austria and Bulgaria. He held several important conferences with President Wilson at which the Italian claims were presented, but Marconi was disappointed in the general outcome as far as Italy was concerned.

Looking back across the war days, the inventor of wireless was caught in a reminiscent mood, as he reflected:

"I am grateful nature gave me a place in science instead of behind a counter. I often thought during the war of the romance of wireless. Messages came to me from Russia, Germany and Austria, intercepted dispatches, and they had come over the Alps, passed through hurricanes of artillery and made their way above all the beauties and miseries of the earth.

"Think of all those millions of words traveling with the speed of light above the earth, day and night carrying with them the destinies of the human race!

"The German talked and we caught his words out of the ether, and so with the Austrian, and the Bolshevik and everybody else. One sat listening to these words and all the time the world was in flames! It suggests the mystery of existence. It lifts thought to incredible heights."

Marconi had seen the calamity of war. He knew such devastation and death were barriers to progress. As a calm, gentle individual, thoughtful of his fellowmen, he became an ardent advocate of peace.

"I am rather depressed at the condition of things," [3] he

[3] March 10, 1919.

said while visiting in London. "It seems to me very bad
after such a war as this that a wave of brutality should be
passing over Europe. It makes one not so much afraid—as
ashamed—ashamed of civilization, of Europe, of human
nature.

"People like to make out that the Russians are not Europeans, but they are. All this wave of brutality, rising in
Russia, Christian Russia, is spreading westward. Think of
all the people who are now stirring up disorder.

"I can't help hoping the League of Nations will save us.
I am very much in favor of the League. I've met President
Wilson and discussed his idea with him, but the rest of the
world will have to help him if the League is really to exist.

"If this noble and grand idea fails, the next war will be
infinitely more terrible than the last one. Civilians will certainly be much more implicated. Cities could be blotted
clean out from the air—I hope men will soon turn their
thoughts away from war."

.   .   .   .   .   .

Wireless emerged from this war, that took a toll of
37,494,186 casualties, a thousandfold more potent than it
entered. Necessity had been the mother of invention. Concentration by research experts throughout the world had
crowded ten years of scientific development into five years
of destruction. The radio telephone, the vacuum tube and
short waves came forth from the battle far more effective
than they were when the bugles sounded. Wireless spread its
tentacles, socially as well as scientifically.

The inventive energy exerted during the conflict over-
flowed into commercial channels and into peaceful entertainment for millions of home-loving people, who might
otherwise seldom hear the best in music, noted educators
and authoritative discussions by prominent men and women,

covering a multitude of topics from politics to the care of babies.

Wireless changed its name to radio! The idea of using radiated energy, which was practically shaken free from the transmitting station's aerial to travel in all directions, in contrast with conduction through the earth's surface or megnetic induction, inspired scientists to recommend the change in nomenclature.

But it would always be *wireless* to Marconi.

"We still have much to learn," remarked the noted Italian, who by 1918 had talked with Australia from Great Britain. "We cannot today even name with certainty the medium through which the electrical waves are transmitted. It is no longer fashionable in scientific circles to speak of the 'ether.' We are forced to fall back upon the vague expression 'space.' "

The Great War had altered many a boundary, many a life and many a thing whether it was electrical or inanimate. The diplomat, the soldier, the craftsman, the scientist, all were changed. Marconi was no exception. One who met him as a youth in a London lodging house in the late '90's crossed his path again near the end of the war, and observed a vast difference—a transformation from youth to manhood under the strain of war: [4]

"The pale youth now is tall and of that firm, high-headed carriage which is given by conviction of success of real importance; but his manner is as unobtrusive, almost shy, his voice is as gently modulated and his words are as modestly considered as they were when all the world was wondering whether he was maniac or genius, and when he was wondering about his various experiments.

"In the old days Marconi was unknown, or if known to any was regarded as a dreamer who possibly might have

[4] Edward Marshall, January 20, 1918.

stumbled onto something big; but probably was merely in a
mental mess. Then he was a supplicator at the doors of
the powerful; now he is powerful in science and in the upper
legislative house of one of the greatest nations fighting for
the freedom of the world."

Marconi was passing the forty-fourth milestone of
his life.

The same foresight he applied to wireless was applied to
world affairs. It was his opinion, if there was to be any freedom to be gained from war, it should be grasped immediately
so mankind would no longer be under the yoke of hatred,
terror and bloodshed. In the wake of the war came a business slump, and out from Italy in 1921 came a warning from
Marconi under the headline, "Only a World Conference of
Business Men Can Avoid Economic Ruin."

But the years would flit through a golden era. The bull
with his arrogant head tossed high would be worshipped as
the symbol of higher prices. Then would come the hurricane of international depression. Money pyramids would
crumble and great empires of business crash like a child's
blocks. A humbled world would cry out for new leadership.
Marconi in posting the storm warning in 1921 also posted
one for 1929: [5]

"Restoration of the world to pre-war economic conditions
may or may not ever be possible, but in my opinion a sine
qua non of any attempt to accomplish it is that it must be
entrusted to men whose business experience fits them to
approach the intricate problem intelligently. Business men
in Europe are not nearly so much concerned about the de-
preciation of their currency as one might suppose.

"What they do want, what they must have, before they
can engage profitably in foreign trade, is a stabilization of
the exchange. . . . Let values be definitely determined and

[5] *New York American*, December 18, 1921.

speedily buyers will come back into the markets of the world, and we shall have taken the first step toward a solution of all the problems which, however independently important they may seem, are actually all co-related and dependent on a solution of the major problem.

"European workmen argue that American labor profited hugely from the war, therefore, the only thing for America to do is to make the money sacrifice involved by canceling the Allied war debt.

"Now, there is room for doubt that such action by the United States would work to the advantage of Europe— capital and labor. It is by no means certain that labor in England or Europe would benefit to the extent of getting back to pre-war conditions.

"Let there be arranged a world conference of business men of proven ability in their own spheres of activity. Let each group have a mandate from its own government that will be authoritative and evidence that it has its government's full support. Out of such a conference, in my opinion, would come a practical, speedy solution of this pressing problem—surely the most urgently needed thing in the world today."

Wireless, too, had pressing problems. It had many devices unknown when the conflict started, and now, the question was, what to do with them; how to capitalize on the rapid expansion as all the new instruments and scientific revelations were turned over to peaceful endeavors.

Marconi hurried back to his laboratory.

PART IV

XIX

ELETTRA—A FLOATING LABORATORY

MARCONI bought a yacht, named it *Elettra* and fitted it for wireless experiments and pleasure trips. Along with wireless he had discovered that work and play can be happily combined. The *Elettra* afforded an ideal combination; as pleasant as it was practical. Proudly he would carry the banner of Italy into some foreign ports where seldom the Italian colors fluttered.

It was 1919. The *Elettra* before the war was the *Rowanski,* so named by its owner the Archduke Stefan of Austria. But when the conflict broke out, she was quickly commandeered by the British Government to serve as a ship flying the flag of the Admiral commanding mine sweepers in the North Sea. Seven hundred and thirty tons burden, with an average speed of twelve knots, she had been built by Ramage and Ferguson of Leith. She had beautiful lines, spacious decks; drew fifteen feet of water, and her eighty-nine-foot masts designed specially to carry the wireless aerials, gave her an appearance of greater speed than she possessed. From stem to stern she measured 220 feet.

Marconi never was a laboratory hugging genius as were Edison and Steinmetz. This yacht gave him the opportunity he had long cherished, to roam the sea in the endless conquest of radio's invisible empire in the sky, and at the same time win relief from the land's constant humdrum and demands on his time.

Once a man turns his back on the coast, however, he is hemmed in by the narrow hull of a ship, and if he is a dynamic, restless individual his patience may be sorely taxed. The man anxious to get things done often becomes impatient when away from his tools. It appeased Marconi's mind while on a pleasure cruise to know his laboratory was just a few steps down the deck from his parlor. Should leisure annoy him—yet he was always asking, "When will I get some leisure?"—he could find plenty of work in his sea-going laboratory. By tapping the aerial wires between the masts he could hear a constant flow of human thoughts wafted across the hemispheres. He could experiment with novel devices; try mystic ideas and hear strange sounds, which to his ears might prove to be a symphony of science drumming away at the mind of man to heed some secret of nature.

He delighted, while at sea, in astronomical calculations and in study of the winds and stars, which were a great attraction to him—freedom from too much buzz of the wireless.

"I like the isolation of the sea," he once remarked, "because I can work better when removed from the land and its interruptions."

Yet it has been said, "in solitude one is least alone." It is then that thoughts run through the mind of a scientist as blissfully as electricity flows through a new-fangled circuit. On the ocean the inventor dreams new dreams. Away from the clamor of the throbbing cities with their blasting motor horns, telephone bells, industrial whistles and business appointments, the mind of the inventor may be renewed to catch a magic vision—the mirage of a novel idea. The change of scene is restful; the talk of people different. Some of the cares and worries of life never leave the land. Obtrusions on the briny deep are likely to be more pleasant than irksome.

Once while coming up the Irish Channel on an ocean liner,

Marconi was talking about wireless and its possibilities when a small, shrill voice interrupted him:

"Oh! Mr. Marconi, come up and see the big ship!"

An electrical diagram under discussion was thrown aside hastily, and the inventor with one youngster on his shoulder and three others clutching at his coat, hurried on deck to look at a disreputable schooner.

Marconi loves little children and delights in their companionship. On another occasion when reporters sought him on the steamer at Queenstown, he was too busy mending a broken doll for a young lady, age six.

Play is one of the best tonics Marconi ever found for work; success was always the spur to further achievements. He had great hopes of finding out new things about wireless once he put to sea.

.   .   .   .   .

Fascinating news about radio progress continued to reach him from the United States. Americans called it "broadcasting," and as a new method of mass communication it was spreading like wildfire. Amateur wireless experimenters thrilled friends and neighbors in plucking music and voices from the air by running a tiny slider across a coil of wire wound on a cereal box or on a rolling pin. Here was something that greatly appealed to the American mind; the radio "craze" swept from coast to coast.

Overnight broadcasting stations sprang up, while quickly assembled "factories" in lofts and electrical plants rushed to build receiving sets to meet the tremendous demand. All America, so it seemed, wanted to eavesdrop on what was flashing through the air. The number of transmitters increased from three to 595 between January 1, 1922 and January 1, 1923.

A new industry was born, offering employment to thousands of persons. A warning was heard that this thing called broadcasting was but a fad, the fancy of which would soon pass as the novelty of listening-in wore off. But it did not; radio deeply embedded itself in the imaginations of the American populace. The ethereal "gold rush" was on; here was a new epoch in American enterprise.

Suddenly there came a realization among those who had rushed to build broadcasting stations that some way had to be found to finance the business. How could so many stations make money in the air? There was no revenue. Would the listeners pay? Could they be taxed? Could each receiver be designed as sort of a coin-box pay-as-you-listen instrument? Hundreds of fantastic ideas were suggested, but it was a most difficult problem to discover a plan of collecting for music cast to the winds and wafted through a medium as free as the air.

By the time 1922 arrived the Western Electric Company had requests to build more than 200 more broadcast transmitters. So foreseeing the high costs of broadcasting, coupled with the eventual necessity of paying the talent and the limited program material available in some communities, the American Telephone and Telegraph Company finally said in effect to those who wanted to own broadcasting stations:

We wonder if you realize how much it costs to operate a broadcasting station? After all you desire to advertise your organization. Why not share some of our broadcasting time? Why not buy from us and sponsor a program of entertainment over station WEAF, in New York?

That solved the problem. Advertising was the keynote. A nominal charge of $100 was placed on a ten-minute talk, and a realtor was the first to take advantage of the offer. Broadcasters were no longer philanthropists; broadcasting became a big business.

The crystal detector set priced at $25.50 was heralded as

The *Elettra*, Marconi's floating laboratory—a research ship of science.

"Radio for Everybody: any member of the family can learn how to use it in a few minutes; it is no bigger than an average hand camera and tuning is as simple as focusing a pair of field glasses."

Then came the magic vacuum tube, the Aladdin's lamp of radio. It fanned the little spark kindled by the pioneer broadcasters into an international flame. The world itself was cartooned wearing earphones, and the broad smile was evidence that something pleasant was being heard, something that entertained and lifted the cares of the day.

No wonder Marconi wanted to visit America; and Americans were anxious to see him, for he started it all.

Proudly the *Elettra*, with Marconi on board, sailed away from the coast of England with her bow pointed westward toward America on her maiden transatlantic voyage. It was 1922 and out of the June air, three hundred miles at sea, Marconi and his Italian crew picked up their first sample of American broadcasting. A barrage of words and melody waved out from the shore to extend a hearty welcome and to entertain for the remainder of the cruise to the port of New York. As he listened to the lively jazz from the metropolis, Marconi remarked with a smile:

"The wireless tells me that New York is a lively place. There is evidence in the development of the radio telephone, in the methods of broadcasting and in the public interest in radio, that the United States is far ahead of Europe."

But what was this thing called broadcasting doing to the solitude and isolation of the sea?

Marconi was still the master of the situation. He could snap a switch and shut it all off. That is one blessing of his invention. Nevertheless, it often adds to the joy and comfort of an ocean voyage to know that overhead there is a flow of Bach, Beethoven and jazz as well as channels cleared for an SOS should occasion arise. Marconi enjoyed tuning in the melodies, for as a boy he had learned to play the piano with agility and perfect tempo; he always liked music.

Life on board the *Elettra,* which the poet D'Annunzio called "the snow-white miracle ship," always proceeded with that clock-like regularity dear to the heart of the wireless wizard, one of whose chief virtues is punctuality. On the voyage from Southampton, via the Azores and Bermuda to New York, breakfast was served precisely at eight o'clock. That did not mean a few minutes before or a few minutes after the ship's bell struck the hour. For Marconi breakfast is invariably a cup of tea, two soft-boiled eggs, bread, butter and marmalade!

To Marconi time is precious. He believes in beginning the day with activity, and punctually; that is the time of day he is usually in the most serious frame of mind. And those long sensitive fingers of his begin to fidget when there is delay.

Meals for the officers and crew are usually served in Italian fashion on the yacht, because the majority of the crew of thirty-one are from Italy.

A breakfast for the crew on the *Elettra* has all the simplicity that legend, tradition and reputation have attributed to the first meal of the people who live along the shores of the Mediterranean. It consists of coffee and bread, the latter crumbled and dropped into the coffee.

Breakfast over, Marconi is free to get on with his work. Off he hurries to the wireless room, his sanctum sanctorum. No one dares disturb anything in that realm. It belongs to Marconi. Every coil, every piece of wire means something to him. In that wireless cabin is up-to-the-minute apparatus, and if it fails to pluck anything from space there is nothing else in the world that can.

The transmitter talks direct to London, no matter where the *Elettra* may be on the Atlantic. It is a fragile-looking ship compared to an ocean liner. However, on the voyage to America it is not so far away from the paths of the grey-hounds of the sea should King Neptune become too ferocious. She can carry fifteen days' supply of coal. Refueling is done at the Azores and Bermuda, if necessary.

One of the rooms in which Marconi works is a smoking room or study, equipped with a serviceable desk. On a table behind him is a large autograph album containing a remarkable collection of signatures of persons who have been his guests on board the yacht. These include in huge, dashing, flourishing writing, the signature of Gabriele d'Annunzio, the Italian poet who, in 1920, also signed the picture of himself that finds a place upon the piano in the same room. Five royal guests, the King and Queen of Italy, the King and Queen of England, and Alfonso, as King of Spain, have autographed pictures in this room. Also Premier Mussolini, who inscribed: "al Senatore Marconi, mago degli spazi, dominatore dell' etere." (To Senatore Marconi, wizard of space, master of the ether.)

Sunset is often the signal for radio men, especially experimenters, to go to work; the end of the evening repast often sends them back to the apparatus. All wireless men like the witching hours of the night. Darkness helps the waves to go further. Erebus brings surprises through the air to Marconi, just as to the amateur tinkering in his workshop. But he seldom followed Edison's example of incessant labor to the extent of ignoring meals.

"My stomach always makes a fuss," he explained with the usual diffidence, "and I find that I can work better if I eat regularly."

When the day's work is finally finished, the inventor retires to a handsome cabin, beautifully equipped in the style of ocean liners and scrupulously clean by virtue of its white enamel. Close to his bed is a speaking tube which communicates with any part of the ship.

Regularity is a paramount factor with this genius. Even at night it is occasionally necessary for him to rise for an important wireless message or test signal. If it is three o'clock in the morning he is there on the minute attired in his dressing gown. Punctuality always!

At eight o'clock precisely another day begins!

Through the morning mist looms the skyline of New York.

The golden-white *Elettra,* the largest Italian yacht that ever crossed the Atlantic, with flags flying, while ships in the harbor tooted and whistled no end of salutes, passed the lower end of Manhattan Island following the route of Hendrik Hudson's *Half Moon* until off the Columbia Yacht Club, at the foot of Eighty-sixth Street, where the anchor splashed.

Reporters flocked to the *Elettra* in small boats. They asked the inventor all sorts of questions, as they always do when he visits America. Following an interrogative volley, Marconi remarked:

"I'm afraid in reportorial enthusiasm I have been credited with saying and doing things I never thought of saying or dreamed of doing. For instance:

"I never predicted scrapping of the submarine cable. If they are ever scrapped it will be in the distant future. Right now I know of no substitute. Wireless and the cables supplement each other. They do not supplant. They meet different needs and conditions.

"And I am not trying to communicate with Mars, or any other such distant point in the universe. Moreover, I have no plans to do so."

He, by this time, knew that New York reporters usually greeted him with visions of a front-page story. He never forgot one occasion when he told them he had nothing to report, but upon the insistence of one reporter who annoyed him, he replied, "I have invented a machine that sees through walls." Papers throughout the world printed the yarn, and Marconi received hundreds of letters condemning such an "eye." Female signatures predominated in the flood of mail, for they protested against the "death knell" of privacy in the home.

Can wireless be made secret? That was always a favorite query of interviewers.

"Scientists cannot employ the words 'finite' or 'absolute' to their investigations and discoveries," replied Marconi. "What we do not know today we may know tomorrow. That is why I am not prepared to say absolute secrecy can be guaranteed with regard to wireless.

"It was twenty-five years ago that I first experimented with regard to communication between two given points without the waves being picked up elsewhere; but then there came the fascinating development of speaking to the world at large by broadcasting in all directions, and I dropped the experiments. During the war I took them up again for the benefit of the Italian navy."

Do you think we will ever be able to hold telephone conversations across the Atlantic?

"That is quite near," answered Marconi, "much nearer than some people think. I will not say that the conversation will be absolutely secret as between speaker and listener. It is my conviction that the human voice will cross the sea. More than that I cannot say."

While he was speaking the *Elettra's* operator picked up a weather report, followed by jazz music from a New Jersey station. It reminded a young woman reporter to ask what the sage of wireless thought of the younger generation.

"I think the younger generation is a great asset to the nation," he replied. "I see no reason to worry about them."

He might have added that he likes to associate with young people because they do not "talk shop," and their spirit of gayety is a relief to him at the end of a busy day.

A reporter inquired if he agreed with the theory that broadcasting would harm newspapers. The idea seemed to amuse him.

"Radio can never take the place of the newspapers," he exclaimed. "Rather do I believe broadcasting encourages newspaper reading. For instance, I listen to some interesting news. I call my wife to share it and discover I cannot find her. She has gone out. If she wants the same news later she must get it from the newspaper and not from the loudspeaker. The newspaper has a distinct advantage; it is a record.

"When a man speaks over the radio he can deny he ever made such a statement, unless a recording is made of the speech. It is not so with the newspaper. The matter is there in black and white. Newspaper clippings can be preserved in a scrapbook. You cannot do that with broadcasting."

Those who observe the owner of the seagoing craft *Elettra* for any length of time, are soon aware that delicacy of hearing is one of his outstanding physical characteristics. Long years of practice in listening for the different notes of his wireless and strange sounds have sharpened his ears to an unbelievable extent. Uncanny is his facility in hearing conversation at a distance and in distinguishing between a multiplicity of sounds.

While in New York he invited twelve guests to dine with him on board the yacht. They were grouped at a long table with five along each side. Two or three were talking in ordinary conversational tone at the end of the table, while Marconi, apparently in abstraction, seemed to be out of earshot. Suddenly he would laugh at the joke at the foot of the table or inject some remark indicating he had heard every word.

How do you like New York? Marconi was asked after he was presented with the John Fritz Medal for engineering distinction.

"I went downtown yesterday," he replied; "returned by way of the subway, and experienced the rather curious sensation of seeing people reading newspaper stories and looking at pictures of me. Also I could hear them discussing Marconi."

What is the sensation?

"Well, the only way I can describe it," he said, "is by saying that it made me hope they didn't recognize me."

A suggestion made by Sir Arthur Conan Doyle that radio might be used to communicate with the spirit world was referred to him.

"I think it would take too long a wave length," he replied laughingly.

But he never casts anything aside labelled, "impossible." He is mindful that since the beginning of wireless, whenever man perceived any queer sounds, he wondered if they were signals from Mars or some other planetary race. Marconi, unlike many other scientists, has never been content to wave the mysterious clicks aside as mere solar eruptions.

"I would not rule out the potency of this, but there is no proof that the signals come from another planet," said Marconi. "We must investigate the matter more thoroughly before we venture a definite explanation. No one can say definitely that abnormal sounds on the wireless originate on the earth or in other worlds.

"Who can affirm signals from Mars? How can I know? How can any one know? Of course, the signals may come from space outside the earth. They may come from the upper reaches of the atmosphere. They may be caused by magnetic disturbances on the sun; they may come from Mars or Venus.

"It may some day be practical to communicate with other planets. It's silly to say that other planets are uninhabited because they have no atmosphere or are so hot or are so different from the earth. If there were no fish in the sea we would say life there is impossible. It is infeasible for man."

The interviewer suggested language difficulties seemed to present an insuperable obstacle.

"Well, it is an obstacle," agreed Marconi, "but I don't think it is insurmountable. You see, one might get through some such message as two plus two equals four and go on repeating it until an answer came back signifying 'yes,' which would be one word. Mathematics must be the same throughout the physical universe. By sticking to mathematics over a number of years one might arrive at speech. It is certainly not beyond the realm of reason."

Marconi then gave a concrete example of the fallibility of coded language once it falls into the clutches of clever men.

"Mark you, during the war the Germans were able within three weeks to decipher British messages and we theirs. No matter what the consonants of the code; no matter what language the dispatch was eventually decoded in, whether English, German, Arabic or Siamese, ultimately experts could interpret them.

"We can communicate by wireless; we can reproduce photographs by wireless—all this within less than a decade. It is not incredible that in the near future lantern slides can be projected by radio. Consider this possibility. Presume there is life on Mars, a language barrier must be overcome.

"By broadcasting a lantern slide showing a tree, an operator on earth, provided we can propagate the right wave lengths, could follow this picture with the word 'tree' repeated many times in international code until the same dots and dashes were repeated by the distant planet. Then following this might be flashed the picture of a man with the caption 'man' repeated. By this method language barriers might be surmounted and intelligent communication established.

"But ask some of my material-minded friends, 'what is the practical advantage of all this; suppose communication is established?' I say the result would be the advancement of scientific knowledge by at least 200 years."

XX

DAWN OF THE RADIO ERA

An ovation awaited Marconi when he came on the stage of the Institute of Radio Engineers in New York, in a setting that made him appear like a real magician. It was June 11, 1922. Queer-looking, skeletonized contraptions were arranged on both sides of the stage. There was also a "baby" wireless outfit, by means of which the wizard would demonstrate how a flying shaft of radio might be hurled in a desired direction.

A crowd was there that night. As always when Marconi is the speaker, thousands were turned away at the entrance of the Engineering Societies building. Though nonplussed at first by the spontaneity of the ovation and its long duration, Marconi warmed up to the technical subject of wireless and won burst after burst of applause.

Heralded as "the master of wireless" he amazed the American engineers, who watched the miniature transmitter shoot its directional rays twenty feet across the length of the footlights. They marveled at one-meter waves in such a performance. A reflector at one side of the stage projected the wave while a horizontal metal rod at the other side caught the impulses, and instantly a clear-sounding note rang from the receiving instrument. When the semicircular reflector, a frame-like apparatus covered with wires, and resembling a bowl cut in half, was turned with its open side toward the receiver the signals were strong and clear. When the open side of the "bowl" was turned away the signals were almost inaudible, revealing the reflector's searchlight effect.

Marconi turned to his manuscript, and looking over the lectern he paused a bit before predicting a revolution in radio was coming.

Very short wave lengths, the same as he had under his control on the stage, were destined to abolish high-power stations with their expensive, cumbersome alternators, lofty towers and acres of aerial wires.

Short waves had a simplicity. Wireless had been following a blind alley for all these years by constantly adhering to the long waves. The pioneers took what looked to be the easiest path—the long waves. Had they paused to experiment thoroughly with short waves the progress of wireless from 1900 to 1920 might have cost millions of dollars less. But they lacked the vacuum tube, so had to do the best they could with existing instruments, the crystal detectors, the sparks and the long waves that would sweep across the seas.

"Short waves have been sadly neglected," said Marconi, "especially in regard to directional wireless and radio-telephony.[1] Some years ago, during the war, I could not help feeling we had perhaps got rather in a rut by confining practically all our researches and tests to long waves. I remembered that during my very early experiments as far back as 1895 and 1896, I had obtained some promising results with waves not more than a few inches long.

"The study of short waves dates from the time of the discovery of electric waves, that is, from the time of the classical experiments of Hertz and his contemporaries. Hertz used short waves. He made use of reflectors to prove their characteristics, and to show among many other things that the waves obeyed the ordinary optical laws of reflection.

"Progress made with long waves was so rapid, so comparatively easy, and so spectacular, that it distracted prac-

[1] Lecture before American Institute of Electrical Engineers and Institute of Radio Engineers, New York, June 20, 1922.

tically all attention and research from the short waves. This I think was regrettable. There are many problems that can be solved, and most useful results to be obtained by, and only by, the use of short waves.

"It may be of historical interest to recall that Sir William Preece described my early tests at a meeting of the British Association for the Advâncement of Science, in September, 1896, and also at a lecture he delivered before the Royal Institution in London on June 4, 1897. I went into the matter more fully on March 3, 1899, in a paper I read before the Institution of Electrical Engineers in London.

"At that lecture I showed how it was possible, by means of short waves, to project the waves in a beam in one direction only, instead of allowing them to spread all around, in such a way that they could not affect any receiver which happened to be out of the angle of the beam's propagation.

"Since these early tests of more than twenty years ago, practically no research work was carried out or published in regard to short waves, as far as I can ascertain. Research along these lines did not appear easy or promising. The use of reflectors of reasonable dimensions implied the use of waves only a few meters in length, which were difficult to produce. The power that could be utilized in them was small. The investigation of the subject was again taken up by me in 1916 in Italy for certain war purposes. I was valuably assisted by Mr. C. S. Franklin of the British Marconi Company. The work was most interesting. It was like going back to the early days of wireless, when one had a perfectly clear field.

"As the result of the success of a series of experiments with the fifteen-meter wave, tests were conducted between Hendon and Birmingham, ninety-seven miles apart. With reflectors at both ends clear speech was exchanged between the two places. A receiver on a ship in Kingstown Harbor picked up a beam from Carnarvon, seventy-eight miles distant. This important fact was also noticed—there was no rapid diminution of signal strength after the ship had passed the horizon line from Carnarvon."

Several days later the *Elettra* steamed up the Hudson to Albany, so that Marconi might visit "the House of Magic" at Schenectady. En route the shore was dotted with Italian flags and people gathered to catch a glimpse of the famous yacht. At one point several monks from a monastery came out on a flat boat in full regalia and waving the Italian colors. Marconi's distinguished friends on board had quite a time inducing him to come on deck to wave a greeting. One of his associates remarked, "He just doesn't care for that sort of thing."

Dignitaries of science welcomed Marconi to Schenectady; there was the mathematical wizard Steinmetz, Dr. Irving Langmuir, noted for his development work on the vacuum tube; Dr. Willis R. Whitney, expert in electrical research, and Dr. W. D. Coolidge, famous for his achievements with cathode ray tubes. They demonstrated their latest wonders, including improved vacuum tubes for radio.

Marconi could see a vast change coming in his wireless as he watched the needles waver across the faces of delicate meters that spoke the electrical language in a most prophetic way. Like tiny fingers the needles beckoned the experts onward while the cherry glow of the filaments inside the "glass bottles" indicated the dawn of a new day in wireless.

Marconi agreed with the American research engineers that these tubes sounded the doom of many old devices. They solved age-old problems. It was evident that the spark and high frequency alternators were on the way out. The crystal detector would no longer be needed. These tubes would send and others would receive. They would make the Marconi dream of ultra-short waves, transoceanic telephony, television and possibly power transmission by wireless come true—some day!

"It is difficult to estimate the enormous influences broadcasting is going to exert on humanity in a hundred directions," said Marconi. "For the first time in the history of the world man is now able to appeal by means of direct speech to a million of his fellows, and there is nothing to prevent an appeal being made to fifty millions of men and women at the same time. Until now it has rarely been possible to speak to more than five or six thousand people packed into some huge hall.

"The limits of the carrying power of the human voice, unaided, are, however, pretty sharply defined. Radiotelephony makes distances more negligible. The day may come when 'the voice of the Government' will no longer be a figure of speech, but a literal truth."

Late in July the *Elettra* sailed for Europe.

Marconi's first marriage, having proved unhappy, was about to terminate. This marriage was dissolved on Marconi's petition by a decision of the Court of Fiume in 1924, which decision was duly confirmed by the Appeal Court of the Kingdom of Italy. The marriage was also annulled by a decision of the "Sacra Romana Rota" (Vatican Court) in 1927. Miss O'Brien married the Marchese Liborio Marignoli immediately after the Fiume decision in 1924.

.   .   .   .   .   .

Despite the predictions of Marconi in regard to short waves, under the impetus of war and in the unsettled aftermath, high power stations were built all around the earth. Lofty towers went skyward near Bordeaux, France; Stavanger, Norway; Mont-Grande in the Argentine; at Bolinas, Cal.; Marion, Mass.; Kahiku, Hawaii; Carnarvon, Wales;

Annapolis, Md.; Tuckerton, N. J., and at Rocky Point on Long Island. Engineers clung to their faith in long waves. They failed to sense the new power of the vacuum tube pumping energy into short waves.

"We are now entering what may be called the field of vibrations," Marconi announced. "The really great forces with which we must deal are locked up in vibrations so gentle that we cannot feel them.

"Science will transform the world within fifty years. Life on this planet will be so changed that we who are here now would have difficulty in recognizing it. Until the end of time, invention and discovery will shower benefits upon the human race at a constantly increasing speed. I see a certain danger to the world in this great progress. The conditions of life will be made so easy that if people are not careful, they will deteriorate. People work now because they are compelled to do so to earn a living—and it is good for them. But it will not much longer be necessary for a person to work more than a fraction of his time to earn a living. Then will come the danger of deterioration."

Radio continued to plunge ahead. Each day brought new wonders. The laboratories were giving to peace and industry the instruments which they had evolved for war.

Aircraft began to wing their way across the ocean, and they carried wireless, notably the United States Naval Flying NC-Boats and the British dirigible R-34 in 1919. It was clearly apparent from these flights that the Marconi invention had a vital role cut out for it in aviation.

Then, on November 2, 1920, station KDKA, Pittsburgh, went on the air with the Harding-Cox election returns.

The description of a prize fight was broadcast in 1921. That indicated possibilities. Woodrow Wilson and Warren G. Harding made the first Presidential use of radio and the microphone. A football game was broadcast in 1922, and by November of that year radio was bold enough to attempt to handle the New York Philharmonic Orchestra.

Wireless was on its way, under the name of broadcasting, and moving rapidly in a direction that Marconi never dreamed of in the '90's.

Donald B. MacMillan, exploring in the Arctic, listened-in on music from Chicago, New York and other centers of life. Cape Town and Calcutta heard Pittsburgh. Marconi, using a thirty-two-meter wave, talked in daylight by voice from his yacht to Syria, 2,100 miles away. From Poldhu, in England, on the 92-meter wave, Marconi was able to transmit his voice to Sydney, Australia, for the first time on May 30, 1924. Big Ben ringing midnight in London boomed through the air of America.

Old principles and practices in wireless were collapsing under the sweeping nature of new short-wave discoveries; the whole technique of long distance communication was changing.

England's sixteen-year-old dream of establishing an Imperial wireless chain came true in 1924 with the Marconi Company's sensational announcement to the Government that it was ready to guarantee a high-speed, all-Empire beam system of communication. Marconi's distinguished research engineer C. S. Franklin had solved numerous short-wave riddles; he had perfected directional aerials and adequate reflectors.

To prove the globe-girdling circuit possible, Poldhu, in October, 1924, using 12-kilowatts of power conducted 32-meter wave length tests with New York, Montreal, Rio de Janeiro, Buenos Aires and Australia. The signals were clear even when daylight covered the entire Atlantic.

"The employment of the *Elettra* for the important experiment, which demonstrated the practicability of short waves working over long distances, reduced the period of preliminary research very substantially," said R. N. Vyvyan, engineer in charge of construction of the beam transmitters. "A moving station for purpose of observation and measurement possesses great advantages over a fixed station where problems of range, directional effects, and other propagation questions require solution. The *Elettra* was able to sail across the path of the beam to ascertain if the signals from Poldhu still traveled in the form of a beam at great distances, and also to measure the intensity of the signals both by night and day over varying distances and with different wave lengths. Many months' investigation were undoubtedly saved by the use of Marconi's yacht for this purpose.

"Mr. C. S. Franklin himself designed the beam aerials and the actual transmitters used. It was due to his careful attention to detail, and profound technical knowledge and experience on short-wave working, that the stations when erected were successful from the start and fulfilled the very severe guarantee that they were called upon to perform." (The stations had to be capable of communication at a speed of 100 words a minute in each direction exclusive of any repetition to ensure accuracy and the aerial system had to be so designed as to concentrate the emitted waves within an angle of 30 degrees.)

Under the spur of American enterprise, radio had made its greatest strides. Just when the broadcasters were boasting of the high popularity of their art as an entertainment factor, already revolutionizing the social aspects of the country, an amusing cable item came under the ocean from Britain.

Marconi was in a London hospital for a slight operation in April, 1926, and it was announced that while recuperating he had complained of being "fed up" with broadcasting. For one day the human race smiled at Marconi. American industrial magnates were shocked with the news that the father of the art was vexed at the activity of the bedside earphones and loudspeakers. It was reported that friends of the inventor, in the American radio circles, asked him to temper the statement lest it have a bad influence on prospective buyers of receivers.

The next day Marconi quickly notified the grinning public that the report was grossly exaggerated; in fact, false in every particular. He had not asked for a phonograph instead of radio. He had not rebelled against music in the air. Perhaps he was weary and merely asked the nurse to turn off the machine so he might slumber.

The march of progress continued.

Facsimile messages, maps and pictures were flashed from New York to Hawaii, 5,136 miles. The picturegram of a check was tossed across the sea from London to be honored and cashed in New York. Byrd and Bennett flew over the North Pole carrying a forty-four-meter transmitter. The dirigible *Norge* followed them into the northern wilderness and sent messages direct from the Pole. All the world tuned in the Dempsey-Tunney fight and the World Series was described on the air for the first time. It was 1926.

Wireless in accomplishing all this did not neglect the mariners.

Disabled in a hurricane 1,724 miles out of New York on January 24, 1926, the British freighter *Antinoe* flashed the SOS from masts that wavered in a vicious sea. The S.S. *President Roosevelt,* one hundred miles away, veered in her course. It was 5:40 o'clock on a cold winter morning.

Mountainous seas were running day after day, waves climbed to a peak of seventy feet, driven by a wind that blew ninety to one hundred miles an hour. Behind the swirling curtain of sleet, snow and fog was the disabled hull of a doomed ship.

Marconi visited with Charles Proteus Steinmetz, electrical wizard, in 1922 at "the House of Magic" in Schenectady. It was Steinmetz who declared, "there are no ether waves; they are electro-magnetic."

The *Roosevelt* reached the position given by the *Antinoe*, but there was no ship; yet the sputter of her wireless was still in the air. The wireless men trained their direction finders on the signals while the skipper followed the bearings. The *Antinoe's* position had been incorrectly reported and she had drifted fifty-eight miles in the wintry blasts of the storm. She was listing thirty-five degrees to starboard.

All lifeboats on the starboard side had been swept away. The port-side boats were stove in and useless. The engine room was flooded. The steering gear was disabled and her navigating bridge crashed by the heavy seas. It was noon, that Sunday, when the *Roosevelt* rode up to the scene, while four hundred and forty persons along her decks watched the hulk roll helpless in the defying waves. Gallant sailors were ready to go over the side, but it meant certain death in such a storm. They could do nothing but stand by.

And that they did for several days, expecting any moment that the distressed vessel would plunge under the waves that pounded and flooded her from stem to stern. At midnight on Wednesday, the sea moderated and a small boat quickly pulled away from the *Roosevelt*. It was a spectacular rescue in the moonlight as the men jumped overboard, one by one, into the lifeboat that carried the entire crew of twenty-five to safety.

That was another triumph for Marconi wireless, and for the radio compass designed to peer through the most blinding snow storm or treacherous squall.

Each achievement at sea brought new honors to the inventor of the humanitarian instruments, and this time it was Spain, which on March 29, 1926, conferred the Plus Ultra Order Gold Medal for "extraordinary service in behalf of mankind."

Bologna was a gay place on June 13, 1926. It was Marconi Day and he had the key to the city.

It seemed from the size of the crowd that all the townsfolk had gathered at the University of Bologna for the grand climax of the festivities—a talk on wireless by Guglielmo Marconi. Never had the old halls echoed with such an ovation as that which greeted the distinguished native son as he appeared in the uniform of an Italian naval officer.

"Since February, 1896, the date of my departure from Bologna, after my first experiment in wireless telegraphy carried out at the Villa Grifone, my life has been spent far from my beloved Bologna," said Marconi. "The force of events has been greater than my will.

"Bologna, the city which gave birth to Galvani and Righi, is always the home of him who has a reverence for study and progress. If in my work I have been carrying on for the last thirty years I have been carried far from Bologna, I hope it has made me no less a worthy son of that city. No greater prize could be conferred upon one who feels the pride of having been born among you in our beloved Bologna. During my eighty-six crossings of the Atlantic, from farthest outposts in Canada, my thoughts have often been carried back here.

"I remember how in both my boyhood and youth I was fascinated by the mathematical hypothesis of Maxwell regarding the electromagnetic theory of light and the brilliant pursuit of such researches made by our great Bolognese physicist, Augusto Righi. For many years I had to face adverse criticisms, and the assurance from many distinguished, as well as ordinary people, that radio-telegraphy would never be in a position to compete seriously with other methods of communication. We Bolognese smile in the face of most difficulties. I was determined that success should crown my efforts eventually.

"In time, by means of the use of thermionic valves, a brilliant conception of Dr. Fleming, perfected by De Forest, Langmuir, and Armstrong in the United States, by Meisner in Germany, and Round and Franklin in England; and by means of the use of balanced tuned circuits, of electric filters, of powerful amplifiers and finally directional radiators, I succeeded in obtaining results such as to ensure regular wireless telegraphy service by day and night between Europe and America. Thus in 1918 I could for the first time in history communicate from England to Australia. To obtain such a result, expensive installation is necessary, yet it was first at the Villa Grifone that I experimented with what has since come to be called beam wireless."

Marconi recalled that in the early days at Bologna it was his intention to develop this method of concentrating the radiation of electric waves in a beam, by means of suitable reflectors. He said that in 1916 he used the first beam system or "fascio" apparatus, utilizing short waves two or three meters in length, and added, "perhaps I may be allowed to claim for this that I was the first fascist in Italy." It was explained that Marconi chose the fascio or Roman bundle to symbolize the concentration of electric waves. The beam was called "the Marconi Fascio system."

With the dawn of 1927 came fulfillment of a prophecy made by Marconi in 1915. The transatlantic radiophone circuit was opened between New York and London. He had declared it would be easy some day, and the press reports indicated he was right:

Scattering words and phrases have been wirelessly telephoned across the Atlantic before, but thousands of words were shot over the distance of 3,000 miles last night and heard apparently with the distinctness of messages over a wire from Times Square to Herald Square. The deluge of words crossed the sea so steadily that the group of auditors on the other side began to complain that it was something of a bore.

Marconi always hit the target of the future with his cautious predictions. He never linked a future possibility with a definite date.

Some one inquired regarding the popularity of a device to permit two persons at opposite ends of a telephone line or radio "see-talk" circuit to view each other as they conversed.

"That seems to be of doubtful utility," replied Marconi. "I can imagine many circumstances, indeed, in which it would be embarrassing to one or both parties."

"This man Marconi could never be accused of talking 'shop,'" remarked an interviewer. "He is not an easy person to lead into conversational lanes of one's own choosing. Quietly, deftly and politely he assumes command of the conversation, and the subject may be changed before one is aware of it. If one would get an idea of Marconi's vision of the future, it must be by piecing together little glimpses which he permits one to have from time to time of that vision—bits of conversation and snatches of pictures which he shows *en passant*.

"But he leaves a distinct imaginary picture of a future world run by wireless. The impression of that future state may be entirely unwarranted by the remarks of the inventor, but an hour or two of conversation with him leaves an indelible impression of a changed world. The outstanding feature of that changed world is its cleanliness; the second, its compactness.

"Marconi's admonition, when discussing the innumerable potentialities, seems most appropriate; 'I must leave to your imagination the uses which can be made of these new powers.'

"'The more a man bends the phenomena of the universe to his will and the more he discovers, the more he will find to discover,'" Marconi once remarked. "Because of this he will realize more and more the infinity of the Infinite."

XXI

REMARRIAGE AND HONEYMOON

Wedding bells pealed a second time for Marconi on June 12, 1927. In the morning of a perfect day the inventor of wireless was married to Countess Maria Cristina Bezzi-Scali, young and beautiful member of an old Roman family.

Marconi had met Maria Cristina at a famous resort of health and fashion in northern Italy, and had at once fallen a victim to her singular beauty and grace.

The young woman had been the reigning belle in Roman society for two years. In a country noted for its dark-eyed and dark-haired women she was conspicuous for her blond hair, fair complexion and blue eyes. Maria Cristina, it seemed from the beginning, had conceived an admiration for the inventor, which had slowly ripened into genuine affection. The parents openly approved of the distinguished suitor, but they made it plain at the outset that they considered a marriage out of the question.

The Bezzi-Scali belonged to the elite of old Papal aristocracy, which in all questions of religious doctrine and practice preserve rigid orthodoxy. In fact, Count Bezzi-Scali, father of the bride, was a brigadier general in the Papal Noble Guard, while her mother was closely related to the Princes Barberini, Orsini and other ancient Roman families.

The case of Marconi's first marriage was, therefore, submitted to the Consistory Court of Westminster and, on

283

appeal, to the Vatican Court of the Holy Roman Rota, in Rome, which accepted Marconi's petition and declared his marriage null and void.

Guglielmo Marconi was happy and so was Cristina Bezzi-Scali.

The Senatore presented his bride-to-be a diamond engagement ring, a pair of diamond and sapphire bracelets and a superb diamond diadem. The bride's gift to him was a sapphire ring, one of the family treasures.

Prince Ludovico Spada Potenziani, Governor of the Eternal City, performed the civil wedding ceremony in the ancient Capitol, where warriors and poets in olden days were crowned. The distinguished bridal couple were received with military honors. They passed into the gorgeous hall, draped with red damask with golden fringe. Prince Potenziani read the articles of the Civil Code establishing reciprocal rights and duties to those who marry. He delivered a short address warmly congratulating the couple, and expressed the hope that the happiness of the marriage would contribute to the further success of that science to which Marconi is the leading exponent.

The ceremony was extremely simple, yet one of pomp and splendor. Only the relatives of the bride and bridegroom and a few intimate friends were present. The witnesses for the bride were Prince Orsini and Marquis Sacchetti, and for the bridegroom, Marquis Giorgio Guglielmi and Marquis Luigi Solari.

Prince Potenziani presented the bride with a bouquet of white roses and a gold pen, wherewith she signed the marriage register. Then every one went to the Bezzi-Scali palace, where hundreds of guests, representing everything that is best in Roman aristocratic, intellectual and political circles were gathering. The newlyweds, smiling and obviously happy, stood in the ante-room and received the congratulations of their friends. One large room was reserved for the display of magnificent presents, which were both numerous and rich.

Three days later, on June 15, the religious ceremony was held at noon. Thus the colorful wedding in the fashionable Church of Santa Maria degli Angeli came as the climax of two years of ardent wooing, which at times must have seemed as utterly hopeless as wireless across the Atlantic in 1896. Cardinal Lucidi performed the ceremony, assisted by members of the Palatine clergy. The witnesses for the bride were Prince Barberini and Marquis Guglielmi and, for the bridegroom, Prince Prospero Colonna and Prince Spada Potenziani.

After the wedding a luncheon was held at the Bezzi-Scali palace, attended by a few close relatives and friends. In the afternoon the couple left for Riete, to spend the first part of their honeymoon in a villa put at their disposal by Prince Potenziani.

Marconi came to New York with his bride in the autumn of 1927. It was his eighty-fifth trip across the Atlantic.

The Marconis steamed into New York on the Italian liner *Conte Biancamano,* and when the big ship was off Fire Island he sent a message to Rome, by the short-wave beam system at two hundred words a minute, and received a quick reply. Those who marveled at the speed were amazed when Marconi said a higher rate had been achieved in laboratory experiments. However, for all practical purposes, from 60 to 100 words a minute is a good average speed for wireless.

Newspaper reporters and photographers overtook him at Quarantine. As usual the news gatherers wanted to know what new magic he had up his sleeve. Cameramen were anxious for pictures of the bride and bridegroom.

What will be your next invention?

"That's a hard one. I can't answer it," smiled Marconi.
What is the chief purpose of your visit to New York?

"When I first came to America years ago, people came to
hear what I might have to say of what might be new in the
field of wireless," he replied. "Now it is just the other way
about. Today I come here to learn something for myself. I
am the student."

Several reporters seeing Marconi for the first time observed that "he looks like an ordinary business man." But
one who had seen him at work in his laboratory on the yacht
in 1922 remarked:

"He looks like a different person when you see him at his
wireless. It is then that you see Marconi the scientist and
not the business man."

"Personally, one of Marconi's remarkable characteristics
is his voice," said a friend. "It is low and soft, with the
caressing quality so distinctively Italian, and he uses it with
slow deliberate gravity which contrasts oddly with his nervous, restless manner.

"So long as he keeps his hat on he is quite like other men.
But when the hat comes off Marconi's personality manifests
itself. The real strength of the man is revealed in the
peculiar shape of his head, and one instantly concludes that
it is the head of a thinker. Yet he has not the observant,
bulging brow of the inventor. All height seems to be directly
in front, with a marked slope toward the back. Behind the
ears it is a flat head—the head of a shrewd man who eats
to live, not one who lives to eat."

A battery of camera lenses were pointed at the inventor;
as he was about to pose on the deck he noticed a group of
chefs gazing at him admiringly; he beckoned to them and
had his picture taken with them, to their delight. He wore
a blue suit, white shirt with purple stripes, purple tie, purple
socks and brown shoes. In the buttonhole of his coat lapel

was the red, green and gold emblem of the Italian Fascisti, of which he is a member.

Do you favor extension of Mussolini's Fascism in America? he was asked.

"I don't want to express any opinion about that, but Fascism is doing a fine work in Italy. Italy, under Benito Mussolini, has turned the corner. His bold, audacious political and financial policies have transformed the country.

"Few people in each country really know the other country. The necessity for a larger and better understanding was never greater than it is today when, under the genial leadership of Mussolini, Italy is giving proof of immense activity in the development of an extensive program in all fields whether political, commercial, scientific or educational."

James J. Walker, New York's dapper and witty mayor, staged a reception for the Marconis at City Hall, welcoming them to the largest Italian city in the world. The mayor praised Marconi for giving an electric spark the power of speech. He concluded by telling the dignified visitor that the Romans had learned to call him Jimmy, and that while he did not want to "indulge in any familiarity, what we feel like doing is to take you by the arm and say, 'Bill, you're welcome!' "

Marconi smiled profusely; thanked the mayor and waved to the crowd, as he and his bride stepped into the car flanked with a motor-cycle escort ready to whisk them to the Ritz Carlton Hotel.

Visit with this Italian gentleman in his suite. It is raining. The streets below are crowded with taxicabs bound for the Grand Central, hotels and business offices, while hundreds of fast-moving umbrellas dot the sidewalks as lunchers hurry back to work.

The inventor has just completed an address to be delivered in the evening before the Institute of Radio Engineers. He draws aside the curtain and as he watches a heavy autumn rain beat against the window he expresses some doubt that many will hear his lecture, despite the fact that the tickets are free. He is assured that the auditorium will be crowded to capacity no matter how inclement the weather. He smiles as a schoolboy wondering what the evening has in store for him.

It is eight o'clock. There is no standing room in the Engineering Societies Building. Crowds are turned away in the drizzling rain. Hundreds who now have radio sets in their homes have gathered to see the originator who has astonished and fascinated all civilization.

Michael I. Pupin steps to the footlights. Marconi's bride is there. The auditorium vibrates with the ovation as Pupin with arms outstretched in welcome, declares:

"Marconi, we love you. We have come to see your boyish smile as much as to hear what you have to say."

Smiling, Marconi bows and steps toward the lectern as tremendous applause greets him. Every one is standing, applauding the master of wireless. He waves a friendly greeting. Many are seeing him for the first time—and they are disappointed if they expected some super-person of Martian stature.

First of all he asked his audience not to think him too visionary "if I say it may be possible that some day electromagnetic waves may also be used for power transmission." From the bewildering processes of evolution he foresaw short waves ready to play a vital role in new triumphs ahead for radio and the science of television, "which is now, I believe, finally emerging from the laboratory." He repeated his warning of 1922 that much of radio's future was bound up in short waves and ultra-short waves.

He recalled how in 1923 an experimental short-wave

transmitter was installed at Poldhu, while he put to sea in the *Elettra* to ascertain the day and night ranges and reliability of signals transmitted on waves less than 100 meters in length. The yacht steamed off in the direction of Morocco and Cape Verde to intercept the 97-meter signals 1,250 nautical miles away in the daylight. There was no trouble from static. The signal strength at night was described as "always astonishing," much stronger than the signals from the powerful long-wave stations at Leafields and Carnarvon, although Poldhu was at times using only one kilowatt. This test was proof for Marconi that long-wave wireless had seen its best day.

"Short waves cannot but enormously assist in rendering more practical the systems of picture and facsimile transmission including television, which are most likely to bring an end to the necessity for Morse code signal transmission on which is based telegraphy as we know it today," said Marconi. "Looking back to our old difficulties, of only a few years ago, the ease and perfection recently achieved by radio, especially in regard to broadcasting, appears little short of miraculous. It shows us what can be done by the combination of a great number of workers all intent on securing improved results. And how many, who began as amateurs, have contributed in one form or another to this progress and this success?

"We are yet, however, in my opinion a very long way from being able to utilize electric waves to anything like their full extent, but we are learning gradually how to use electric waves and how to utilize space. Thereby humanity has gained a new force, a new weapon which knows no frontiers, a new method for which distance is no obstacle, a force destined to promote peace by enabling us better to fulfill what has always been essentially a human need—that of communicating with one another."

Twenty-eight years ago, Marconi on his first visit to New York jokingly remarked that a taxi cost him four times as much as a London cab.

This time a grand Isotta-Fraschini motor was waiting on Forty-third Street, where a crowd gathered to admire the shining black foreign car in front of *The New York Times*. Marconi and his bride having been the luncheon guests of Adolph S. Ochs, the publisher, returned to the car but the chauffeur was missing. They waited but a minute, and walked slowly toward Broadway, and at the so-called "cross-roads of the world" mingled unrecognized in the noonday crowds—too modest to wait in the motor car under the gaze of a curious throng until the driver could be found.

The next day the Marchese and Marchesa set sail for Italy; wireless was calling!

Shortly after his return, Cyril Clemens, President of the International Mark Twain Society, was in Rome to present the Mark Twain Medal to Marconi for having "knit the whole world in bonds of cultured peace."

In the words of Mr. Clemens, he put on his long tail coat, brushed off his top hat, and leisurely drove across the Tiber by the bridge of San Angelo to the Italian Academy, a glorious old two-story palace, exceedingly handsome, classic in design and beautifully executed in all its smallest details.

"Informing the guide that I had an appointment with his Excellency, I rose greatly in his estimation, and he now could not do enough for me," said Mr. Clemens, "whereas before, I must confess, he had eyed me somewhat suspiciously. He conducted me to the office of Marconi's secretary, a pleasant young man who spoke English well, and with as high admiration for his chief as a member of the old guard entertained for Napoleon.

"It was not long before a number of gentlemen came into

The Marchesa and Marchese Marconi at Cowes for the Royal Regatta.

the room; the secretary introduced me to a tall distinguished-looking man with a monocle, Aristide Sartorio, vice-president of the Italian Academy. After the introductions were over, Mr. Sartorio said that they would like to show me some of the Academy before Marconi sent for us, so he led the way towards a glorious marble stairway. At the top of the stairs we found ourselves in a magnificent chamber, all the walls and ceilings of which were covered with fresco paintings done by Raphael and his school.

"Another long chamber even more magnificent, formerly the banqueting hall, when the building was a palace, is now used for official meetings. What other Academy in the whole world meets in an apartment with the walls and ceilings decorated by Raphael himself! Next we proceeded to the other rooms all of which were likewise frescoed by great masters of the Renaissance. What particularly struck me about these rooms and, in fact, about all those of the Academy, was the wonderful state of preservation of the paintings: as fresh and clear as though painted the day before. The inlaid marble floors were so magnificent that one had a decided hesitancy about treading them.

"After we had been looking for some minutes, an official announced that Marconi was ready to receive us," continued Mr. Clemens. "Hastily we went down the steps, and I was somewhat puzzled at the celerity so suddenly developed by these learned and stately individuals, when Professor Marpicati, the Chancellor, whispered, 'The Senatore hates above all things to be kept waiting: the presentation was arranged for eleven o'clock sharp and it is now three minutes after the hour.'

"At the foot of the stairway was a tremendous door half opened before which the others stood aside so that I could go in first. I found myself in a long, richly furnished room; on my left was a row of splendid windows opening on a gar-

den in front of the Academy, and on my right a wall decorated with what appeared to be Beauvais tapestries, depict-
ing a Medieval king going hunting.

"Standing at the other end of the chamber behind a small
mahogany desk, where he had evidently been working up to
the last second, was Guglielmo Marconi, President of the
Italian Academy, and the inventor and perfector of wireless
telegraphy, smiling pleasantly, with his right hand extended.
His youthfulness especially struck me, for already a third of
a century had elapsed since he made his great invention, yet
his hair was still quite brown, and his face unwrinkled—
a man of medium height with a fine Roman face and an
unusually strong and expressive mouth. As we were shaking hands the other officers of the Society grouped themselves around us. . . . I then presented the silver medal and
Marconi expressed appreciation of the honor, after which
in an informal talk he spoke of his delight at the wit and
conversation of Mark Twain, alongside of whom he once
sat at a dinner."

At Trento, on September 11, 1930, Marconi addressed a
meeting of the Italian Society for the Progress of Science,
discussing in particular the phenomena encountered in wireless. Recalling the first transatlantic signal, he confessed,
despite his faith in wireless to span long distance, "there
was lacking a rational theory explaining how these electric
radiations could follow the curvature of the earth and reach
most distant countries.

"Several physicists and mathematicians (among them
Lord Rayleigh, who in 1903 read a paper on the matter before the Royal Society of London), referring to the results
I had obtained at distances of several thousands of kilometers, demonstrated by calculation that such results could
not be explained by the phenomenon of diffraction pure and
simple.

"Other experiments which I was able to carry out in the Atlantic on the S.S. *Philadelphia* in 1902, enabled me to discover another phenomenon of importance—that with waves of about 2,000 meters in length the distances over which messages could be sent were several times greater during the night. This indicated either an absorption by sunlight of the energy of the electric waves, or variation in the conditions which permitted the waves to reach the greater distances.

"The mathematician Sir Oliver Heaviside in England and the physicist Kennelly in America were the first to put forward the hypothesis at once universally accepted, that at a certain height (100 miles or more above the earth) there must exist a state of ionization of the atmosphere, or a conductive layer, constituting a kind of envelope concentric to the surface of the globe. This envelope was capable of reflecting or deflecting the electric waves in such a manner as to compel them to follow the curvature of the earth, impeding their radiation and their loss into infinite space. . . . This hypothesis approximates to the more modern ideas which not only suppose the existence of manifold zones and layers capable of reflecting or bending the electric waves, but also that these zones vary in height and distances from the earth at different hours of the day, with the seasons, and according to their ionization or composition due in turn to the effects of light, to the electric and magnetic activity of the sun and perhaps to other causes still unknown. The determination of the height of the reflecting or refracting layers has been, and continues to be, the object of laborious study on the part of patient investigators."

Patience—that was a keynote. Nature had clung tenaciously to its ethereal secrets. But patience was one of Marconi's virtues; here was a man with a highly strung nervous system, nevertheless, painstaking with experimental

detail and noted for keen ability to concentrate and to remember. He never forgot those tiny waves he first encountered in the '90's.

Wireless surges through his life like the recurrent phrase
in a symphony.

PART V

XXII

SALUTED BY ALL THE WORLD

THERE is no such thing as a summary of Marconi's achievement. There never will be, for as radio progresses as a symbol of doom for racial isolation, it spreads like the branches of a great tree of which Marconi's conception is the roots and the trunk is his work. Nature nurtures the invisible attributes of the Creator just as she does the oak.

In the words of the late H. D. Arnold: [1] "Nature has pointed us to many if not all the principles which we use in our art. . . .

"Research is not constructing and manipulating; it is not observing and accumulating data; it is not merely investigating or experimenting; it is not 'getting facts'; although each of these activities may have an indispensable part to play in it. Research is the effort of the mind to comprehend relationships which no one has previously known. And in its finest exemplifications it is practical as well as theoretical; trending always toward worthwhile relationships—demanding common sense as well as uncommon ability. . . . To have ideas and to share them—that makes civilization."

Guglielmo Marconi lived up to these ideals. As an interpreter of Nature, rich in common sense and uncommon ability, he shared his ideas and brought nations ear to ear as neighbors. In the vast emptiness of space between the hemi-

[1] Director of Research, Bell Telephone Laboratories, in lecture on "Research in Communication," Lowell Institute, January 5, 1932.

spheres he demonstrated "that in great matters the world is more and more becoming a single organism." Wireless stimulates human solidarity.

Does this man Marconi really know the science of wireless or did he just happen to stumble upon it; stub a toe that actuated a scientific nerve, and then become internationally famous through publicity of a most spectacular kind? Indeed not!

He knows wireless, radio, broadcasting, radiocasting or anything one might call it, from A to Z. He answers questions pertaining to wireless as quick as a flash. There is no pondering over the answers. For example, he is asked what fields of radio he considers most fertile for the amateur experimenter and young engineer out of college. His ready reply is, "Short waves, directive transmission and television."

Marconi, the Edison of his field, in mood is quiet and modest. He has a calm, softly pitched voice and talks slowly with no show of egomania. When addressing a public gathering or delivering an after-dinner speech his words are carefully chosen. On the radio he is easily recognized by a characteristic of his speech; he drops the "g" of words ending in "ing."

When he replies to questions a swift-running analysis of every problem is apparent. It is noticeable that he rarely expresses an opinion on anything but wireless although he relates observations and cites facts in other fields. His memory is remarkable. He recalls names, dates, events and incidents of thirty years ago as if imprinted on his mind only yesterday. Minute details of wireless trip glibly out of his memory.

His manner is reserved, his carriage erect and his bearing confident. He impresses one as a man possessed of a great idea—an all-absorbing thought from the contemplation of which he detaches himself with difficulty.

Rudyard Kipling might have had Marconi in mind when he wrote:

If you can dream—and not make dreams your master.

What of the future? he was asked.

"I live and work in the present," he answered quietly.

And do you never dream of the future?

"Yes, I dream sometimes."

Of a world run by wireless?

"Perhaps, but I live in the present and work in the present; that is sufficient."

Seeing Marconi for the first time, a reporter remarked: "I suppose he is highly technical; talking only ohms, watts and volts." But not so. While discussing experiments on the 15-meter wave some one inquired, "How many kilocycles is that?"

Marconi smiled shyly like a schoolboy who missed a lesson, and replied, "Oh! offhand I don't know how many."

There is no bluff in Marconi's make-up, nor does he conceal what he doesn't know in a maze of technical terms to baffle a layman.

He has neither the volatility of the Italian nor the cheery cordiality of the Irishman. He is of an intensely nervous and energetic temperament, easily rattled by trifles when in the stress of work or by miscarriage of his plans. He smokes cigarette after cigarette and holds it limply between the lips as he talks.

Patience and acute observation are two parts of his make-up. If the door to the room creaks a bit or opens slightly, nervously his head turns quickly—like that of a lion hearing a rustle in the African grass. Adverse criticism does not bother him. He is determined to get the best results. He listens to praise and enjoys it because he is Italian. He listens to praise and forgets it because he is partly Celtic.

.   .   .   .   .   .

Electricity is a celestial gift with power to lift the life of man higher than any of us have yet dared to dream about. That is the way Dr. Pupin put it, and he added, "when man has achieved control of that power, the miracles of the present age will seem insignificant in comparison and man may at last achieve an existence akin to that of the Olympian gods."

Radio from 1927 to 1930 gave inklings of miracles ahead, but of paramount importance man was warned by science that he must have the faith to penetrate "the mysterious veil which covers the face of the space-time entity behind which is found the throne of a divinity which created the infinite and filled it with energy granules of the tiniest, liveliest sort."

The image of a woman's face, that of Mrs. Mia Howe, flickered across the sea in 1928 from London to New York in a telecast by John L. Baird. Herbert Hoover speaking in Washington was seen on a screen in New York. Outdoor scenes were televised and color television introduced. The Byrd Expedition went into secluded Antarctica for a flight over the South Pole. Radio gave instantaneous contact with New York, 11,000 miles away.

King George V welcoming delegates to a London Naval Conference was heard in his first world-wide broadcast. German and Dutch programs began to find their way to America. Premier Hamaguchi of Japan sent greetings to the United States in the first rebroadcast from the Orient. Benito Mussolini, Italian Premier, speaking into a microphone on his desk at the Palazzo Venezia in Rome, was heard distinctly throughout the world in a plea for peace.

Norway's celebration of the 900th anniversary of the introduction of Christianity in that country crossed the Atlantic. Provisional President Uriburu of the Argentine Republic addressed the North American people from Buenos Aires. The English Derby was described on the wings of short waves so all America could eavesdrop on the race at Epsom Downs. Spain and Siam joined the international radio circuit with special programs. From Vienna music of the Philharmonic Orchestra was wafted westward across Europe and the Atlantic to entertain an American audience.

News of all this progress delighted Marconi but another event of great significance to him, and possibly to the world was in prospect.

Science and mankind had cause to rejoice with the fifty-six-year-old inventor on July 20, 1930, when he received congratulations from all quarters of the globe on the birth of his daughter Elettra. Authorities on heredity and genius assert that a man's ability is transmitted through his daughters, not through his sons. The grandsons—the sons of Marconi's daughters—will have this in their favor.

The scientist's wife gave birth to a daughter, her first born, at the Villa of Prince Odescalchi at Civita Vecchia. Marconi had rented this country house which is on the edge of the sea, about an hour by motor from Rome. Queen Elena consented to be the godmother of the child named Maria Elettra Elena Anna. The first name is that of the mother, the second that of the yacht, the third that of the Italian Queen, and the fourth after her paternal and maternal grandmothers.

Ten days later the babe was christened in the beautiful Villa Odescalchi. Cardinal Pacelli, the Papal Secretary of

State, performed the ceremony and conveyed a special blessing from the Pope. After the christening, refreshments were served to numerous distinguished guests in the extensive park of pine, cypress and eucalyptus trees. Through the vista the *Elettra*, all gay with bunting, could be seen at anchor.

Within a short time Marconi was back on the deck to continue the experiments with short waves which were setting the stage for radio to accomplish one of the greatest triumphs of his life as far as personal satisfaction was concerned. Having supervised the erection of a powerful shortwave station in Vatican City, he was invited to participate in the inaugural ceremony, it being his honor to present Pope Pius XI with the microphone through which he might speak to a countless audience in all parts of Christendom.

It was late in the afternoon in Italy; noontime in New York on February 12, 1931. For the first time a Pope departed from the limited means of communication by encyclical letters to speak into a gold-mounted microphone to many millions of an unseen audience that eavesdropped on the most globe-girdling broadcast ever attempted.

Senatore Marconi, introducing the Pontiff, said:

"It is my very great honor and privilege to announce to you that within a very few moments the Supreme Pontiff, his Holiness, Pius XI, will inaugurate this radio station of the State of the Vatican City. The electric waves will carry his august words of peace and benediction throughout the world.

"For nearly twenty centuries the Roman Pontiffs have given their inspired messages to all people, but this is the first time in history that the living voice of the Pope will have been heard simultaneously in all parts of the globe.

"With the help of Almighty God, who places such mysterious forces of nature at mankind's disposal, I have been able to prepare this instrument that will give to the faithful throughout the world the consolation of hearing the voice of the Holy Father."

Turning to the Pope, he said:

"Holy Father, I have today the happiness of consigning to your Holiness the work entrusted to me. Its completion is now consecrated by your august presence.

"Be pleased, I pray you, to let your voice be heard all over the world."

And it was in an instant!

As news the occasion was evaluated as "the crowning miracle, thus far, in man's transmission of human speech by radio."

Later, in reviewing this historic event, Marconi recalled:

"At the Jubilee of Pope Leo XIII in Rome, in 1903, the Pontiff's benediction was more or less clearly heard throughout St. Peter's in which some 50,000 were massed. But now it is possible to speak to an audience of a million, five millions, or twenty millions, if need be, and every unit of that audience may be comfortably seated at home, or at sea in a ship or in a train or flying in an airplane separated from the speaker by tens or hundreds of miles.

"The developments made in wireless during the last few years destroy one's belief in the boundary of possibilities. Even to me they seem romantic and strange—or they would seem so, did I not know the scientific principles involved— and I can quite understand that the uninitiated must regard the developments in wireless as something bordering upon the supernatural. I think I may say that the people will cease to wonder at wireless. The only wonder will be that there was ever a time when it was unknown."

The King of Italy had made Marconi a Marquis on June 18, 1929, and Pope Pius made him a member of the Pontifical Academy of Science on February 12, 1931, further conferring the Grand Cross of the Order of Pius XI.

The King of Italy added to the honors by decorating him with Knight of the Grand Cross of the Order of Saints Maurice and Lazarus, a distinction second only to the Order of the Annunziata, on January 15, 1832.

The city of Philadelphia awarded him the famous John Scott medal on March 10, 1932, and England, on May 3, 1932, presented the Kelvin medal, one of the most highly prized of the engineering profession, awarded triennially in memory of Baron William Thompson Kelvin, British scientist.

Radio now international in scope was ready to honor its inventor in the most far-flung, cosmopolitan salute ever given to any human in the history of civilization. Fourteen nations and insular possessions on four continents were invited to participate in world-wide festivities marking the thirtieth anniversary of the first transatlantic signal. The "ether" on December 12, 1931, vibrated with voices of diplomats, scientists and communication chiefs, as their words couched in native tongues praised the Italian genius and crowned him the undisputed Monarch of Space.

What a miraculous change had come over wireless in thirty years!

In contrast with the feeble letter "S" of 1901 fame, this program of 1931 was switched from country to country in no more time than required to make the average telephone connection.

From New York to Washington to London to Brussels; from Paris to Berlin to Rome to Warsaw; from Rio to Tokyo to Manila to Caracas; from Buenos Aires to Honolulu to Ottawa and Montreal and back to New York, the listeners of the United States were transported by ear through the medium of the greatest radio hook-up ever arranged. The ethereal envelope of the earth pulsed in honor of Marconi.

As one portion of the program was completed, the pickup point was switched off, another plug was inserted in the main control board at New York, and another country, thousands of miles away, was pouring its words and music into the American homes. Even the radio operators, in the habit of conversing with distant points of the globe, were visibly excited.

Marconi, in the London studios of the British Broadcasting Corporation, was plainly affected by the demonstration of what his life-work had made possible. His words came haltingly at times, as he sought to express his feelings, and to recall that it was chiefly in America that the announcement of his first transoceanic signal met with belief.

"The announcement of our success," said Marconi, actuating the London microphone, "was received with scepticism by most scientists, principally in Europe, but not so in America. Practically all the great American scientists believed in me, and the American Institute of Electrical Engineers was the first scientific body to endorse my statement.

"Naturally at this time my thoughts go back to the moment thirty years ago, when instead of sitting in a comfortable room in London sending signals which I know will be received and understood on the other side of the Atlantic, I was standing in a bitter cold room on the top of a hill in Newfoundland, wondering if I should be able to hear the simple letter 'S' transmitted from England.

"From the time of my earliest experience, I was always convinced that radio signals would some day be sent across the great distances of the earth, and that transatlantic radio would be feasible. My first problem, however, was to prove that waves could be sent across the ocean and be detected on the other side."

After recounting his experiences in Newfoundland, the inventor continued: "The fact of getting radio signals right across the Atlantic may properly be considered a discovery of cardinal importance. Although we already had the waves and the means, more or less, of detecting them at short distances, nobody knew or could have foreseen that in the electric waves we possessed means of instantaneously transmitting communication and broadcasting intelligence to the ends of the earth.

"No other forces produced by man have ever been perceived or detected without the aid of artificial conductors over a distance in any way approaching that which separates Europe and America.

"I am happy to know Mr. Kemp and Mr. Paget who were with me at Newfoundland are at my side again at this moment.[2] I wish to send my cordial greetings to all of you who are interested in radio. I feel sure you form the major portion of the great American public."

Then came the most dramatic moment of the broadcast —the reproduction in Morse code of Marconi's pioneer transatlantic signal. The difference effected by thirty years was strikingly illustrated.

"Perhaps it will interest you," said Marconi, "if I now repeat the Morse signal of the letter 'S' as I first heard it across the Atlantic in 1901."

The master touched the key and the "S" girdled the earth as a sharp, vigorous signal compared to the faint three dots which ears were strained to catch thirty years ago.

Marconi added, "Good afternoon, my American friends," and with that the program switched back to New York, where Dr. Michael I. Pupin was waiting at the microphone.

"No message carried by electric waves from Europe to

[2] George S. Kemp, died January 2, 1933, in Southampton, England, at age of seventy-five.

America had deeper meaning," said Pupin in reminiscence
of the first transoceanic signal. "Marconi alone understood
its full significance; to him alone the message announced the
early dawn of a new epoch of transoceanic communications.
This awakened in his prophetic mind the vision which
guided his great efforts along the steep and arduous path
which led to the greater triumphs in the radio art.

"Few of us understood the full meaning of Galileo's simple experiments of 300 years ago, when from the leaning
tower of Pisa he dropped little weights and from their motion derived the laws which guide the motion of the planetary system.

"Few of us understand the full meaning of Marconi's
vision. But just as all of us know and admire the sublime
courage with which Galileo defended his new science, so we
admire Marconi's sublime courage which enabled him to
transform his vision of thirty years ago into the beautiful
reality of our present radio. Italy can be justly proud of
her two great sons Galileo and Marconi."

It was a long jump from New York to Manila, but radio
made the leap in a flash and Vice-Governor G. C. Butte
came on the air:

"The 13,000,000 people of the Philippine Islands bid you
good-morning in Manila. [It was noon of another day in
New York.] Beyond the green fields and through the fronds
of the distant palms, we can see the flaming tropical sun
just above the horizon. It is Sunday morning. The deep-
voiced church bells are calling the people to early mass. My
radio audience in Europe and the Americas is hearing my
voice yesterday. Surely Marconi's invention has annihilated
time and distance.

"The Philippine people are indebted to him in a great
degree. Our emerald isles extend more than 1,200 miles
from north to south. They are isolated by long stretches of

water. Wireless is the only means by which a large fraction of our people keep in immediate touch with the capital and the outside world.

"I want to thank Mr. Marconi because his invention has banished all fear of that menace to inter-island navigation, the tropical typhoon. . . . It has done more than any other scientific agency to spread and to deepen the universal consciousness of the brotherhood of man."

Up from the Argentine came the next voice. Octavio Pico, Minister of the Interior, was speaking:

"Today with rapid communication to all parts of the world, and within speaking distance of nine-tenths of all the telephones in existence, Argentina is better able to play her part in science and commerce, and to contribute to the harmonious welfare of all mankind than ever before. All the nations of the world owe a tribute of admiration not only to the illustrious inventor, but to his predecessors, who by their notable labors contributed to this magnificent realization of which the present and future generations will take advantage of the more intimate relationship between the nations of the earth."

The tables were turned on May 14, 1932, and Marconi participated in another international broadcast—this time in praise of a fellow inventor, on the Centennial of the telegraph's invention.

"It is pleasant to find it recorded that although Morse's early years as an inventor were full of labor and the inevitable disappointments of pioneering, he reaped to the full success of his work in later life," said Marconi. "I would pledge my own tribute to his memory by saying that I am sure he would have rejoiced in the knowledge that it is on the foundation of his invention that we are building a bridge of peace and friendship across the Atlantic with radio. He would be happy to know that he has enabled the people of

the two countries he knew so well—America and England—
to exchange messages and greetings of good will both by
the written and the spoken word."

.   .   .   .   .   .

"The man who invents a new machine makes millions.[3] Maxwell and Hertz, who laid the basis of what is radio, made only
reputations. . . . Neither Maxwell nor Hertz had the faintest
inkling that his discoveries would enrich the world with a new
means of communication and with broadcasting. What should be
their reward, were they still alive?"

[3] *The New York Times,* February 11, 1934.

XXIII

ENTRANCED BY TINY WAVES

NATURE imposes limitations on the ears and eyes, but man accepting the challenge is always trying to reinforce them to hear and see things outside their normal range by inventing instruments that detect the invisible and inaudible. The very sight of the ruddy Mars prods the star-gazer to wonder if some day man will communicate with celestial neighbors on a light beam or on some other magic channel. He dreams of interplanetary broadcasts. And when he hears flashes from explorers in the north polar and Antarctic regions his imagination is stirred, and he wonders what those areas of the earth really look like; he dreams of television.

Scientists are now talking about hearing light! Radio is leading communication engineers close to the fringes of that spectrum. Tiny Hertzian waves are a scientific rainbow of promise arched across the infinite domain of the research expert.

Marconi was one of the first to be entranced by this "rainbow" in the ether. He pioneered across the wireless trails that lead from the long waves, some measuring 30,000 meters from crest to crest, to the ultra-short waves or mere ripples only a few centimeters in length. Down the wavelength scale the men of radio have plunged, approaching closer and closer to the infra-red ray, the ultra-violet ray, the X-ray and the gamma rays of radium. That's light; radio is encroaching upon its frontiers.

The micro-wave is the future of radio!

The short wave (150-10 meters) that hops-skips-and-jumps around the earth with strange effects, tantalized scientists for a decade or more.

Why should an airplane's 33-meter SOS over the Pacific be heard in New York amid the skyscrapers but not in California? Why should a message from London find South Africa or China but absolutely miss Brussels and ignore Paris?

Such erratic performances, compared with the more stable long waves, mystified even Marconi and aroused the curiosity of those restless souls who must learn the secret of inconsistency before they can sleep a good sleep. Evidence that the Heaviside layer or "mirror" reflected the truant short waves back to the earth, causing a skip effect, was partial relief for their inquisitive minds. But solution of that riddle led only to further study.

Radio men set out to chart the short waves just as a mariner charts the routes of the sea. They catalogued every wave and distinguished between those that jump through daylight and those that can be entrusted to sneak like a flash through the night's regions of darkness. The analysis disclosed that some of the waves revel in sunlight; others more owl-like hoot their messages only at night. So man had to cope with several variable factors utterly out of his control; the trickery of day and night and the knavery of the billowing "mirror."

With no hope of ever being able to govern these natural mischief-makers, Marconi and others sought ways and means to operate wireless in harmony with them. Unable to harness nature they would cooperate, and that they did, although the task was not easy. Few days offer the same atmospheric conditions and the lofty "mirror" is quite unstable. Just a sun spot on the face of Old Sol often calls for quick scientific maneuvering if world-wide wireless is not to be overpowered and faded out.

Marconi built reflectors, wire-like aerials to shoot the waves in desired directions. For instance, if London wants to chat with Calcutta when that zone is in darkness, aerials designed to fling the waves in that direction are used to project specific wave lengths. If Canada is the goal and the Atlantic basks in sunlight still different aerials and another assortment of waves are called into play. Soon Marconi short-wave beams were encircling the earth with telephony and high-speed dots and dashes that rat-a-tat-tat between the hemispheres like the rapid fire of a machine gun.

As Marconi and his staff studied the results, they observed that short waves told tales on space. The wireless experts also became experts in prognosticating magnetic storms that frequently bombard the broadcasts in nature's brazen attempt to obliterate the flow of dots and dashes. Now, for example, if King Edward decides he would like to speak to his far-flung colonies, the radio men would probably be consulted for a forecast of atmospheric conditions. They can inform his Majesty, usually at least two weeks in advance, whether or not "the ether" on the day of his choice would be sprayed with static from some magnetic "blizzard." And with such advice the monarch would probably shift his speech to a clearer date on radio's calendar.

It was natural after all this conquest of short waves that the mind of Marconi buzzed with new ideas. He turned to the ultra-short wave (10 to 1 meter). And when he glimpsed beyond the frontier of 1 meter he was in the realm of microwaves, measured in centimeters! So here were two new things to work with, ultra-short waves and micro waves.

Marconi was converging on the province of light. Possibly Nikola Tesla was right after all in his declaration, "light can be nothing else than a sound wave in the ether; and the shorter the waves the more penetrative they will be." Certainly these miniature radio waves act in many ways like light; to some degree they obey the law of optics. Therefore, scientists were quick to label them "quasi-optical" because they seemed to travel only as far as the eye could see to the horizon. Some one with a dramatic flair called micro waves "dark light."

Stretched out before the eyes of man, as far as the eye could see, lay a vast field for experimentation. There was evidence of inventive opportunities galore. So bewildering with possibilities for expansion was the ultra-short wave that Marconi as well as other research pioneers rushed to develop new and more sensitive instruments to capture them for useful purposes. Tiny detector and amplifier tubes were devised no bigger than an acorn and just about that shape. Short duralumin rods were erected as pipe-like aerials from which the "baby" waves could hop into space.

Experimenters went sky-high; to the towers of skyscrapers, up in airplanes and to mountain tops, because if these waves did travel only as far as the eye sees then the higher the aerial rod and antenna the greater the range. Marconi went to sea with the *Elettra* to study ultra-short impulses flashed out from the Italian coast; other experimenters cruised city streets with mobile receivers to learn all they could about the technique of ruling this mystic dominion of science.

They found that the micro wave has little or no affinity for Mother Earth, while the ultra-short wave does, although that was not the early belief. There seem, however, to be fewer sky-wave phenomena below 2 meters. Such signals over a short distance apparently hover close to the ground, and with the horizon as a springboard leap off into space on a straight line. Even the Heaviside "mirror" does not seem to reflect micro waves as it does the waves of longer length. On the other hand, the very fact that radio engineers in London have intercepted 9-meter broadcasts from a 5-watt police patrol car cruising a street in a Mississippi Valley town, showed along with other long-distance pickups, that ultra-short waves are by no means strictly quasi-optical.

Some are inclined to believe, however, that micro waves, measured in centimeters, do go on and on into the infinite traveling as straight a line as light. Visionaries base their hope for interplanetary communication on these "freak" waves that dash away from the globe. They argue if these electric waves are almost like light, and light comes from the stars, then what is to stop radio from straying that far from the earth, provided, of course, sufficient power is used?

Now suppose a straight stick is placed on a library globe. It touches only a comparatively small area of the sphere, the ends go off into space. That is believed to be a "picture" of micro waves. Therefore, if man wants to intercept the signals over greater distances he must climb up on lofty pinnacles to pluck them from space because the ethereal "stick" doesn't bend. And if he wishes to relay the messages further or "bend" them around the earth from city to city he may have to use booster stations to relay them at different angles. For example, two such automatic stations might be needed to "bend" a two- or one-meter television wave from New York to Philadelphia, and that is only ninety miles. Those ultra-short and micro waves are going some place in a hurry and man must call upon his ingenuity if he is to outwit them and confine them to earthly performances.

Both the ultra-short and micro wave are more potent on an unobstructed path. That again follows the law of optics. The height of the aerial and antenna above earthly objects is more important than the height above the ground. Trees, electric wires, buildings and mountains are "death" to the ultra-short impulses. All objects seem to absorb and reflect the tiny waves, splashing them like light. Even a steam radiator in a room near an ultra-short-wave receiver will absorb or "shield" the signals; so will a kitchen stove. The "dead spot" caused by a skyscraper, even by a three-story structure or a bridge may well be imagined.

An airplane up 4,000 feet and 100 miles away can hear a 5-meter message; also at 3,000 feet; but after the plane drops to 1,000 feet the signals fluctuate rapidly and become more erratic than ever between 400 feet and the ground.

Marconi and other experimenters in various parts of the world are convinced by their investigations that the ultra-short wave is diffracted and refracted as well as reflected. Otherwise, what explains why the signals are audible, even faintly, far below the line of sight? A receiver atop Mt. Washington in New Hampshire, 6,290 feet above sea level, 284 miles from New York, and 37,600 feet below the line of sight, intercepted 6.8-meter and 4.9-meter signals projected into space from a skyscraper. It seems that these waves are diffused just the same as twilight. Technicians like to call it "atmospheric refraction." To explain it they point to the fact that a star appearing on the horizon, is actually thirty-five minutes below it. Otherwise, how could 7.3-meter waves from Rochester, N. Y., be detected in England and on the Pacific coast? How could amateurs talk across the country and the Atlantic on ultra-short waves?

Furthermore, the miniature waves seem to travel in a substantially horizontal direction. The wave-front moves in a plane nearly vertical, and since the upper parts travel faster than the lower, because of atmospheric conditions, the tendency is for the wave to "bend" slightly toward the earth. There is probably an advantage in that the energy is diffused, for it may often provide signals on the "shadow" sides of buildings and hills in much the same way that light passes through a window not facing the sun.

When it was first observed that the ultra-short wave apparently balked at the curvature of the earth, experimenters of a mathematical turn of mind figured that at last there was plenty of room in space for all sorts of radio stations; and for every television aspirant to establish a station. For example, it was estimated, if a 3-meter signal would cover only thirty miles on earth, then, Boston, Albany, New York, Philadelphia, Washington and numerous communities in between, as well as others across the countryside, could use the same channel without interference caused by overlapping. Whether this theory holds is still problematical, for between two New England hilltops 100 miles apart, $2\frac{1}{2}$-meter signals have established reliable communication.

Nevertheless, micro waves are heralded as the promised land—radio's Utopia—despite the fact that television requires a much wider channel than sound broadcasts, if the image is to appear in detail. Normally the little waves do not fade. They are generally oblivious to static; even a lightning storm does not blockade them. Then they are ideal for television because a picture distorted by fading might be gruesome or it might be ugly if streaked and freckled by static. The "baby" waves are less dependent upon seasonal influences than are the longer waves. Also they are "delicate" to handle, and how to pump high power into them is a puzzle of the first magnitude. So far they have performed their magic with the power of only a few watts. What might they do should 50,000 watts be injected into their arteries? But to get that power flowing across ultra-short-wave channels is a real trick; to control such energy in a tiny wave is no simple task. These things all taunt and haunt the engineers.

Marconi, too, in his sixties, was teased from any possibility of leisure, by these unanswered riddles. Fascinated by the opportunities, his after-the-World-War research was concentrated on the little waves which he beheld in his early experiments, but the devices needed to make them "jump through the hoop" at that time were missing. Into what niche of wireless could he fit this wondrous "dark light"? That was the question and Marconi was among those determined to find the answer.

"The general belief is that with electromagnetic waves under one meter in length, usually referred to as quasi-optical, communication is possible only when the transmitter and receiver are within visual range of each other," explained Marconi; "and that consequently their usefulness is defined by that condition.[1]

"Long experience, however, has taught me not always to believe in the limitations indicated by purely theoretical considerations or even by calculations. These—as we well know—are often based on insufficient knowledge of all the relevant factors. I believe, in spite of adverse forecasts, in trying new lines of research, however unpromising they may seem at first sight."

These words reveal the resolute Marconi spirit of the '90's still very much alive. Years failed to dim the ardor, the patience required for this man to unwind the invisible threads of science and spin them into a practical service for mankind.

"It was about eighteen months ago," said the inventor, "I decided again to take up the systematic investigation of the properties and characteristics of the very short waves in view of the palpable advantages which they seemed to offer —i.e., the small dimensions of the radiators, receivers and reflectors necessary for radiating and receiving a considerable amount of electrical energy—and in view also of the

[1] Lecture, December 2, 1932, at Royal Institution of Great Britain.

fact that they do not suffer interference from natural electrical disturbances. It was, of course, obvious that these investigations would be facilitated if it were possible efficiently to utilize more power at the transmitter and more reliable receivers than those available for the tests in 1919-24."

Marconi summoned his personal assistants, G. A. Mathieu of short-wave beam receiver fame, and G. A. Isted. Vacuum tubes were developed to function on a half-meter wave and less. New circuits were evolved to meet the extraordinary conditions. An instrument was designed to measure waves as short as a millimeter. And when the mechanism for working the modernized wireless was ready, the practical-minded Marconi and his engineers instituted a thorough investigation under actual operating conditions along the Italian coast. He had used reflectors before, but now radical changes had been made in their design in order to master the tiny waves.

The first test was conducted in 1931 between Santa Margherita and Sestri Levante, near Genoa, a distance of twelve miles over water. The elevation of the two instruments was capable of giving a direct line of vision across twenty-four miles.

Marconi was more anxious than ever to test the distance capabilities of the miniature waves, and with that purpose as the incentive he went to sea on board the *Elettra* with a single reflector unit installed astern of the main deck.[2]

The Santa Margherita signals were still perceivable twenty-eight miles away, well beyond the optical range, and notwithstanding the curvature of the earth. The signals began to lose their strength noticeably at 11 miles from Santa Margherita, that is, before reaching the optical limit, but after passing that position they gradually decreased in in-

[2] July, 1932.

tensity until no longer audible. Beyond 22 miles, how-ever, the signals suffered a deep fading. Up to 18 miles, speech was 90 per cent intelligible, but from 20 miles until the signals could no longer be heard, tone Morse signals only could be clearly identified.

Then the apparatus at Santa Margherita was taken to Rocca di Papa, 12 miles southeast of Rome at a height of 750 meters above sea level and about 15 miles inland. As the *Elettra* moved toward the island of Sardinia, Marconi observed and logged reception. The signals vanished at the 110-mile mark.

When the yacht arrived at Golfo Aranci, Sardinia, the ultra-short wave instruments were installed on the tower of a signal station at Cape Figari, 340 meters above sea level. The signals from Rocca di Papa were heard clearly at times over 168 miles, while the optical distance or theoretical horizon, considering the height of the two places was approximately 72 miles. The average signal strength was superior before sunset than after.

"It is interesting to add that at Cape Figari the angle of reception was investigated several times by tilting the reflector, and it was found that the waves from the distant station reached the receiving experimental station from a horizontal direction," said Marconi. "I feel that I may say that some of the practical possibilities of a hitherto unexplored range of electrical waves have been investigated, and a new technique developed, which is bound to extend very considerably the already vast field of the applications of electric waves to radio communications.

"The permanent and practical use of micro waves will be, in my opinion, a new and economical means of reliable radio communication, free from electrical disturbances, eminently suitable for use between islands, and to and from islands and the mainland, and also between other places separated by moderate distances. The new system is unaffected by fog, and offers a high degree of secrecy, by virtue, principally, of its sharp directive qualities.

"Its strategic uses in wartime are obvious, no less than its practical value to navies and aircraft, insofar as the communications can be confined to any desired direction. The fact, however, that the distance of propagation of these waves appears to be limited, suggests other advantages in wartime, besides greatly reducing the possibility of mutual interference between distant stations.

"In regard to the limited range of propagation of these micro waves, the last word has not yet been said," warned Marconi. "It has already been shown that they can travel round a portion of the earth's curvature, to distances greater than had been expected, and I cannot help recalling that at the very time when I first succeeded in proving that electric waves could be sent and received across the Atlantic Ocean in 1901, distinguished mathematicians were of the opinion that the distance of communications, by means of electric waves, would be limited to a distance of only about 165 miles.

"In any case, the new system is now available for advantageously replacing optical or light signaling in all its long-distance applications, as for example, between signaling stations along coasts, or between forts constructed along a frontier, and in general will be found advantageous in many cases where the erection and maintenance of an ordinary telephone or cable circuit is difficult, or too expensive.

"Other applications such as broadcasting and television are already under consideration, and the study of the new fields of application for these so far unutilized electric waves will, I feel sure, soon bring about the design of greatly improved methods and apparatus."

With this complete account of his work to date, Marconi

returned to Italy and to the *Elettra,* "to try new lines of research, however unpromising at first sight."

So successful had been his investigations that the Vatican authorities decided to adopt the new system for telephonic communication on about 60-centimeter waves between the Vatican City and the Papal summer residence at Castel Gandolfo, about fifteen miles from Rome.

The unique installation, the first of its kind in the world, was presented by Marconi to Pope Pius XI in a broadcast heard throughout America as well as Europe.[3]

"Our first word shall be for you, Signor Marchese Marconi," said the Pontiff, "and it will be a word of congratulation for the continuous successes that Divine Providence and divine goodness have reserved for your researches and applications in this field."

The Marchese replied: "This first practical application of micro waves fills my heart both as an Italian and a scientist with pride and hope for the future. May my modest work contribute to the achievement of true Christian peace in the world."

Radio engineers throughout the world had by this time accepted the challenge of micro waves. Just as the English Channel had dared Captain Webb to swim it, Marconi to leap it by wireless and Bleriot to fly across, so it offered an ideal opportunity across which to "spin" a micro-ray radiophone line.

The Straits of Dover between Lympne and St. Inglevert, a distance of 56 kilometers, was chosen for experiments, using 18-centimeter waves. The tests began in March 1931, and after five years of service W. L. McPherson and E. H. Ullrich, engineers of the International Telephone & Telegraph Company, summarized their observations as follows:[4]

[3] February 11, 1933.   [4] *Electrical Communication,* April, 1936.

(1) The most stable micro-ray conditions coincide with very stable atmospheric conditions as judged by thermometer and barometer.

(2) Given stability of temperature and pressure, the actual values seem to have no importance.

(3) Given stable temperature and pressure: rain, hail, snow, or fog, do not affect the link.

(4) No definite relation between the electrical state of the atmosphere (potential gradient) and micro-ray stability has been found. Excellent operation has been obtained during thundery periods, but there is no information as to the general atmospheric stability at the time.

(5) A high wind is almost invariably accompanied by good micro-ray transmission.

(6) Sudden changes in temperature are usually accompanied by micro-ray fading; likewise sudden barometric changes. Rapid fluctuations in temperature occur much more frequently on hot days than on cold days; fading is more pronounced during the summer months than in winter.

(7) The settling of a heavy bank of fog has been accompanied by very severe and rapid fading, followed by stability when the fog bank has ceased to move.

(8) During the summer, extremely violent fades of very short duration—1 to 2 minutes—have been noticed.

(9) During the summer, fading at audio frequency seems to occur both in broad daylight and in darkness.

(10) Ultra-short waves of 6 meters length are much stabler than micro-rays over optical paths across the Straits of Dover.

(11) In noisy locations micro-rays have the advantage over ultra-short waves of being much less affected by "man-made static."

(12) Micro-ray communication is much more private than ultra-short waves.

It will be recalled that when Marconi first encountered the tiny waves before the turn of the century, "the ether" was all the rage; it helped to account for some of the mystery in wireless. To envisage such a medium assisted the layman, and scientists too for that matter, to understand how messages could be sent through the air. But now with the return of ultra-short waves to prominence, scientists

Marconi ultra-short wave reflector or radio "searchlight" on top of the Vatican station "beams" a 56-centimeter wave across a distance of about fifteen miles.

because of their advance knowledge of radio, were beginning to discard the ether theory. Even Marconi, it was noticed, refrained from using the term "ether." He spoke of Hertzian or electromagnetic waves.

The one-hundredth anniversary of Clerk Maxwell's birth was marked by the scientific world "digging a grave for the theory of a luminiferous ether," but at the same time honoring Maxwell's mathematical genius. That supreme "paradox of Victorian science and yet a triumph of the scientific imagination" was at an end. The ether was gone.

Science, however, will always remember Maxwell for the necessary and convenient fiction his mathematical mind spun to help physicists in the days before they realized "there are no ether waves," as Charles Proteus Steinmetz put it. The waves are electromagnetic wafted in an unfathomed field of force which modern men of science contend extends throughout space.

Marconi had an intuition that the micro waves might be made to penetrate solid bodies just as other wireless waves; he was not satisfied with the experiments to date. He would chase the little waves further, beyond the horizon.

Into the Tyrrhenian Sea sailed the *Elettra* to conduct tests with inland Italy.

On August 14, 1933, Marconi mounted the rostrum of the Royal Academy in Rome with the surprise announcement that both radiophone and telegraphic signals had been exchanged with Santa Margherita 94 miles away. And while the *Elettra* was anchored at Porto Santo Stefano, 161 miles from Santa Margherita, faint code signals on the 60-centimeter wave were intercepted on the yacht, although two mountain promontories intervened, indicating that opaque objects do not block the waves. He did not hazard a guess as to what caused the waves to "bend," because he planned other experiments in an effort to determine definitely the laws governing the propagation of the micro waves.

Marconi was at "the gateway to television."

.   .   .   .   .   .

". . . mankind is at the very beginning of its existence; on the astronomical time scale it has lived only a few brief moments, and has only just begun to notice the cosmos outside itself. It is, perhaps hardly likely to interpret its surroundings aright in the first few moments its eyes are open."—SIR JAMES JEANS.

XXIV

MARCONI LOOKS INTO THE FUTURE

GUGLIELMO MARCONI is welcomed in friendship wherever he goes. Buckingham Palace, the Quirinal, the palatial residences of Presidents, the imperial palaces of emperors are on his calling list. And that, too, includes the White House. He has hobnobbed with the grandees of the world.

The strong-willed, precocious inventor face to face with the smiling, magnetic personality of Franklin D. Roosevelt draws quite a contrast. It is easy to picture Mr. Roosevelt leading the conversation while Marconi, modest, diplomatic and softly spoken, answered briefly with dignity and almost chilly reserve. Yet should the genial Mr. Roosevelt inquire of Italy and wireless then that boyish Marconi smile might reveal a friendliness and warmth; Italy and wireless strike a responsive chord.

Alongside the Presidents of this century, Marconi lacks the joviality of a Taft; the outward aggressiveness and glorious gusto of a Theodore Roosevelt. In dress he is more like Coolidge; more like Coolidge in speech, and in the fact that trifles are likely to stir his wrath. The stoical Marconi could never organize his time to be like a Herbert Hoover, yet he could leave just as "cold" an impression on the average man. Marconi is more like Woodrow Wilson; more of the student; ladies and orchids appealed to both. The second marriage of both was most romantic.

Marconi seems always possessed with an air of mystery, which lifts when talking with such men of science as Millikan or Compton. He can sit and smoke with these philosophers, apparently forgetting himself and his work for the moment.

But this man of wireless does not have the mathematical mind of a Steinmetz. His simple calculations are from dreams, instinct and practical experiments, never from the slide-rule or involved equations. He is creative; a man of intuition and logical imagination. He invents with ingenuity, without fixed formula or ready-made ideas. Never is he immersed in technicalities.

Marconi is much more the aristocrat than Edison. People encountering him for the first time naturally approach with imaginative impressions of what a wizard of wireless might look like and how such an electrical mesmerist might act. Marconi seems to sense these strange conceptions that grant him a bewitching superiority. And rightly or wrongly people who meet him sense a lofty manner. He is deceptively complex. This more than anything else helps to make Marconi sort of a highbrow, fantastic person in whom there is a great deal of the blue blood.

Should he desire, and he often does, he finds it easy to slip behind the mystic curtain people visualize between him and them. Meeting odd people is no happy knack for him. At mass interviews he usually acts bored and restless, nervous and anxious to go on to something else. To some this is evidence of snobbishness, unless one succeeds in penetrating that hermitical air of his. He relishes only first-rate people around him and only a few of them at a time. For him "a crowd is not company."

Marconi might be described as a fashionable, scientific intellectual, possessed of multifarious interests, with wireless always omnipotent. He belongs to the intelligentsia of old Rome, yet he is ever eager to get away from the social whirl to learn by experiment. Electrical devices in existence are merely tools with which to dig out the secrets of space. He is not one to invent the tools. He merely uses them to create, to stir immensities that call for a new order of things and still newer instruments. He revolutionizes. Men of a more complex mathematical mind apply their skill to invent the gadgets and machines for which his genius reveals the need. In this way Marconi places fingerposts to fame along the highways of science just as Maxwell and Hertz did before him.

Then old theories are ripped asunder; old wireless structures tumble. His discoveries rock even the foundations and shake out of the electrical circuits old devices, which for years seemed indispensable. In this way Marconi has been the beacon light of wireless; invincibly he typifies his inventions. He personifies wireless; it is his namesake.

He is a searcher in the skies for information, for new scientific clues; never in coils and vacuum tubes. They are but the telescopes of science through which he hopefully reaches out across the universe. He has that superb faculty of seeing great meanings in little things, which other men of research are likely to skip as trivial or insignificant. Anything appearing futile on its face only arouses his curiosity to learn what it is all about. His aim has always been to know everything about everything in wireless.

He seems to have a multiplicity of eyes, yet he has only one. Coupled with his keen perception is an imagination that foresees new wonders in radio. Constantly this fires him with impatience to bottle up something new. Time alone overwhelms him. Possibly a bit enviously, he hopes beyond hope to harness space completely for wireless; to give television to mankind, to light homes and run factories by radio power. Nothing can divert him from it. Nothing except his end of Time.

His vision always leads him on, but it was like reaching

out to touch the moon to ever hope to catch up with all he could see in the silver ball of science. He could but point the way for the next generation.

"Mankind is on the verge of discoveries quite as momentous as the discovery of fire," exclaimed Marconi.[1] "Who knows where the future will take us?"

With regard to the transmission of power——?

"I must leave that to your imagination," he quickly rejoined. "The beam system may be adopted for transmission of power. Employing the beam, power can be sent in fixed parallel lines. Without the beam system the power spreads out as an open fan and most of it is wasted. Again, much of it could be stolen by Tom, Dick or Harry who cared to put up the proper receiving set for utilizing it."

Will we have one or more great power stations with numberless parallel beams carrying power through the air to a definite destination?

"There is much to be done before a practical solution of the power transmission problem," he continued. "It is a far cry to the time when all the power man requires for his needs will be delivered to him through the air in full force and at the exact spot where he requires it. A great deal is still to be done before such a thing can become an actual fact, but I believe it is coming.

"I can hardly conceive of power being so transmitted over a range which would carry it beyond the curvature of the earth from the point of generation; beyond what might be termed the point-blank range, there would be too great a loss of energy through diffusion and reflection. But up to perhaps 25 miles, where economic considerations permit, electric power will, I believe, some day be carried without wires."

[1] Address of welcome at opening congress of scientists at the Royal Italian Academy in Rome, October 12, 1931.

Wireless power transmission is discarded by many as fanciful, chiefly, because the very nature of radio is to spread its cargo in all directions, and even in beam form to be absorbed quickly leaving only a fraction of power to serve a useful purpose. Marconi, however, was never so skeptical.

Once he projected a short wave 11,000 miles from the *Elettra* at Genoa to Sydney, Australia. There the signal was intercepted, amplified and local currents were caused to actuate circuits in which electricity flowed to light an electric lamp. On another occasion he touched a switch in Rome, thereby flooding with light the figure of Christ that juts into the sky above Rio de Janeiro, on a mountain peak 3,000 feet above the level of that beautiful harbor.

This was not power transmission by radio as some were quick to interpret. Energy traveling across the sea is too feeble to light directly a lamp. It is merely, as in this instance, the signal for strong local currents to turn on the illumination.

There are visionaries, however, bold enough to suggest the day will come when homes will be heated and lighted by radio power. To get electricity will be like turning on a radio set to hear music. Micro waves may warm the body but not the air in the dwelling.

Already ultra-short waves are used to create artificial fevers in the body to fight various diseases. And the impulses can be so controlled that they can cook the white of an egg while the yolk remains uncooked, or the yolk while the white is unaffected. Professor F. L. Hopwood, member of the Grand Council of the British Empire Cancer Campaign, reported this discovery to the London congress of the Institute of Radiology in 1933.

This ability of radio to act as an internal poultice foreshadows a new weapon in the war on bacteria and disease. Medicinal radio has become a most important and interesting field of research. Medical scientists wonder if certain membranes and tissues of the human body as well as malignant growths might be affected by micro waves of different lengths. This branch of science is called radiothermy and radiotherapy.

.   .   .   .   . .

Out of the morning mist of an Indian summer day in 1933 the Italian liner *Conte di Savoia* proudly nosed up the Hudson River to her pier at the foot of Forty-sixth Street, having brought Marchese Marconi and his charming wife into port completing his eighty-seventh transatlantic voyage.

"I am, of course, very glad to be back in the country which has been so encouraging to me in my work, and so hospitable," said Senatore Marconi to the newsmen. "It has been a long time since my last visit. I greatly look forward to seeing everything at the Century of Progress Exposition in Chicago, and especially the exhibitions of radio progress."

He came down the gangplank, stepped into a limousine and was whisked across the city under motorcycle escort to his hotel. But like every sightseer he was soon on the street again bound for Radio City in Rockefeller Centre, built since his last visit to New York. On the fifty-third floor of the newest skyscraper he met a group of radio editors to whom he declared with a smile, "I am here to have Americans put me wise, as you say, on what is taking place."

It was late in the afternoon; tea-time, so Marconi invited his guests to a party. At one end of the long table, designed for a Board of Directors meeting, was the silver kettle; at the other end the coffee urn for Americans who might prefer Java to Oolong. Marconi, always a perfect host, is extremely thoughtful and considerate of the welfare of those around him.

With a china cup and saucer in one hand, and a cigarette in the other, he walked around the room chatting and becoming acquainted with newcomers. It was suggested that the Senatore sit in a large chair at the head of the table.

"Oh, no," he said. "I'll use one of these regular chairs; they are more efficient."

The inventor was in a gay mood; his first hours in New York were to him a tonic, like the June days for a schoolboy aware that the bell is silenced for vacation. His secretary whispered that he seldom saw the Senatore in that spirit. The problems that always seem to occupy his mind and veil him in an air of mystery apparently vanished, leaving him free for an hour or two. Marconi was enjoying the occasion; his smiles and humor told the story.

He stood up, made a brief, informal speech on how happy he was to be in the United States; recalled the encouragement he had found on the American side of the sea; confessed he had much to learn about wireless—and then invited questions.

Will it be possible to talk across the Atlantic on ultrashort waves? he was asked.

Recalling how early predictions relative to wireless had gone astray, he replied: "If we succeed in sending micro waves over long distances we may revolutionize the whole art of radio. And I stake my reputation on it—the micro waves are not affected by static. I have listened to them in thunder storms, but the static did not bother reception. We use a short receiving element (antenna)," he said, holding up a table fork to illustrate the length of the antenna rod or wire.

"Curious as it may seem, day and night do not seem to influence these waves. We might think daylight would hinder them, and darkness increase their range as in the case of longer waves, but no. We are puzzled for an explanation. Further research may solve the mystery."

Are the micro waves useful in television?

"They will no doubt be utilized in image transmission," Marconi continued. "The importance of television, however, is problematical. I believe conveyance of information by sound is more important than conveyance by sight. For example, if one wants to sell stock in London he prefers to get the information across the sea as quickly as possible, and doesn't care to see a television picture of the man who takes the order at the other end.

"We must remember that animals can see, and some have eyes superior to those of man, but man can express thoughts in words and thereby convey information. Speech gives man tremendous power not possessed by animals no matter how sharp their vision. Think what broadcasting has done. A politician can reach a vast audience. What he says is likely to be more important and more appealing than his picture. Broadcasting will survive, despite television. They will supplement each other—sound and sight together.

"We must cheapen the transmission of television pictures, which is at present a rather expensive process. I do not share the opinion that television will kill the motion picture. The relation between television and the films will be the same as exists between wireless and the talking machine. Television and radio will tell us about things that are taking place, but this will not appeal to every one.

"The secrets of extremely short waves greatly intrigue my curiosity. The fact that they are not influenced by static is a factor of great importance in television. It makes possible clear, distinct pictures. They will not have the appearance of 'rain' which streaked the early motion pictures. Blank spots and distortions in television pictures are not generally present when ultra-short waves are utilized.

"I am known as a man who deals in cold scientific facts and practicalities," said the inventor, "not in Utopian fantasies. As to the talk of a saturation point—a limit of radio progress—there is no limit to distance, hence there can be no limit to wireless development.

"I believe the next twenty-five years will see developments in wireless quite as important as those marked on the pages of the first quarter of this century. Looking into the future I am confident of the perfection of television or motion pictures by radio. Both have been accomplished in a small way."

When bulletins from Rome had indicated Marconi had succeeded in "bending" miniature waves there was much conjecture in American engineering circles as to whether he had actually bent the waves by means of reflectors or other devices, or whether the waves had been reflected by nature from the Heaviside "roof." Apropos of this he was asked if the waves penetrated mountains or merely glided over the tops.

"You've got me there," said the inventor. "I really do not know. They may be reflected from the Heaviside surface as are other short waves. But we must continue to investigate before being sure."

How far down in the ethereal spectrum can you go?

"Oh, we haven't plumbed the depth yet," he replied. "We have used waves less than a centimeter in length. That radio region offers great opportunity for experimentation. We have much to learn about micro waves."

Taught by experience that the financial contributions of business go hand in hand with science, if an invention such as television is to be lifted from the stage of an electrical toy to that of a world-wide industry, Marconi said:

"The money aspect of the development of radio must not be forgotten. For example, my first experiment in wireless across the Atlantic cost more than $200,000. Governments are not so constituted that they can afford to encourage something which has not yet been proved worthwhile. A great deal of credit must be given to business men who had the faith to put money into the development of wireless. Scientists cannot get along without money to back them."

Some one shyly announced that he wanted to ask, what he termed foolish question No. 1, and good-naturedly the inventor said he would try to answer it.

Have you ever sent messages to other planets?

"I've sent lots of messages that never got anywhere," chuckled Marconi.

A young executive, alert to an old trick of rescuing a busy man from a crowd, stepped into the room, touched Marconi on the shoulder and whispered: "You are wanted on the telephone, Senatore."

That ended the tea party.

"Marconi is the same old Marconi; he doesn't change," remarked a veteran American business man as he left the party scene. "Fame never spoiled him; he is always just as boyish. No man in the world has such a conception of wireless, and I mean that sincerely. There is nothing in wireless too simple for Marconi to devote time and attention. That's a big secret of his success. In the little things he finds clues for big things.

"I have been with him at Cannes, in London and in Paris; I have crossed the Atlantic with him, and have been with him on the *Elettra*. Marconi has the uncanny sense of discovering a need. That was also characteristic of Edison. Marconi ably points out the need for certain instruments, and then his men like Mathieu carry it out. That is a powerful combination if geared to function properly.

"Men of wireless really never knew Marconi. He never mingled with them socially. They knew him only in an engineering way. He is surrounded usually by his own coterie of people. He never likes large social affairs. He attends them only because he believes it is politic. In his own quiet way he prefers a good party within his own little circle, and is at times quite frivolous.

"He holds himself aloof, and that is well demonstrated by the fact that I have seen him at dinner in the Savoy with his wife, and during the evening no one would go over to interrupt with a greeting or shake hands, as certainly would be the case should he try to dine in public in New York. While visiting in America he is 'hounded' to death, and he telephoned to say he would like to steal away to my home in the suburbs and hide. He cares nothing for ostentation.

"His second wife is from the Roman aristocracy; and I think this lovely lady's greatest fear is that some of her husband's prominent friends may think she has 'high-hatted' them because she fails to recognize them; she is very near-sighted."

Marconi had not been long in New York before editorialists observed that he had lost none of the optimism and courage that imbued him a generation ago and that ultimately enabled him to realize "the long cherished dream of remote peoples bridging the ocean with waves carrying their thoughts."

In looking ahead, *The New York Times* recalled:

When Marconi sent the letter "S" across the Atlantic it was in the face of the best scientific opinion of the day. His waves were like those of light, he was told. Who ever saw in New York a glare in London? The curving earth raised a mountain of water that cut it off. If now we talk and telegraph through space around the world, it is because something urged a divining inventor to experiment in spite of theory. We know that if we can signal across the ocean it is partly because intangible mirrors in the sky collectively known as the "ionosphere," reflect our waves to their destination and thus circumvent the curving earth.

Radio engineering is now faced with a situation not unlike that which Marconi overcame in his early transatlantic experiments. Crowded as the ether is with waves that carry images, voices and code messages, the engineers have been driven to find new paths. From waves measuring yards and even miles from crest to crest they turn to ripples of less than a foot. We have lately heard much of micro-wave transmission. Again the impossibilities are stressed. The short waves are so readily absorbed by buildings and mountains that signaling over vast distances seems hopeless. But not to Marconi.

The solution of the problem is to be found not on earth but in the heavens. Just as he divined the mirror in the sky early in the century, so he divines that it will serve him again. He turns his beams upward and lets the mirror on high carry his micro-waves to ever greater distances until at last he is convinced that ultimately they can be made to reach any destination on earth.

It is not that the principle is daringly new but that it is applied with such success in the face of familiar opposition. What the outcome may be Marconi himself will not venture to predict. "It is dangerous to put limits on wireless," he says. The point is that so little is known about those ever-rising and ever-falling mirrors in the sky that there is still room for Marconis in the young science of radio engineering, still room for the imaginative experimenter to fly in the face of scientific theory.

.   .   .   .   .   .

As the final September sunset of 1933 faded in New York an express train dipped through a tunnel under the Hudson River bound on a night run toward the West, speeding the inventor of wireless and his wife in a private car to A Century of Progress Exposition in Chicago, where he was dined and honored; Northwestern University conferred a Doctor of Science degree.

"Marconi Day" at the exposition was designated in tribute to the distinguished visitor, and on that occasion the Western Society of Engineers invited Marconi for luncheon. Just as the engineers were seated a note came from President Roosevelt, who was also a guest of the Exposition on that day, inviting Marconi to pay him a brief call. The

Senatore excused himself, and some twenty minutes later returned. His face wore a puzzled expression; as he sat down at the luncheon table he turned to Dr. Arthur H. Compton, and exclaimed:

"Where did I meet that man? Mr. Roosevelt described the exact details of a meeting in 1917, but for the life of me I cannot remember the occasion."

It was apparent that on the earlier occasion of their meeting, when Marconi was visiting the United States on behalf of the Italian Government, there was no reason for him to remember an Under-Secretary of the Navy, who was one of the many guests at a reception in his honor, whereas, to the Under-Secretary Franklin D. Roosevelt, the inventor of wireless was the man of the hour.

A week later Marconi returned to Manhattan Island stopping off en route at Niagara Falls to marvel at the thunderous cataract for the fourth time, and to show it to the Marchesa for the first time.

Back in New York he was conducted on a tour of Radio City; through the elaborate broadcasting studios and backstage of the magnificent Music Hall. To the showman who pointed out the features, Marconi did not appear to be impressed. His mind seemed to be looking ahead—to something even greater? Or was he puzzled at the vast outlay of money in this field of radio which might change overnight and render much of it obsolete?

To the chief engineer who described the nerve centre of the broadcasting system Marconi gave the impression of being perplexed; when a novel device was explained, the only word he found to express surprise was, "indeed," with an exclamation point. It all seemed as if modern radio had run ahead of Marconi. But had it?

Possibly he was comparing the present wonders with the future in which he could see new marvels for micro waves.

Perhaps again he wondered at the American extravagance and audacity in such a nebula as radio; possibly he marveled at the courage and optimism of the Americans. And well he might, for all of his triumphs had emerged from apparatus extremely simple compared to this electrical temple of modern broadcasting—a citadel that would long tower as a monument to the American spirit of progress in the face of a devastating business depression.

He was enthused about it all the next day when met in his private suite at the Ritz. A dapper man, who looked more as if he had come from London than from Rome, smart, handsome and perfectly groomed in a double-breasted blue suit, a starched collar and a purple tie with pocket handkerchief to match, slipped into the room through a French door.

Marchese Marconi calmly approached his guest, shook hands, and commented on the sunshine, but every move was guarded with a formal mask behind which he awaited questions, for he was aware the motive of the meeting was an interview. He was on the defensive. Having met him before, there was no expectation that he would manufacture the conversation. His answers are generally brief, of the "yes" or "no" variety; the reporter seeking a story soon begins to wonder if he will get enough news to cover one typewritten page.

"Please sit down here," invited Marconi pointing to a sofa, and he was careful to sit on the right to keep his good eye toward his guest.

A clipping from the morning paper on his arrival in New York the day before was handed to him to "break the ice." He donned a monocle and quickly scanned the column commenting on the reporter's accuracy. His smile revealed he was pleased—that he enjoys seeing his name in print—he turned from the clipping with a sheepish smile, confessing he had been too busy to read the morning paper earlier.

The inducement for Marconi to talk is to turn to the past; reminiscences of his triumphs in wireless are a lure to conversation. In the light of his glories he is seen as Marconi the man and not the scientist or Italian Senatore. The cold reserve begins to melt. He becomes more friendly. But should an interviewer seek to lead him into the role of prophecy, with a gesture and a puzzled frown he waves the future aside. The present too he shuns. He almost gives the impression that he is so busy with his experiments that the rest of the world's activities are a mystery to him. For instance, if one should ask him if Fascism would be good in the United States, he would not answer the question directly, but might dispense with it briefly by commenting upon its success in Italy.

He never belonged to any political party, but when he saw Fascism saving Italy he said, "I am a Fascista by conviction. Fascism is a regime of strength necessary for the salvation of Italy."

He likes the past because he is sure of it. It is definite. The present is too fleeting to catch with accuracy; Marconi cherishes accuracy and precision. The future to him is powerfully full of promise; if only there were more of it, for even if granted three score and ten years, he knows it is too short. Wireless, the task of his youth cannot be completed in a lifetime; it is destined to go on from generation to generation.

To get off the subject of wireless an interviewer runs the risk of terminating the visit, but taking this chance, to see another side of him, he was asked, "How is your little daughter Elettra?"

The cool smile of the inventor immediately changed; Marconi had that same warm, fond smile of any proud father as the little girl was mentioned. Wireless might be in his mind but Elettra was in his heart.

"I must give you one of her pictures," he said standing up and then returning to the sofa to add, "I forgot, my wife has gone out and I don't know where she put them."

No matter the topic under discussion, whether it be his golden-haired daughter, his floating laboratory or wireless, not the faintest spark of southern fire flares up within him. For a man decorated by kings and governments; for a successful inventor whose name will live throughout the ages, Marconi appears the least joyous of men. His features are melancholy. Despite his record achievements he seems to be racing with time, aware that it will win the race, but with the pace of a champion he maintains in his sixties the stride of his youth on the track of scientific research.

What did your mother and father think when you first experimented with wireless? he was asked.

"Mother encouraged me; she had faith in what I was doing," he reminisced. "Father was skeptical until I got results," and he smiled as he recalled the triumph of youth in convincing his parent that there was something to wireless after all. "I'll tell you, if you set your heart and soul in a thing you can do it."

A glance at his wrist watch reminded him of a luncheon engagement at Radio City, and whether it be for luncheon or for a banquet, to catch a train or board an ocean liner, Marconi likes to be there a few minutes ahead of time. Time seems to prod him and he becomes uneasy as the clock approaches the hour of an appointment. If he ever happens to be late, even a few minutes, he is apologetic the minute he enters the room. The interview concluded, he accompanied his visitor into the hall to the elevator, shook hands and said, "I shall expect to see you next week when I return from Washington."

That afternoon he left Manhattan Island again and

stopped off at Camden, N. J., to be amazed at Dr. Vladimir Kosma Zworykin's television; then on to the national capital with his wife to dine with President Roosevelt at the White House; to Indiana for an honorary degree, Doctor of Laws from Notre Dame; then across the Rockies to Hollywood to see how movies are filmed.

The broad Pacific was near at hand; it looked enticing and when the Japanese steamer *Chichibu Maru* sailed through the Golden Gate on November 2, the Marchese and Marchesa Marconi were on board bound for Yokohama en route around the globe to Italy. He abandoned his plans to return to New York; new ideas about a "radio lighthouse" were buzzing in his mind. He was anxious to get back home at 11 Via Condotti in an historic part of old Rome; back on the *Elettra's* deck.

Via Condotti is a narrow street running through the heart of the city from the Corso Umberto I, the main thorough-fare, up to the Piazza di Spagna, the background of which is formed by the great Spanish steps leading up to the Pincio Hill, one of the seven hills of the Eternal City.

The first house on the right of the stairs, about a block from Marconi's home, is where the poet Keats died. At the top of the stairs is the French Academy.

The Bezzi-Scali Palace, where Marconi at present lives, is an ordinary façade with a portico leading into the court-yard from the narrow Via Condotti, noted for its elegant shops; it is quite an English-American center. Marconi's typical Roman apartment has spacious rooms, darkened by shutters which keep out the summer sun while stone steps and tiled floors add to the cooling effect.

.   .   .   .   .   .

The comforts of home could not win Marconi from his laboratory, even under the glare of a mid-summer sun; on

July 30, 1934, a new application of micro-wave radio—a safety system for ships to permit blind navigation in a fog was demonstrated to a large group of Italian and British marine experts. The *Elettra* steamed into the port of Sestri Levante, sailing in a narrow space between two floating buoys, piloted by the indications of the new instrument and without being guided by any landmarks. To guard against the navigator being influenced by the ordinary indicators the yacht's bridge was screened making it impossible to see ahead. With absolute accuracy the skipper placed the craft on the line that ran into port, followed the mark unerringly until the ship was safely berthed in the harbor.

If the yacht deviated to the slightest degree from the safe course the deviation was instantly signaled by the instruments on a panel that informed the navigator whether the shift had been to the right or left. Constantly it was possible to determine the *Elettra's* exact position from the wireless "lighthouse."

The transmitting apparatus comprised two small short-wave outfits described as "twin 'searchlights' on a single mounting with a dark zone between the two beams." Each of the beams, right and left, had distinctive characteristics. The right-hand beam flashed signals of a low-pitched tone on a 60-centimeter wave.

The left-hand beam transmitted a note of much higher pitch. By having the two notes in exactly opposite phase a zone of silence was created in a central zone between the beams. That "dark" area was where the two notes canceled out.

To guide the ship the system was swung from left to right of the center line similarly to the manner a searchlight seeks an object on the water. The beam sounded a low note when swinging to the right and a high note when swinging to the left. The change of tone took place when the zone of

Eva Barrett Photo.

Proud Italian parents—Marconi, his wife (the former Countess
Cristina Bezzi-Scali) and daughter Maria Elettra Elena Anna.

silence coincided with the line of entrance to the harbor. It was necessary that the beams swing back and forth, for if the signal was fixed the pilot might assume he was in the silent zone, in case the apparatus failed to operate.

The yacht's installation consisted of a receiving set, loudspeaker and a galvanometer the quadrant of which was painted half red and half green. When the vessel entered the area of the radio beam a succession of rapid clicks was heard and the galvanometer's needle shifted to the red or green section of the quadrant as the ship moved to the right or to the left, respectively, of the hypothetical line leading into the harbor.

In demonstrating the operation of the equipment, Marconi saw fit to make adjustments, and he picked up some hand tools which he used as an expert. Dr. Arthur H. Compton, who was standing near by, commented that he evidently did much of his experimental work with his own hands.

"Yes," said Marconi, "how else can one think?"

After watching him on board the *Elettra*, Dr. Compton later remarked that it would be difficult to ascribe his success to any one personal attribute.

"In my judgment," he said, "it is rather the fine balance of technical knowledge and skill with an appreciation of the economic and personal factors involved that have made it possible for Marconi to continue to occupy a leading place in the application of the highly refined science to human needs."

To which Dr. Robert A. Millikan added, "I have known Senatore Marconi slightly for the past thirty-three years, and have had rather intimate association with him on a number of occasions within the past five years. I regard him as a man of excellent poise and judgment. He is a man who has contributed in an altogether outstanding way both to our scientific and to our industrial developments. In addition to all this, he is a human being of great friendliness and of the finest sort of human sympathy and much personal charm."

After the "radio lighthouse" demonstration, Marconi was free to devote attention to other applications of micro waves. He flew to London and secreted himself in his laboratory. News reports had it that television was whirlpooling in his mind. War interrupted.

Premier Benito Mussolini of Italy sent hordes of black-shirted troops into Ethiopia in the autumn of 1935. Marconi made a hurried trip across the ocean to Brazil to inaugurate a radio station, while reports intimated he went on a mission to arrange a loan for Mussolini. Within a month he was back in Rome with rumors attracting front-page notice that he had invented a "wireless death-ray" designed to plummet airplanes from the skies and to stop motor cars on the highways.

The story circulated afar. Scientists were doubtful but imaginative writers thrived upon it. They recalled how ever since wireless became a reality "engineers have been racking their brains to discover a way of concentrating radio waves in long, thin pencils." Nevertheless, success so far has not been conspicuous. Even the Marconi western beam from England widens out across the Atlantic into a cone that embraces the North American continent. Some one has written that "the energy required at the source of a deadly radio beam could not be much less that that of Niagara Falls."

"I prefer to think of the lives that have been saved by wireless," said Marconi, "rather than the uses to which it might be put in wartime."

From the powerful station 2RO, Rome, he went on the air for a broadcast to America, and as an introduction to his plea for American sympathy for his country's position, scouted the reports of a machine to paralyze aircraft:[2]

"If you are eager to hear from me about an alleged new invention by which I could stop motor engines at great distance, or do worse tricks than that, then let me reassure you at once by saying that you may fly to your heart's content as there will be no stopping you—for the present, at any rate."

Turning to the war issues, Marconi said in part:

"Europe is just emerging from the narrowest escape it has had for the last seventeen years from another clash, the horrors of which would have eclipsed all the horrors of the Great War. . . . You Americans, who, luckily for yourselves, are outside the League of Nations and breathe the free, invigorating air of two oceans and of great spaces, somewhat different from the confined atmosphere of Lake Geneva, will be able to form your own unbiased opinions, and you won't fail to recognize the justice of Italy's claim."

The Marchesa Cristina Marconi also went on the air in an international broadcast, the theme of which was high praise for the state of Italian women under fascism.[3] Expressing "great faith in women's mission in life," the Marchesa said there were 5,000,000 working women in Italy "on an absolute equality with men—equal work, equal pay."

"It is only since the advent of Mussolini that all professions have been open to women," she explained. . . . "As a rule Italian women are not politically minded, but they play their full share in our constructive human effort. They proved that throughout the Italian-Abyssinian conflict."

Those were the busy days for the Italian people; Marconi was seen in the news pictures with the Grand Council at the head of which sat Benito Mussolini. While Italian radio tossed lines of communications across the Mediterranean to

[2] October 30, 1935.   [3] June 15, 1936.

Marshal Pietro Badoglio's troops in Ethiopia, and the waves in other directions protested against "the economic conditions most unjustly inflicted upon Italy," radio in other lands also played new roles befitting modern times.

A million-dollar television field test was initiated in New York from atop the lofty Empire State Building; in London images were dancing across the rooftops from Alexandra Palace. It was the evolution of a new industry.

And on the high seas wireless was advancing too. Great Britain's 1,004 foot, 80,733 ton super-liner R.M.S. *Queen Mary* sped proudly into New York harbor boasting ultra-modern radio instruments, which proved their multiplex efficiency by broadcasting and sending messages all the way across the sea. The eight separate lines of communication, four in and four out, all working at the same time independently of each other, were never silent. The fourteen radio operators were busy day and night. Even the passengers in any one of 500 staterooms might pick up an ordinary telephone and talk by radiophone with friends in towns far distant. In fact, while one man was chatting with Cape Town, South Africa, another was talking with Chicago.

Old-timers marveled at the equipment; just the touch of a tiny switch turned the conversation into ethereal jargon sometimes called "scrambled speech," yet those talking were unaware that their words were being wabbled and all mixed up so no one might eavesdrop. Everything about this modern marine radio seemed so complex, yet so simple in performance. The veterans on board reminisced and compared the old with the new; they recalled the *Titanic* and how radio and ships had changed. Marconi naturally came into the conversation and a pioneer, associated with him since the inception of the Marconi Company, was asked to what forces he attributed Marconi's success.

"Chiefly to his instinctive intuition as to what was wanted and how to arrive at the solution," he replied.

"Also to the fact that he had a company with plenty of capital behind him, and that the success or otherwise of the company depended upon the rapid development of wireless in the early days. With this money behind him he had the courage to launch out on great experiments such as the development of transatlantic wireless in the early part of the century.

"The fact that the organization was named the Marconi Company added enormously to his prestige and has always kept his name prominently before the world. The most interesting period in the life of the company passed, in my opinion when cables obtained control of wireless in England and the Marconi Company became practically a manufacturing organization.

"Marconi deserved all the praise he received in the early days, but since the World War he has contributed very little himself to wireless development, either in invention, design or construction. . . . Marconi is a curious man."

The famous "instinctive intuition," however, was very much alive.

Did he expect television? Yes! Did he see any limitations to wireless? No! Impossible solutions of wireless mysteries, climatic, atmospheric or otherwise? No!

Wireless to him was no riddle. Time was the all important element in the solution. To him there was one great problem, the most persistent ever placed before the thought of man. That was life itself!

Life to Marconi was an impenetrable secret. He declared life "would be truly frightening were it not for faith." Never in all his research had he glimpsed the slightest clue to explain the mystery of humanity's origin and the future.

"If we consider what science already has enabled men to know—the immensity of space, the fantastic philosophy of the stars, the infinite smallness of the composition of atoms, the macrocosm and microcosm whereby we succeed only in creating outlines and translating a measure into numbers without our minds being able to form any concrete idea of it—we remain astounded by the enormous machinery of the universe," said Marconi.[4]

"If, then, we pass toward the consideration of the phenomena of life, this sentiment is accentuated. The complexity of the different organs, which all work out in coordinated and determinate functions, the constant preoccupation for the conservation of the species, man's marvelous adaptation of his constitution to surroundings, the transmission of instincts, the mechanism of thought and reasoning, and, lastly the spectre of death, place man, who wishes to explain the tormenting mystery, before a book closed with seven seals."

Marconi had reached an age where he was beginning to philosophize—to look back.

Youth dreams of the future—the road ahead. Age dreams of the past—the long road back. The one leads on to progress; the other into hazy reveries, into the land of memory.

With a tinge of sadness, like saying farewell to an old friend, Marconi saw Poldhu, the scene of the transatlantic triumph, close after twenty-two years of continuous service, having flashed its final message to Spain, curiously enough the land from which Columbus sailed westward as did Poldhu's famous three dots.

There was a time when the skies were "painted with unnumbered sparks." But no more. He saw them pass unobtrusively from the heavens. Gone is the awe-inspiring

[4] Lecture before the International Congress of Electro-Radio Biology, at Venice, Italy, September 10, 1934.

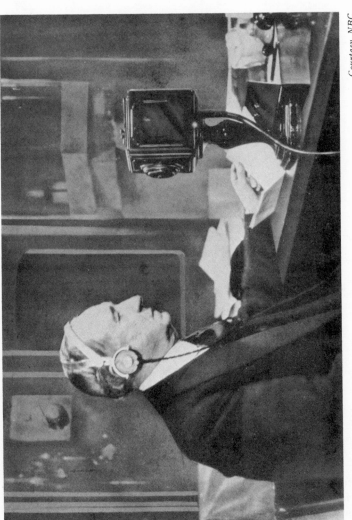

Marconi as he appears in 1937, broadcasting from his yacht *Elettra*.

apparatus of old. There are few crashing, cracking sparks; no electric flames leaping across wide-open gaps. The long waves upon the crests of which Marconi and the pioneers wafted wireless to victory have lost much of their glory Short waves are the thing.

The ships which first flashed wireless from their masts no longer sail the seas. Erosion and corrosion worked by Time and the restless ocean are destructive. They leave only memory, ever fading.

Wireless has changed. Softly glowing vacuum tubes silently broadcast a rhapsody of words across the world without as much as a blink. Silence in a vacuum has made wireless more mysterious. Behind it all is the dream of a youth and the romance of a famous spark.

Enlivened by constant progress, refreshed by invention, wireless is ever young. New instruments are being continually hooked into the circuits often before those in use indicate any signs of electrical fatigue. Against such a background it is rather difficult to realize that age gradually wears away the human equation that first figured out the miracles.

The destiny of the men of wireless also decrees they too must drop one by one out of the "circuits." Gone are Maxwell, Hertz, Edison, Preece, Righi, Fessenden and Pupin. Only Branly, Lodge, Fleming, Tesla and Marconi remain in 1937 as the grand old men of wireless. The irony is that their science pulses with greater vigor with the years while Time turns them gray, etches wrinkles across their brows and slows their tempo of life. Challenged by television, they suddenly realize it is not for them; they see new champions entering the arena.

It was in the winter of 1935, word flashed around the world that Marchesa Marconi declared her husband "very,

very tired." He had been working too hard; his strength failed him. Under doctor's orders he went to a London nursing home for "a few weeks' complete rest."

The Marchese, himself, within a month, wirelessed friends in America he was "laid up and unwell." A two months' rest renewed his strength and he became anxious to get back beyond the Alps. He boarded the Rome Express, on which an old associate met him at the Gare du Nord, traveling as far as Gare de Lyon with him.

"He was as charming as usual, but is beginning to look a good deal aged," he remarked of Marconi as the locomotive raced on toward the Italian frontier.

Time was creeping up on him just as it had done so often on his instruments of magic. But Marconi without wireless or wireless without Marconi—that could never be! Throughout the ages it seems the *Elettra* will sail on and on into the infinite with her white and golden bow gently dipping with the swells of Time as it moves across the ethereal sea toward the westerly sun. On the bridge Marconi can be seen waving his Italian naval cap in farewell to earthly waters. Surely there must be more of wireless out there in the infinite, far off in unfathomed space across which all wireless waves endlessly surge against unseen shores from which no traveler has yet returned.

So the *Elettra*, with Italy's colors proudly flying at her masthead will some day vanish beyond the curvature of the earth. Only on the uncharted sea of "the ether" will Guglielmo Marconi find the rest which the enchanted world of wireless denied him.

Nothing in wireless lives long. Science moves swiftly, ever changing, ever progressing, but as Time turns each new page one name is penned afresh—MARCONI. Silhouetted against the historic past he goes on, ever toiling, ever search-

ing for new truths in wireless. The spark of his genius will
leap forever across the skies.

> *Who says Italia holds a dying race*
> *And all the glory of her line is spent?*
> *This western world is still her monument*
> *No less than when the Genoese did trace*
> *The trackless ocean and Spain's banner place*
> *Upon our strand. For, hark! the air is rent*
> *With strange turmoil, a mystic hail is sent*
> *To us by her last born who conquers space!*

WILLIAM ASPENWALL BRADLEY.

MARCONI HONORS

1897 Italian Knighthood.
1902 Knight of the Russian Order of St. Anne.
1905 Knight of the Civil Order of Savoy.
       Knight of the Italian Order of Workers.
1912 Grand Cross of the Spanish Order of Alfonso XII.
       Medal of the African War (Italy).
       Grand Cross of the Order of the Crown of Italy.
1914 Knight Grand Cross of the Royal Victorian Order.
       Senatore of the Kingdom of Italy.
1919 Military Cross for World War Service.
1929 Spanish Order of "Plus Ultra."
       Created Italian Marquis by H. M. the King of Italy.
1931 Knight Grand Cross of the Order of Menelik, Abyssinia.
       Grand Cross of the Order of Pius, Vatican City State.
       Grand Cross of the Sovereign Military Order of Malta.
1932 Grand Cross of the Italian Order of St. Maurice and St.
          Lazarus.
1933 Grand Cross of the Japanese Order of the Rising Sun.
1935 Grand Cross of the Brazilian Order of the Southern Cross.
1936 Grand Cross of the Chinese Order of the Jade.
       Rear Admiral of the Italian Naval Reserve (June 20).
Honorary Citizenships: Rome, Milan, Florence, Leghorn, Pisa,
   Genova, Bari, Rieti, Civitavecchia, San Francisco, Calif., Rio
   di Janeiro.

HONORARY DEGREES

Doctor of Engineering: University of Bologna, University of
   Pisa.
Doctor of Science: Oxford University, Cambridge University.
Doctor of Law: Glasgow University; Aberdeen University; Liver-
   pool University; University of Pennsylvania; Louisiana Uni-
   versity; Columbia University; Notre Dame University; Loyola
   University; Northwestern University.

Doctor of Physics: Rio di Janeiro University.
Professor of Electro-magnetic Waves at the Rome University.

PRINCIPAL AWARDS

Nobel Prize for Physics, 1909.
Albert Medals, Royal Society of Arts (London).
Gold Medal, Institute of Radio Engineers (New York).
Gold Medal, Franklin Institute (Philadelphia).
John Fritz Medal (awarded jointly by Institutes of Electrical
  Engineers and Mining Engineers for achievement in applied
  science, United States, with the motivation "for the invention
  of Wireless Telegraphy").
Gold Medal, University of Bologna (awarded at Silver Jubilee of
  invention of wireless).
John Scott Medal (Philadelphia).
Silver Medal (International Mark Twain Society).
Kelvin Medal, Institution of Civil Engineers, London.
Goethe Medal, presented by President Paul von Hindenburg
  (Germany in 1932).
Gold Medal, Royal Society of Rome.
Gold Medal, Royal Academy of Science (Turin, Italy).
Gold Medal, Italian Society of Science.
Gold Medal, New York Electrical Society.
Gold Tablet, Italian Institute of Electrical Engineers.
Gold Medals from the cities of Bologna, Florence, Venice, Madrid.
Gold Tablet by the survivors of S.S. *Titanic*.
Gold Medal and Diploma of the Veteran Wireless Operators Asso-
  ciation, New York.
Medal "Gustave Trasenter," Liège Belgium.
Medal "Exner," Vienna.
Diploma of Merit in Science by the Pontificia Accademia Tibe-
  rina, Rome.
Tablet "Viani" by the Humanitarian Society, Milan.

INDEX

American Institute of Electrical Engineers, Marconi dinner celebrating first transatlantic wireless, 112–117

America's Cup races, first reported by wireless, 76–81

Anglo-American Telegraph Company, opposition to wireless, 103–104, 108–109

Antinoe, S.S., flashes SOS, 278–279

Beam wireless. *See* Marconi beam

Bezzi-Scali, Countess Maria Cristina, marriage to Marconi, 283–285

Binns, John R., Marconi operator S.S. *Republic,* 166–174

Bologna, Marconi's home at, 19–21; honors Marconi, 142–143, 279–281

Branly, Edouard, develops coherer, 16–19, 230; comments on Marconi's work, 18–19

Bride, Harold, Marconi operator S.S. *Titanic,* 186–196

Broadcasting, first opera, 174–175; the "craze" spreads, 259–261; America greets Marconi by, 261–262; pioneer events in, 274–277, 300–301; international salute to Marconi, 304–309

Cables, influence of wireless upon, 57–58, 87, 103–109, 129, 151–155, 161–162

Cape Cod, Marconi's experiments on, 94–95, 138–142

Carlo Alberto, S.S., Marconi experiments on, 133

Carpathia, S.S., rescue ship in *Titanic* disaster, 186–198

Children, Marconi's, 151, 301

Clemens, Cyril, presents Mark Twain Medal to Marconi, 290–291

Clifden, Ireland, Marconi station at, 155; tests radiophone, 235

Coherer, development and operation of, 16–17; Marconi's use of, 16–19; Popoff's use of, 44

Compton, Dr. Arthur H., recollection of Marconi, 337, 343

Cottam, Harold, Marconi operator S.S. *Carpathia,* 190–193

Crookes, Sir William, prophecy of wireless, 45–46, 230

Crystal detector, development of, 146–147

Davis, Jameson, aid to Marconi, 49–51

de Forest, Dr. Lee, invents audion, 153; broadcasts Metropolitan Opera, 174–175

Direction finder, Marconi discusses, 199–200; locates S.S. *Antinoe* in distress, 278–279

Distress call, first use of, 67; first American ship to use, 146; adoption of CQD and SOS, 165; use in *Republic* disaster, 165–174; use by *Titanic,* 186–203; flashed by the *Volturno,* 220–224; the *Antinoe's* call, 278–279

Dolbear, Professor A. E., comments on first transatlantic wireless, 105

Edison, Thomas Alva, discovery of etheric force, 27–31; his wireless patent, 29–31; friendship for Marconi, 30–31, 248; discovers "Edison Effect," 45; comment on first transatlantic wireless, 113

Edison Effect, discovery of, 45

Electrolytic detector, invention of, 146

Electromagnetic waves. *See* Hertzian waves

Elettra, Marconi's floating laboratory, 257–258; Marconi's life on

for his success, 25–26, 33–39, 346–
347; Edison's friendship for, 30–31,
113; early assistants of, 34–35;
why he left Italy for England, 48;
comments on his early tests in England, 51–55; the New York *World*
appraises, 53; explains his wireless
magic, 53–55; Preece's tribute, 55,
82–83; describes regatta by wireless, 60–61; flashes bulletins for
Queen Victoria, 61–62; his foresight in wireless, 62–67; honored by
Italy, 68–69; sends first wireless
across English Channel, 70–75; his
patent No. 7777, 73–74, 91–92;
first visit to America, 76–83; reports *America's* Cup races by wireless, 76–83; New York reporters'
opinions of, 77–81; first transatlantic experiments, 87–102; as he
appeared in 1901, 88–89; impressions of 88–89, 110–111, 144–146,
282, 286, 297–300, 334–335, 338–
339, 343–344, 350; develops
tuning, 90–93; comments on first
transoceanic wireless, 94–101; tribute to Hertz, 99–100; world-wide
recognition, 104–118; Pupin's faith
in, 104–105, 198–199, 202, 306–307;
Lodge's tribute to, 106–107; comments on wireless vs. cables, 107–
108, 161–162; honored by American Institute of Electrical Engineers, 112–118; Tesla's comment on
113; discusses wireless progress,
114–117; the *New York Times'*
tribute to, 117–118, 335–336; experiments on S.S. *Philadelphia*,
125–127, 130; observes sun's effect
on wireless, 130, 293; tests at Glace
Bay, 132–138; develops magnetic
detector, 132–133; opens station on
Cape Cod, 138–142; an impression
of him in 1903, 142–143; Bologna
honors him, 142–143, 279–281; develops directional aërial, 150; marries Beatrice O'Brien, 151; three
children and dates of birth, 151;
defends his patents, 154, 227–234,
238–239; inaugurates first transatlantic commercial service, 154–161;
Maxim's tribute, 159–160; Hewitt's
comment, 160–161; comments on
Republic disaster, 170–171; discusses science, 175, 282; opens Col-

tano station, 176–179; as seen by a
fellow worker, 179, 346–347; compared to Edison and others, 179,
325, 334–335; comments on wireless in *Titanic* disaster, 193–195;
outlines the wireless compass,
199–201; honored by Spain,
201, 279; lectures on wireless in New York, 201–202, 270–
273, 288–289; personal characteristics, 202–203; testifies at hearings
on English political wireless "scandal," 204–217; honors conferred on,
210–211, 235–236, 352–353; loses
eye in accident, 217–219; London
press comment on, 225–226; sum-
marizes wireless progress to 1913,
226; discusses rôle of inventors,
226; outlines radiophone possibilities, 235, 241–242, 265, 273–274; his
part in World War, 237–254; discusses radio use in war, 243–245;
reviews Italy's rôle in World War,
246–248; at Peace Conference, 250;
as he appeared at end of war, 252–
253; sees need for world economic
conference, 253–254; buys yacht
Elettra, 257–258; life on board
Elettra, 261–264; talks with reporters, 264–269; discusses communication with Mars, 267–269;
lectures on short waves, 270–273,
288–290, 316–328; visits "the
House of Magic," 273; first marriage dissolved, 274; recalls early
experiments, 280–281, 292–294;
first marriage annulled by Rota,
283–284; second marriage, 283–
285; a 1927 interview with, 285–
287; comments on Mussolini, 287;
comments on wireless power transmission, 288, 328–329; discusses
television, 288, 332–333; presented
Mark Twain Medal, 290–292;
daughter born, 301; presents radio
station to Vatican, 302–304, 321;
international salute to, 304–309;
ultra-short wave research, 310–313,
316–324, 331–334; interviewed in
1932 on the future of radio, 331–
334, 338–340; inspects Radio City,
337–338; his home in Rome, 341–
342; demonstrates radio navigation
system, 342–343; Compton's tribute, 343–344; comments on wire-

less "death ray," 344; his observations of life, 347–348

Marconi, Luigi, birth, 6; association with Guglielmo, 11–13
Marconi beam, development of, 276–277
Marconi "scandal." *See* "Political"
Marconi Wireless Telegraph Company, purchase of Edison's wireless patent, 30; organization of, 51; German competition with, 147–148; sells coastal stations to British Post Office, 162
Marconigrams, the first paid, 58
Marescalchi Palace, home of Marconi, 21
Mark Twain Medal, presented to Marconi, 290–292
Marriage, Marconi's, with Beatrice O'Brien, 151; with Countess Bezzi-Scali, 283–285
Mars, Marconi discusses communication with, 267–269
Martin, T. C., comments on Marconi and transatlantic wireless, 106, 113
Mathieu, G. A., Marconi engineer, 318, 334
Maxim, Hiram, tribute to Marconi, 159–160
Maxwell, James Clerk, his rôle in wireless, 15, 41–42, 230, 331
Micro waves, research in, 310–321; use across English Channel, 321–322; possibilities in television, 332–333; use in wireless "lighthouse," 342–343
Millikan, Dr. Robert A., tribute to Marconi, 343–344
Mussolini, Benito, Marconi's comment on, 287

Newfoundland, Marconi's first transatlantic tests in, 87–102; Marconi as seen there, 110–111; Marconi discusses experiments in, 112
New York Electrical Society, Marconi lecture at, 201–203
New York Times, comments on first transatlantic wireless, 99–101, 105–106; comments on wireless vs. cables, 108, 129; tribute to Marconi, 117–118, 335–336; receives press wireless across Atlantic, 156;

receives first message from Coltano, 176–177; Marconi's visit to, 292

O'Brien, Lady Beatrice, marries Marconi, 151; marriage dissolved, 274; second marriage, 274
Onesti, Calzecchi, his work with coherer, 16, 44
Opera, first broadcast, 174–175

Paget, P. W., assists Marconi in Newfoundland, 94–98, 306
Parkin, Sir George R., describes first west-east transatlantic wireless, 135–138
Patents, significance of No. 7777, 73–74, 91; Marconi's defense of, 154, 227–234, 238–239
Philadelphia, S.S., Marconi's experiments on, 122–131, 293
Phillips, John George, Marconi operator S.S. *Titanic,* 186–196
Poldhu, site of first transatlantic wireless station, 89–90; early transatlantic tests from, 93–102; experiments with S.S. *Philadelphia,* 122–131; tests with Glace Bay, 132–138
"Political" scandal, in England, 204–217; Marconi's testimony, 208–211; press comment, 213–215
Pontecchio, Marconi's home at, 9, 12–13, 22–23; birthplace of wireless, 12–24, 38–39
Popoff, Alexander, his experiments with coherer, 44–45, 230
Preece, Sir William, his rôle in wireless, 32; Marconi's meeting with, 48–50; his appraisal of Marconi, 55; reviews radio progress in 1901, 82–83
Press service, for ships, 140; first transoceanic, 154–162
Pupin, Michael I., comments on first transatlantic wireless, 104–105; tribute to Marconi, 198–199, 202, 306–307; greets Marconi, 288

Radio, Marconi lectures on short waves, 270–274, 288–289; progress after World War, 274–276; first flashes from North Pole, 278; development 1927–30, 300–301; world-wide salute to Marconi by, 304–308; ultra-short wave re-

HISTORY OF BROADCASTING:
Radio To Television
An Arno Press/New York Times Collection

Archer, Gleason L.
Big Business and Radio. 1939.

Archer, Gleason L.
History of Radio to 1926. 1938.

Arnheim, Rudolf.
Radio. 1936.

Blacklisting: Two Key Documents. 1952–1956.

Cantril, Hadley and Gordon W. Allport.
The Psychology of Radio. 1935.

Codel, Martin, editor.
Radio and Its Future. 1930.

Cooper, Isabella M.
Bibliography on Educational Broadcasting. 1942.

Dinsdale, Alfred.
First Principles of Television. 1932.

Dunlap, Orrin E., Jr.
Marconi: The Man and His Wireless. 1938.

Dunlap, Orrin E., Jr.
The Outlook for Television. 1932.

Fahie, J. J.
A History of Wireless Telegraphy. 1901.

Federal Communications Commission.
Annual Reports of the Federal Communications Commission.
1934/1935–1955.

Federal Radio Commission.
Annual Reports of the Federal Radio Commission. 1927–1933.

Frost, S. E., Jr.
Education's Own Stations. 1937.

Grandin, Thomas.
The Political Use of the Radio. 1939.

Harlow, Alvin.
Old Wires and New Waves. 1936.

Hettinger, Herman S.
A Decade of Radio Advertising. 1933.

Huth, Arno.
Radio Today: The Present State of Broadcasting. 1942.

Jome, Hiram L.
Economics of the Radio Industry. 1925.

Lazarsfeld, Paul F.
Radio and the Printed Page. 1940.

Lumley, Frederick H.
Measurement in Radio. 1934.

Maclaurin, W. Rupert.
Invention and Innovation in the Radio Industry. 1949.

Radio: Selected A.A.P.S.S. Surveys. 1929–1941.

Rose, Cornelia B., Jr.
National Policy for Radio Broadcasting. 1940.

Rothafel, Samuel L. and Raymond Francis Yates.
Broadcasting: Its New Day. 1925.

Schubert, Paul.
The Electric Word: The Rise of Radio. 1928.

Studies in the Control of Radio: Nos. 1–6. 1940–1948.

Summers, Harrison B., editor.
Radio Censorship. 1939.

Summers, Harrison B., editor.
**A Thirty-Year History of Programs Carried on
National Radio Networks in the United States, 1926–1956.** 1958.

Waldrop, Frank C. and Joseph Borkin.
Television: A Struggle for Power. 1938.

White, Llewellyn.
The American Radio. 1947.

World Broadcast Advertising: Four Reports. 1930–1932.